# Theories of Welfare

Also by Anthony Forder:
'Concepts in Social Administration: a Framework for Analysis'

# Theories of Welfare

Anthony Forder
Terry Caslin
Geoffrey Ponton
Sandra Walklate

Routledge & Kegan Paul
London, Boston, Melbourne and Henley

First published in 1984
by Routledge & Kegan Paul plc
39 Store Street, London WC1E 7DD, England
9 Park Street, Boston, Mass. 02108, USA
464 St Kilda Road, Melbourne,
Victoria 3004, Australia and
Broadway House, Newtown Road,
Henley-on-Thames, Oxon RG9 1EN, England
Printed in Great Britain
by St Edmundsbury Press, Bury St Edmunds, Suffolk

Library of Congress Cataloging in Publication Data

Main entry under title:
Theories of welfare.

   Includes bibliographies and indexes.
   1. Social service - addresses, essays, lectures.
2. Social policy - Addresses, essays, lectures. 3. Economic policy - Addresses, essays, lectures. 4. Public
welfare - Addresses, essays, lectures. 5. Poverty -
Addresses, essays, lectures. I.Forder, Anthony.
HV40.T475    1984         361'.001         84-8199

ISBN 0-7100-9625-9 (pbk)

# Contents

# Illustrations

FIGURES

TABLES

# Chapter 1

# The social sciences and welfare
## Anthony Forder

The purpose of this book is to aid beginning students of
social administration by presenting brief critical
accounts of various theories which are referred to in the
literature of the subject and by showing the extent to
which they are relevant to the study of social policy and
the social services.  The purpose of this chapter is to
clarify some initial issues.  First, it presents a brief
account of the problem presented by the multi-disciplinary
nature of social administration.  Second, it looks at the
nature and status of the social sciences.  Third, it considers alternative views of the nature of 'welfare' and
their ideological implications.  'Ideology' here means a
system of beliefs, which is used to guide and validate
actions.  Finally, it describes the position adopted by
the writers for the purposes of the book.

   Social administration as an academic subject is the
study of certain collective activities undertaken by governments, voluntary organisations or, in some cases, by
commercial organisations with government support, whose
ostensible aim is to improve the welfare of the people of
a nation-state.  Human behaviour generally and these
activities in particular are the subject of a range of
disciplines known collectively as the social sciences.
The full understanding of any particular human activity
requires the application of all these disciplines.  For
example, to understand fully higher education as a social
service, sociology may be needed to explain its role in
the preparation and maintenance of an elite, economics to
evaluate the costs and benefits of its contribution to
economic prosperity, political studies to understand the
implications of its peculiar forms of administration,
social history to explain how these have arisen, and
finally psychology and philosophy to evaluate its educational processes.

These different social sciences have a common origin in
philosophy and at one time it was not unusual to find a
single person who was regarded as a distinguished contri-
butor to two or more disciplines.   However, a process of
specialisation and professionalisation has led to the
development of spearate disciplines focusing on different
aspects of human behaviour.   Although the established
boundaries between disciplines were largely arbitrary in
origin, they have become deeper and more rigid with time.
Differences of language, conceptualisation and methodology
have all helped to make communication more difficult and
professionalisation has created a reluctance to overcome
those difficulties.

In these circumstances students of a multi-disciplinary
subject like social administration are faced with two
major problems.   Their studies have to be broad and they
are in danger of trying to apply or criticise theories of
which their knowledge is superficial, although they may
not realise this.   Second, they may have considerable
difficulty in grasping how the theories and conclusions of
one discipline relate to those of others.   This book
cannot solve those problems, but it may make students more
aware of the issues involved.

THE SOCIAL SCIENCES AS 'SCIENCE'

The term 'social science' originated in the nineteenth
century because many people believed that the methods of
the physical sciences could be applied to the study of
human behaviour with similar productive results.   Its
adoption was an attempt to by-pass what has proved to be
an enduring controversy, whether the social sciences are
or can indeed be 'scientific'.   Answering that question
has involved consideration of three different issues.

First, there has been a need for a clearer understanding of the nature of the scientific method employed by
physical scientists.   The scientific status of the social
sciences has often been measured against an idealised
picture of the processes and results of the physical sciences.

Second, physical scientists seem to have been relatively successful in achieving a measure of objectivity in
their work, in that the observations and experiments on
which conclusions are based can be verified independently
by other observers and do not seem to be directly affected

by the values of the scientists themselves.   It is not
clear whether this is possible or even desirable for those
who study human behaviour.

Third, the social sciences are concerned with phenomena
of even greater complexity than those in the physical sciences with less possibility of controlling variables in
the situation in which observation takes place.

Each of these three issues will be discussed in turn
before looking at different concepts of the nature of
social welfare.

THE LOGIC AND PROCESSES OF SCIENCE

From the seventeenth century to the mid-twentieth century
it was generally accepted that science was concerned with
the discovery of truth in the sense of verifiable facts or
propositions.   It was believed to do this by the process
of induction, that is to say, the development of universal
theories or laws from the observation of numerous singular
events.   These theories were then tested by further
observations and experiments.   The aim was to discover
'laws' which were universal, general and precise.   The
laws were to be universal in that they were true in all
places and at all times;   they were to be general in the
sense that the same law could explain a wide range of
phenomena;   and they were to be precise in that the
effects could be precisely calculated and measured.   The
ideal example was Newton's law of gravity which appeared
to fulfil all these conditions.   It has been against this
view of science, generally called 'positivism' or 'logical
positivism', that much of the argument has been conducted
about whether there can be a true 'science' of human
behaviour.

Since the nineteenth century physical scientists have
become less confidently optimistic about the ability of
science to explain everything.   They have been extraordi-
narily successful in expanding the boundaries of knowledge
and in developing theories that cover wider and wider
ranges of phenomena (for example the assimilation of laws
governing matter and energy).   But the mysteries have
also been extended.   They have had to recognise that some
events may be unpredictable except in terms of the laws of
probability, and some events may be unknowable because the
process of observing them changes them.

This change in attitude among scientists has found its parallel in new theories about the logic and methods of science, particularly those of Karl Popper and Thomas Kuhn, both of whom greatly admire the achievements of science.

Popper was a philosopher and he started his first major work, 'The Logic of Scientific Discovery' (1934 and 1959), from a logical fallacy that had long been recognised as being embedded in the theory of induction.   It is logically impossible to confirm the truth of a generalisation through individual instances, however numerous, since the possibility of an exception can never be excluded.   Thus if science was founded on induction, its logical basis was extremely insecure.   Another difficulty in the theory of induction is that random observation rarely, if ever, leads to useful generalisations, but rather to confusion. Observation needs to be systematic before it can produce useful results.   Systematic observation requires some theoretical framework to indicate which observations are relevant.   Popper dealt with the first problem by standing the theory of induction on its head.   He pointed out that whilst it is never possible to prove a generalisation from numerous singular instances, it only requires one conclusively accepted negative instance to falsify it. Thus he proposed that the logic of empirical science lies in a deductive process in which one begins with the statement of a generalisation and deduces consequences from it which one then tries to falsify.   Failure to falsify the proposition does not prove it to be true so there can be no certainty.   After all, even Newton's law of gravity was eventually falsified as a universal law and was superseded by Einstein's theory of relativity.   But it is the very process of testing out the theory that extends its applications, gives its predictions more precision, and eventually locates the counter-instances that lead to its supersession by a theory with wider explanatory power.

Thus Popper proposed that the most useful way of distinguishing science from non-science was the principle of falsifiability - 'it must be possible for an empirical scientific system to be refuted by experience' (1959, p. 41, original italics).   Unlike the more extreme supporters of the theory of induction, the logical positivists, he did not consider that unprovable or unfalsifiable statements were meaningless.   Not only might such statements be true, but they could also at a later stage lead to propositions that were falsifiable (like the first atomic theories).   Such statements were, however, so long as they remained unfalsifiable, unproductive scientifically.

Popper believed that there can be no certainty in the search for truth.   But this did not lead him to the view that there are no criteria by which one can judge one theory against another.   First, one would prefer a theory that had not been falsified to one that had been falsified. Second, theories should be preferred that provided greater opportunities for falsification.   This might be because of their greater precision, or because of the wider range of phenomena with which they deal.   In this sense boldness and improbability were virtues in a theory, provided the theory was falsifiable and had not been falsified.

Kuhn, in 'The Structure of Scientific Revolutions' (1962) started from a different perspective from Popper, that of a historian of science.   Indeed, it is an interesting fact that despite the relationship between the two books Kuhn, the later writer, makes no reference to Popper in the whole of the book, even in the 1970 edition.   Like Popper, Kuhn was in profound disagreement with the traditional account of empirical science, but in his case not with the account of its logic, but of its processes and procedures.   Kuhn starts with the concept of what he calls 'normal science, the activity in which most scientists inevitably spend almost all their time' (p. 5).   In normal science, scientists are not engaged in seeking new theories, or even new knowledge that will falsify accepted theories.   They are working as members of a scientific community which shares and is committed to a particular 'paradigm' or model of the world or that part of it which concerns them.   Each paradigm has its own rules which determine the phenomena to which attention should be given, the methods which will produce valid results and the criteria by which results should be evaluated.   The paradigm and its rules are learnt together by new members as they undertake the educational process that inducts them into the community.   Their work consists in solving a series of problems or puzzles whose framework and solution are determined by the paradigm within which they are working.   Indeed, if an experiment produces a result which is inconsistent with the paradigm, this is seen, at least initially, not as a failure of the theory but as a failure of the scientist.   The puzzles, which often require great ingenuity to solve, include such work as the calculation of predicted constants, filling in the gaps in the periodic table of elements by finding new ones, exploiting new applications of the paradigm, and extending it to solve existing anomalies.   Although this approach is in some ways very narrow, it seems to provide the opportunity and the incentive to study a range of phenomena

at a depth that has been very productive.   Much of this
study would never have been undertaken if belief in the
paradigm had not given scientists a real hope of achieving success.

   Before a field of study becomes the subject of 'normal
science' there will be a period that Kuhn describes as
'pre-paradigmatic' - although this is something of a mis-
nomer.   Instead of a single dominant paradigm, there are
numerous competing schools and sub-schools.   Each of
these supports some paradigm which explains a particular
cluster of phenomena and plays down the importance of
others which it cannot explain.   The paradigms supported
by different schools often draw strength from their
attachment to a particular metaphysical or philosophical
theory, beyond the reach of scientific proof at least at
that particular period.   When eventually a dominant paradigm emerges, it will often draw together elements from
different competing schools and will be accepted because
it explains a much wider range of relevant phenomena,
although rarely all of them.

   The acceptance of any particular dominant paradigm in a
field of science is not immutable.   Sooner or later there
is likely to be, in Kuhn's phrase, 'a scientific revolution', in which the dominant paradigm is succeeded by a
new one, as, for example, Newton's laws were succeeded by
Einstein's theory of relativity.   The period before the
new paradigm is accepted is normally one of confusion or
crisis due to a more acute awareness of the nature and
importance of the phenomena that cannot be explained by
the dominant paradigm.   This period of confusion has many
similarities to the pre-paradigmatic period, but is often
comparatively short.   The new paradigm often draws in
elements of earlier rejected paradigms as well as of its
immediate predecessor.   It is accepted, like its predecessor, because it can explain a wider range of relevant
phenomena, although never all of them.   Kuhn points out
that the new paradigm often originates from the mind of a
comparatively young man, or someone from a different field
of study who has been less conditioned by the socialising
processes that determine entry into the relevant scientific community.

   Because Kuhn and Popper are studying different aspects
of scientific process, they do not appear to be wholly
consistent with one another.   Thus the procedures which
Popper seems to expect to follow from the logic of science
are not the same as the procedures of Kuhn's 'normal sci-

ence'.   Nevertheless, both reject the traditional view of
science as induction and as proceeding to the discovery of
'laws' which are true and can be known to be true in an
absolute sense.   In this way both present a view of science that is less idealistic than the traditional view.


## OBJECTIVITY IN THE STUDY OF HUMAN BEHAVIOUR

If the work of Popper and Kuhn raises doubts about the
possibility of discovering 'truth' in the physical sciences, in the social sciences that possibility is made even
more remote by the difficulty of achieving objectivity in
the study of human behaviour.   This difficulty takes two
forms.   First, there is the problem of whether the unre-
liability of human observation can be counteracted by con-
firmation from independent observers.   Second, and perhaps more fundamental, is the question of whether the
observation and interpretation of human behaviour can be
made independently of the values held by the observer.

In considering each of these questions in turn it is
useful to begin with the views of Max Weber (1881-1961).
Weber saw the subject of social science as 'social action'
which he defined in the following way:

> In 'action' is included all human behaviour when and
> insofar as the acting individual attaches a subjective
> meaning to it. ... Action is social insofar as, by
> virtue of the subjective meaning attached to it by the
> acting individual (or individuals), it takes account of
> the behaviour of others and is thereby oriented in its
> course. (Weber, 1947, p. 20)

In stressing 'the subjective meaning' of action, Weber is
distinguishing the social scientist's interest in behaviour from that of, say, the physiologist.   To the physiologist observing a man walking, it is the physical processes involved that are important.   To the social scientist it is the meaning of the action that is important,
including the actor's intentions and motivation.

This definition of the subject of social science
involves considerable problems for its validation.   As
Weber pointed out, the subjective meaning of an action for
the actor is not a fact that is open to verification.   It
is only observable by one person, the actor himself, and
his observation may be in error or deliberately misrepor-
ted.   So in Weber's view social science will always

depend to some extent on the insight of the investigator
into the meaning of what he is observing, whether he is
studying individual behaviour or the culture of a society.
But the insight of the investigator also has its subjective elements which make it in turn unverifiable, so
social science can never, in Weber's view, attain the
objectivity of the physical sciences.

Behavioural scientists in psychology and other disciplines have disputed Weber's argument.   They accept that
mental states are objectively unknowable, but have deduced
from this that social science can only be truly scientific
if it confines its studies to overt behaviour.   'Overt
behaviour' can include the actor's statements about his
mental state, provided these are not taken as evidence of
the true nature of that state.   Behaviourists do not
necessarily deny that private psychic states exist and
influence behaviour, but they do believe that the only
sound procedure for achieving reliable knowledge of individual and social action is through the controlled study
of overt behaviour.

Ernest Nagel (b. 1901), who defends the logical position of behaviourists, takes what may be regarded as an
intermediate position between them and Weber.   He argues
that the empathy of the social scientist with the actors
in a social process may be 'heuristically important in his
efforts to *invent* suitable hypotheses to explain the process' but this 'does not annul the need for objective evidence, assessed in accordance with logical principles
that are common to all controlled enquiries, to support
his imputation of subjective states to those human agents'
(Nagel, 1961, p. 44).   However, this still leaves open
the possibility that a social science informed by the
principles of behavioural science will fail to study the
issues of greatest significance to human beings.

The objectivity of the social sciences is also problematic in another sense, namely whether there are objective
truths that are separable from the values of those who
observe and analyse phenomena.   Weber, despite his belief
that full objectivity is impossible because of the importance of insight, was still a firm advocate of a scientific
sociology.   He considered that an essential condition of
this was to make a clear distinction between facts and
values.   'By "value judgements" are to be understood ...
practical evaluations of the unsatisfactory or satisfactory character of phenomena subject to our influence'
(1949, p. 1).   Such judgements, in Weber's view (with

which there is very wide agreement), inevitably involve an
element of subjectivity so that ultimately they cannot be
refuted.   Facts, on the other hand, are all those phenomena which are ascertainable by observation, or logical
argument based on observation, and which are objectively
verifiable and therefore refutable.   Weber did not regard
value-judgements and moral commitment in the social scientist as unimportant.   But he considered that the social
scientist whould not disguise his value-judgements as
facts, giving them an authority to which they are not en-
titled.   So, while the social scientist may make recommendations about policy, he should distinguish clearly
between the value-judgements that prescribe ends from the
facts that determine means.

Most of those who defend Weber's point of view recognise that it may be very difficult in practice to distinguish between facts and values, but believe that this is
possible in principle.   Nagel (1961), for example, takes
this point of view.   He suggests that while individuals,
or even schools of thought, may err in this respect, the
ultimate protection lies in the openness of debate and the
scrutiny of many eyes.   But this hardly meets the argument of Karl Mannheim (1893-1947).   Mannheim (1936)
examines the concept of ideology as an influence on social
theory.   He concludes that all social theory is developed
out of the social situation of those who expound it and is
influenced by their values.   We have to accept, in Mannheim's view:

> that there are spheres of thought in which it is impos-
> sible to conceive of absolute truth existing indepen-
> dently of the values and position of the subject and
> unrelated to the social context ... for what is intel-
> ligible in history can be formulated only with refer-
> ence to problems and conceptual constructions which
> themselves arise in the flux of historical experience.
> (pp. 70-1)

If this is true, fact and value cannot be distinguished by
bringing to bear on social theories the scrutiny of many
social scientists if they themselves are influenced by a
common situation.

A more radical interpretation of Mannheim's view is
that even the attempt to develop a value-free social science results in an ideological bias in favour of the
status quo.   It will do so because social science can
only study human behaviour as it is at present, constrained

by its existing environment.    But a value-free social
science leaves little room for a critique of that environment (e.g. Galtung, 1977).

Even if one does not accept Mannheim's position, it is
clear that to evaluate theories it is essential to understand the historical and ideological context in which they
have arisen.

First of all one must take into account the general
climate of thought in the period in which the theory
arises.    Thus the nineteenth century was characterised by
a belief in the value of scientific rationalism in the
solution of problems, in contrast to an earlier emphasis
on religious faith and the acceptance of traditional ways.
In industrialising societies, feudal and aristocratic
structures tended to break up to be replaced by political
democracy and a capitalist economy.    There was an emphasis on the individual as the primary unit of society,
whose welfare was its primary objective - an issue discussed further in the next section.    Theories may be positively influenced by the climate of thought, or negatively
influenced by the desire to present a competing view.

Second, theories arise because of concern about specific problems that have become important.    The problems of
industrialisation and urbanisation influenced the direction of economic and sociological theory in the nineteenth
century.    The massive unemployment of the inter-war years
stimulated Keynes to work out his general theory of
employment.

Third, theories are developed as a result of a process
of argument between protagonists of competing paradigms.
Thus the arguments of a theorist can often only be fully
grasped in the context of the case he is opposing.

Finally individuals may be influenced by their own
personal experiences in the phenomena that they choose to
regard as important.    This is perhaps the least important
of the various social influences on the evolution of
social science theories, since its acceptability to
others, and therefore its promulgation, cannot depend on
the validity of this subjective element.

THE COMPLEXITY OF HUMAN BEHAVIOUR

Another problem in the social sciences is that of dealing
with the complexity of human behaviour and the influences
on it, in such a way as to separate out particular causes
and effects.   The wide range of different kinds of behaviour, the lack of obvious regularities of universal application and the large number of different influences from
the physical environment to social custom and individual
inheritance all make it particularly difficult to provide
explanations that are universal, general and precise.
Moreoever, this complexity is compounded by the practical
difficulties of and the ethical objections to controlled
experiments.   Ultimately most empirical work in the
social sciences has to take place outside a laboratory and
in the real world in which the importance of factors that
are not the prime interest of investigators have to be
guessed.   They are constantly in a situation in which the
unexpected is always liable to interfere, and in which the
subjects of study are particularly likely to change their
behaviour just because they are under study.

Weber (1949) saw the most successful solution to this
problem adopted by social scientists as the development of
what he called 'ideal types':

> An ideal type is formed by the *accentuation* of one or
> more points of view and by the synthesis of a great
> many diffuse, discrete, more or less present and occa-
> sionally absent *concrete individual* phenomena which are
> arranged according to those one-sidedly emphasized
> viewpoints into a unified analytical construct. (p. 90,
> original italics)

Weber gives as an example of an ideal type the picture of
the working of the market economy presented by the classical* economists and described in chapter 2 of this book.

There are certain ambiguities in Weber's use of 'ideal
type' (Runciman, 1972) and the term more commonly used
today is 'model'.   A model can be described as a picture
of the real world which is simplified by making assumptions

* In chapter 2 a distinction is made between 'classical'
and 'neo-classical' economists.   In this chapter both
terms are used in appropriate contexts for the benefit of
those who read or re-read this introductory chapter after
chapter 2, but the distinction is not important for understanding the issues discussed here.

about the nature or lack of importance of those factors or
influences which are not the focus of the investigator's
attention.   For example, neo-classical economists make
assumptions about the psychology of consumers and producers which clearly ignore the complexity of human motivation and individual variability although these would
undoubtedly be relevant to the consideration of many if
not all individual transactions.   Equally, they assume
that economic transactions can be analysed without reference to historically developed social relationships.

Such models serve three main purposes.   They provide a
framework for selecting and organising information in a
way that makes it comprehensible.   They also have a
heuristic function by suggesting possible relationships
that may be worth further exploration.   Third, some
models may be sufficiently specific to make it possible to
predict the probably consequences of certain actions or
changes.   For example, the neo-classical economic model
predicts that 'all things being equal' an increase in the
supply of a commodity like wheat, will lead to a fall in
price.   Such predictive models are often called
'theories' and the two terms are sometimes used inter-
changeably.

By the development of models it is often possible to
identify important general influences on human behaviour
in particular types of situation.   But these general
propositions are almost never universal and rarely precise, so they are always readily open to dispute.   Moreover, the validity of the explanations generated by the
models will depend on the extent to which the simplifying
assumptions are appropriate to the purposes that the model
is intended to serve.   This is a major criticism levelled
at many models and theories in the social sciences.   For
example, Maslow (1954) has criticised behaviourist models
of human behaviour on the grounds that they exclude consideration of some of its most significant aspects such as
the intention of an actor in a situation.

At first sight this looks like a purely practical problem that is soluble in principle, even if it is difficult
and will take a long time.   This may be so, but in the
meanwhile the simplifying assumptions built into the
models often have value implications and are strongly
influenced by the values of those who put them forward.
These value assumptions are often disguised by the apparent objectivity of the presentation of the model.   For
example, the simple neo-classical economic model assumes

that consumers are primarily motivated to 'maximise their satisfactions' and producers to 'maximise profits'.   This assumption involves, in our present state of knowledge, a value-judgement about human nature.   The model based on this assumption is then used to predict and ultimately to justify a competitive economic market against other systems of production and distribution.   But it has been argued by Marx among others that the existence of a competitive economic market itself encourages people to conform to the stereotype assumed in the model.   Thus the initial value-judgement about human nature becomes a crucial issue in the evaluation of a theory that is often claimed to be value-free.

It is important to notice that the models themselves in modern social science generally start from an initial disciplinary simplification.   Thus psychologists, economists and sociologists tend to ignore the facts and theories that are the concern of the others.   Disciplinary boundaries have particularly serious implications for social science as a whole because of their rigidity.   The followers of each discipline tend to develop their own professional culture with its own language and its own history of ideas.   In this way the boundaries become barriers, so that disciplines tend to develop in mutual ignorance.   Alternative theories within a discipline tend to result in argument;   thesis begets antithesis and this creates the possibility of synthesis.   But if the theories are in different disciplines potential conflicts and potential contributions will often go unrecognised, so development will be stultified and there will be no possibility of resolving conflicts.

The problem of disciplinary barriers has been less serious in the development of marxist theory than elsewhere in the social sciences.   Marx included in his theoretical work economics, sociology and political science in a single model with a fair measure of consistency. Indeed marxists consider that such disciplinary divisions themselves have ideological implications.   For the belief that economic, political and social processes can be separately studied implicitly supports the independence of the economic system from political control.   It helps to disguise the way economic power is exercised through political and social processes and even that the economic market itself involves the exercise of power.   Marx's theories are radical theories when contrasted with other theories developed in the separate disciplines.   So in the chapters that follow this a constant underlying motif will be the interplay between the perspectives of marxism and of non-marxist disciplines.

In the light of these arguments what can be said about the scientific nature of the social sciences?

As has been indicated, the theories of both Popper and Kuhn present a less idealistic view of the natural sciences than the traditional view;  in that sense they can be used to lessen the distance between the social sciences and the natural sciences.   But neither offers much encouragement to the view that the differences between the two are only matters of degree, unless one is convinced that fact and value are distinguishable in the social sciences.

Kuhn's theory presents a clear analogy between the present position of the social sciences and the pre-paradigmatic period that precedes 'normal science'. There is a similar competition between competing schools offering alternative paradigms, that emphasize particular clusters of phenomena.   Each school gains its strength from a more fundamental ideological perspective, like the metaphysical theories on which scientific schools draw. Thus, by drawing this parallel, Kuhn's theory gives some hope that the social sciences may discover paradigms that are sufficiently convincing to enable 'normal science' to take place.   But would this, in fact, be desirable, if acceptance of a dominant paradigm involved also acceptance of a dominant value system?   In that case the narrowness of 'normal science' might be more than a handicap.   It might be a disaster.   It may be one thing to use the paradigms of Newton and Einstein to guide human beings on a journey to the stars, and quite another to use a social science paradigm to guide the people of a state to a man-designed utopia.

Similarly, Popper's criterion of falsifiability gives some hope of progress towards a better understanding of human behaviour, since even in the pre-paradigmatic state some propositions can be devised which are falsifiable. But if the most important propositions are inextricably linked with issues of value, which are by definition unfalsifiable, progress towards a consensus on the appropriateness of particular paradigms may be limited.

CONCEPTS OF SOCIAL WELFARE

'Social welfare' is a value concept.   It implies a desirable end, the definition of which requires a value-
judgement.   Those who put forward theories about how to
achieve social welfare are, therefore, likely to have
different ideas about what social welfare consists of and
its relationship to individual welfare.   So some arguments that are ostensibly about the means of achieving
social welfare may be complicated by implicit or explicit
disagreements about ends.

There are two broad approaches to the definition of
social welfare.   In the individualist tradition social
welfare is no more than the sum of the welfare of individuals.   In reaction to this, other definitions see
social welfare as in some sense more than or different
from the sum of individual welfare.

The individualistic tradition has its roots in the
eighteenth century 'enlightenment', was dominant in the
nineteenth century and is probably the basis of the most
prevalent attitudes in the Western world today.

The concept of individualism is used with many meanings
which are united by a common emphasis on the importance of
the individual as the fundamental unit of society.   Lukes
(1973) has attempted to separate the many strands of meaning incorporated into the concept of individualism by
different theorists.   He distinguishes four ideals and
six doctrines.

The four ideals are:

the dignity of human beings - individuals' right to
    respect as persons;

autonomy - the right (and responsibility) of individuals
    to make their own decisions;

privacy;

self-development - the right (and responsibility) of
    individuals to develop their own potential.

All these ideals are relevant to the concept of welfare.

The doctrines are more to do with methodological issues
than with values as such, but often have important impli-

cations for the conclusions drawn about the nature of welfare.   Two of the doctrines are of particular importance
for the social sciences as a whole.   First, methodological individualism proposes that no explanation of social
phenomena can be wholly adequate unless it is grounded in
an understanding of individual behaviour.   Second, much
social science theorising makes use of 'the concept of the
abstract individual':   generalised individuals, whose
interests, wants, purposes and needs are given prior to
the social situation within which they are placed.   For
example, much economic theorising is based on the concept
of abstract individuals who are constantly trying to maximise their satisfactions.   Society and the economy set
the scene within which they seek these ends, but are not
seen as taking a part in the formation of these basic
drives.

Lukes argues that the ideals and the doctrines are not
logically dependent on one another - one can believe in
the ideals without having to accept any of the doctrines.
Their connection is historical in that both the ideals and
the doctrines helped in breaking earlier modes of thought
that supported organismic views about institutions such as
the church and the state.

In considering the concept of social welfare in the
individualistic tradition, it is useful to begin with its
place in the work of two philosophers of the eighteenth
and nineteenth centuries - the utilitarian Jeremy Bentham
(1748-1831) and the liberal J.S. Mill (1806-73).

The touchstone of utilitarian philosophy was the fundamental importance of rational action in the achievement of
desirable ends.   Its most enduring and most disturbing
physical manifestation today is in the old British prisons
built in the mid-nineteenth century to Jeremy Bentham's
design.   In these prisons galleries of cells radiating
from a central point enable a single man at that centre to
keep under observation every cell door in the building.

Utilitarians started from the concept of an abstract
individual motivated primarily or even solely by the
search for pleasure and the avoidance of pain.   Individual welfare, therefore, consisted in the 'maximisation of
satisfactions' in these terms.   'Social welfare' was the
sum of individual satisfactions.   Bentham himself talked
of the objective of government as 'the greatest happiness
of the greatest number'.   In his later years, however, he
refined this to 'the greatest happiness', recognising the

danger of interpreting the phrase to justify the exploitation of a minority by a powerful majority (Bhikhu Parekh,
1973, pp. 16-17).

Since satisfactions are by nature subjectively determined, utilitarians generally saw individuals as being the
best judges of their own welfare, and this lead them to
emphasise freedom of choice and individual liberty.  But
individuals were not necessarily regarded as the best
judges of the means to achieve that welfare and the emphasis on rationality could lead to an over-riding belief in
the judgement of the expert.  Hence Jeremy Bentham's in-
humane prisons.  Nevertheless, Bentham and the utilitarians generally greatly distrusted absolute power.  They
believed in representative democracy and the accountability of government to a popular electorate.

If satisfactions are subjective and not readily measurable, any attempt to evaluate changes in social welfare by
calculating changes in individual welfare is very difficult or even impossible.  It is somewhat easier if one
confines one's attention to 'economic' welfare, because
then growth in the economy becomes virtually synonymous
with an increase in social welfare.  However, Bentham
and other utilitarians were prepared to advocate some re-
distribution of wealth on the grounds that the benefits to
the poor who received an addition to their income would be
greater than the loss to the wealthy from whom it was
taken.  However, greater economic equality was not given
much priority.  Bentham, for example, was strongly influenced by his recognition that the loss of rights and
status could be a cause of much pain.  He thought for
this reason that existing rights should be protected and
redistributive taxation limited to death duties.  He also
feared that government action to increase equality would
result in a slower or negative growth in the economy on
which he put a higher weight (Bhikhu Parakh, 1973, pp. 36
and 41).

J.S. Mill began his career as a philosopher as a utilitarian, and indeed may have considered himself such to the
end.  But his contribution changed the whole emphasis of
individualism by his stress on the importance of liberty.
To the utilitarians, liberty was important as a means
towards the maximisation of satisfactions, and as has been
seen they were not averse to making it subject to rationality as a principle.  Mill valued liberty primarily
because of its relationship to the development of individuality, and because of its contribution to social progress.

In considering the question of liberty, Mill started from utilitarian acceptance of representative democracy, but he considered this to be insufficient on its own.   He was afraid of the deadening hand of custom and public opinion in enforcing conformity on people and denying their essential nature.   Indeed, he feared that political democracy might reinforce that deadening hand.   His view of the essential nature of human beings is well expressed in this passage (p. 123):

> He who lets the world, or his own portion of it, choose his plan of life for him has no need of any other faculty than the ape-like one of imitation.   He who chooses his plan for himself employs all his faculties. ... Human nature is not a machine to be built after a model, and set to do exactly the work prescribed for it, but a tree, which requires to grow and develop itself on all sides according to the tendency of the living forces which make it a living thing.

It is from this basis that he states his central position that 'the only purpose for which power can rightfully be exercised over any member of a civilised community, against his will, is to prevent harm to others.   His own good, whether physical or moral, is not a sufficient warrant' (p. 69).

To Mill, the development of one's own faculties, particularly to choose and to plan, will hopefully result in both happiness and pleasure but it is more important than either.

In a rather different way Mill considered that liberty contributes to social progress through freedom of debate. Without such freedom of debate, new ideas could not find expression, and the 'deadening hand of custom' would be reinforced.

Mainstream philosophy, psychology and economics, in so far as they have been concerned with welfare, have all tended to define it in individualistic terms based on or closely related to liberal or utilitarian philosophy.

In philosophy, Mill's propositions on liberty are generally accepted as fundamental (Timms and Watson, 1976, 1978:  Watons, 1980), although room is left for the positive concept of the 'rights' of others as well as the negative concept of avoiding harm to others in justifying limits on individual liberty.   Unsatisfactory aspects of

'the greatest happiness' and 'the maximisation of satisfactions' are corrected but replaced by similarly individualistic concepts.   For example Brandt (1976) develops
the idea of 'rational preference' as the basis of individual welfare.   An individual's welfare is increased if
action taken by himself or others results in a situation
that he prefers to alternative situations that could
result from other actions.   The concept of preference
leaves open the possibility that a person may prefer an
altruistic alternative despite a reduction in his own
personal happiness or satisfaction.   The preference must
be 'rational' in the sense that the choice must be made as
a result of correct knowledge and beliefs, when the subject has all the relevant factors in mind and he is not in
some abnormal state of mind (e.g. anger, depression or
elation).

Psychology, by the nature of its focus of study and the
consequential models that it derives, will tend to be
based on methodological individualism which may incorporate a concept of an abstract individual.   Behaviourists,
for example, in an attempt to achieve objectivity and a
value-free science, assume that the individual responds to
his environment in a utilitarian manner, and in consequence their findings tend to support the utilitarian view
of human nature.   Maslow (1954), on the other hand, has
reacted against the behaviourist view of human beings and
constructed a theory of personality development which
still uses an abstract individual, but a more complex one.
Maslow's theory is that human beings have a hierarchy of
needs.   The satisfaction of lower needs normally results
in the emergence of other needs and, therefore, other
motivations for action.   In simple terms, if human beings
have satisfied their physiological needs - hunger and
thirst for example - they will seek to gratify their need
for safety and security.   These, when satisfied in turn,
are succeeded by the need for love, affection and belong-
ingness, then for self-respect and self-esteem, then knowledge, understanding and aesthetic satisfaction.   At the
point at which the need for love emerges, other individuals become particularly important in personal development, but the final goal is a form of self-actualisation
in which individuals become relatively independent of the
opinions, and to some extent even the actions of others.
Their strength is produced by the earlier satisfaction of
lower needs which makes them clear in their evaluation of
the world about them and firm in their own self-image.
In Maslow's view, each individual starts life with a positive urge towards self-actualisation, which he contrasts

to the passive response to the environment implicit in
behaviourism.   This urge may be stunted by negative
experiences and unfulfilled needs which leave the person
stranded on a lower level of development.

Classical and neo-classical economics are based on a
utilitarian abstract individual (Lukes's doctrine of economic individualism), and welfare is defined in utilitarian terms - the maximisation of satisfactions.   Generally
despairing of the possibility of making comparisons
between the satisfactions of different people, or perhaps
being unwilling to face the radical implications of making
such comparisons, economists place great emphasis on
growth in the economy as a measure of social welfare.
Individual liberty is also highly valued and capitalism is
often defended as a bulwark of liberty as well as an
effective agent of growth.

Most individualistic definitions of social welfare have
something to say about the sort of society which will promote individual welfare.   For example, they tend to
favour constitutional limitations on the exercise of power
and the existence of representative democracy.   However,
they tend to neglect the extent to which cultural and
structural factors in society may determine what gives
happiness or satisfaction to individuals within it.   For
example, a culture which encourages competitive display
will tend to ensure that individual satisfaction is
derived from material goods.   Similarly, if Mill's
liberty requires a competitive economic market to ensure
its continuance as Hayek would maintain (1944), then that
in itself will help to determine how that liberty is used.
Both Bentham and Mill recognised this, but neither could
incorporate the idea into their scale of values.

Critics of individualism often accept the ideals of
individualism, although with qualifications, but reject
some or all of the doctrines.   The most consistent attacks
are on the concept of 'the abstract individual', since it
is considered unrealistic to base any model on the concept
of an individual whose interests, wants, purposes or needs
are independent of the situation into which he or she has
been socialised.   The point has already been made in a
different form in discussing the idea of an objective
social science.   The doctrine or methodological individualism has also been attacked on the grounds that social
institutions cannot be understood solely in terms of the
behaviour of individuals within them.   This alternative
'holistic' view assumes that social institutions are more

than the sum of their parts.   Social structures and
social processes have a constraining influence on individual behaviour which is not wholly dependent on the responses of the individuals concerned and cannot therefore be
wholly explained in terms of such individual behaviour.

Alternative approaches, therefore, see social welfare
as being something different from merely the sum of individual satisfactions expressed through individual choice.
Somehow the nature of the social interaction engendered by
the culture and the structure of society has to be included as an additional element.

These criticisms of individualism are evident throughout the discipline of sociology.   Nisbet (1967) has suggested that sociological traditions can best be understood
as part of a more general reaction against the extreme
individualism of nineteenth-century social thought.   This
reaction took both a conservative and radical form.

In the conservative reaction, society was seen as a
system in which like a biological organism, the parts with
their separate functions all serve to maintain the system
as a whole.   With this view of society, social welfare
becomes synonymous with the smooth running of the system
and its successful adaptation to changes in its environment.   Individuals must be enabled to play an effective
part in the system.   Effectiveness usually demands willingness, since compulsory labour is often inefficiently
performed, and willingness requires a broad consensus on
values.   On the whole the functionalist theories that
adopt this paradigm (see chapter 5) have little to say
about individual welfare as such except that it is seen as
subservient to the needs of society as a whole, that it
depends on a sense of integration into society and that
the nature of individual welfare must depend on the broad
consensus on values within the society.   If competition
and inequality are accepted within that consensus, then
they are acceptable within the system, provided that they
take place within agreed rules that limit their potentially
negative effects.   It is in this acceptance of current
values and current structure that the conservatism of functionalist theories lies

The radical reaction to individualism saw conflicts of
interest built into the structure of most societies and
looked towards a more positive ideal of a co-operative
society.   The conflicts of interest were seen as coming
primarily from inequalities of economic power which were

reflected in and supported by political power and an
appropriate ideology.   Thus economic equality is seen as
being of supreme importance in the determination of social
welfare.   Liberty is seen as too limited a concept if the
individuals lack the economic and political means to
influence and control their own environment.   Even the
accountability of representative democracy becomes inadequate unless individuals are able to influence decisions
actively.   Thus individual welfare is seen in terms of
the development of individual potential in a context of
social co-operation and an egalitarian social structure.

Finally, perhaps one should mention the newer environmentalist view which sees social and individual welfare as
being bound up with the relationship between human beings
and their natural environment.   The recent prominence of
this view has come about because of a new awareness of the
ease with which the ecological balance of the world can be
and is being permanently upset.   In particular, there has
been a recognition of natural limits to industrial growth.
Environmentalists lay emphasis on longer-term intergenerational aspects of social welfare, which are completely
neglected in individualist definitions.   Indeed this
approach to welfare finds little place in any current
social science theories although economists have paid some
attention to the problem.

To sum up, there are two broad ways of defining social
welfare.   The first, based on methodological individualism, sees social welfare as being no more than the sum of
individual welfare.   The second proposes that social welfare has to take into account that the individual always
exists in a social context that influences his view of
welfare as well as the means by which he pursues it.   So
the evaluation of social welfare requires an evaluation of
the social context as well as adding up individual satisfactions.

Within each of these broad definitions certain values
may be differently stressed, such as personal satisfaction
or self-development;   competition or co-operation;   political or economic democracy;   stability or change;
liberty, equality or economic growth.

## THE POSITION TAKEN BY THE AUTHORS

These philosophical and methodological issues have been
very briefly presented, at the risk of oversimplification,

partly to encourage further reading which will be discussed at the end of this chapter, and partly to set the background for the position taken by the authors in this book.

First of all we see no need here to come to a conclusion about whether a value-free social science may ultimately be possible, although we doubt that possibility. However, we are convinced that none of the theories discussed in this book can be regarded as value-free. Value-judgements are implicitly or explicitly incorporated into the assumptions on which they are based, in the selection of the phenomena that are regarded as important, and in judgements about the balance of evidence in favour of one theory or another.   All this is consistent with a view that the social sciences can be regarded as being in a pre-paradigmatic state.   Taking this view, we have tried to be as explicit as possible both about the social context in which theories have arisen, and about the assumptions of fact and value that underlie them.

Second, we have taken the view that while none of the theories presented can explain all the phenomena within their purview, each can explain some phenomena more convincingly than other competing theories.   Each theory provides a different perspective on some of the same phenomena and needs to be taken into account even if ultimately it is regarded as having validity in a very limited area.   In this sense, each theory must be taken seriously and cannot be dismissed purely on ideological grounds.

Third, our assessment of the theories will be influenced by our own values and particularly our views about the nature of welfare.   Broadly, we would accept a definition of welfare that is consistent with the radical reaction to individualism.   In our view this incorporates beneficial elements of the individualistic tradition, particularly the individualist ideals.   But it also transcends individualism by its emphasis on the extension of liberty and political accountability to freedom to participate in the control of the wider environment including economic processes, with an emphasis on co-operation and economic equality over competition and growth.

FURTHER READING

In following up this chapter the student has to decide whether to go to the originals or to read about them.

If he goes to the originals, they are often tough reading - though not always - and he may have a good deal of difficulty in deciding how to select the passages that are relevant to a particular issue, and how much credence to give to what they say.  On the other hand, he may be saved from an oversimplified and even misleading summary of their views - a criticism that may be applied to this text.  A useful compromise may be a selection of readings with comments such as that of Brodbeck (1968).

If the student decides to read about the authors and their views, he has a choice between general texts, such as Pratt (1978) and Lessnoff (1974), or books about particular authors like Magee (1973) on Popper or Ten (1980) on Mill.  The latter will help to put a particular work within the context of the author's total output, but they are frequently written by admirers who may make light of other people's criticisms.  The former set out the wider arguments, and therefore give a wider perspective.  To help students I have marked books in the bibliography that I found particularly useful or interesting with one asterisk, and with two asterisks those that I thought were relatively easy to read.  Pratt and Lessnoff have only one asterisk because, although they were recommended to me for general reading, I cannot claim to have done more than look through them fairly quickly.

BIBLIOGRAPHY

* Brandt, R.B. (1976), The Concept of Welfare, in Timms and Watson (1976).
* Brodbeck, M. (ed.) (1968), 'Readings in the Philosophy of the Social Sciences', New York, Macmillan.
* Galtung, J. (1977), 'Methodology and Ideology: Theories and Methods of Social Research Vol. 1', Copenhagen, Christian Ejlers, Basic Social Science Monographs from the Institute of Peace Research, Oslo.
Hayek, F.A. (1944), 'The Road to Serfdom', London, Routledge & Kegan Paul.
** Kuhn, T.S. (1962), 'The Structure of Scientific Revolutions', Chicago University Press.
* Lessnoff, M. (1974), 'The Structure of Social Science: Philosophical Introduction', London, Allen & Unwin.

** Lukes, S. (1973), 'Individualism', Oxford, Blackwell.
** Magee, B. (1973), 'Popper', Glasgow, Fontana.
Mannheim, K. (1936), 'Ideology and Utopia: an introduction
    to the sociology of knowledge', London, Routledge &
    Kegan Paul.
Maslow, A.H. (1954), 'Motivation and Personality', New
    York, Harper & Row, 2nd edn, 1970.
** Mill, J.S. (1859), 'On Liberty', quotations from
    Penguin edn, Harmondsworth, 1974.
Nagel, E. (1961), 'The Structure of Science', New York,
    Harcourt, Brace & World and London, Routledge & Kegan
    Paul.   Extracts reproduced in Brodbeck (1968) to which
    page numbers refer.
* Nisbet, R.H. (1967 and 1970), 'The Sociological Tradi-
    tion', London, Heinemann.
Parekh, B. (ed.) (1973), 'Bentham's Political Thought',
    London, Croom Helm.
** Popper, K.R. (1959), 'The Logic of Scientific Dis-
    covery', London, Hutchinson.   First published in
    Vienna in 1934.
* Pratt, V. (1978), 'The Philosophy of the Social Scien-
    ces', London, Methven.
** Runciman, W.G. (1972), 'Critique of Max Weber's Philos-
    ophy of Social Science', Cambridge University Press.
Simmonds, A.P. (1978), 'Karl Mannheim's Sociology of Know-
    ledge', Oxford University Press.
** Ten, C.L. (1980), 'Mill on Liberty', Oxford, Clarendon
    Press.
Timms, N., and Watson, D. (eds) (1976), 'Talking about
    Welfare', London, Routledge & Kegan Paul.
Timms, N., and Watson, D. (eds) (1978), 'Philosophy in
    Social Work', London, Routledge & Kegan Paul.
Watson, D. (1980), 'Caring for Strangers: an introduction
    to practical philosophy for students of social admin-
    istration', London, Routledge & Kegan Paul.
Weber, M. (1947), 'The Theory of Social and Economic
    Organisation', New York, Oxford University Press.
    Extracts reproduced in Brodbeck (1968) to which all
    page numbers refer.
Weber, M. (1949), 'The Methodology of the Social Sciences',
    New York, The Free Press.

# Neo-classical and micro-economic theory

## Anthony Forder

Economics is the social science that has concentrated on
the study of the processes of exchange, and more particularly those exchanges that are mediated by money.    In
other words, in societies in which there is a complex
specialisation of labour in the production and distribution of goods and services, economics looks at how these
processes are organised and how they work.    Macro-
economics is concerned with large-scale economic phenomena
that apply at national and supra-national level, for
example general recessions and expansions of economic
activity.    Micro-economics is concerned with the processes
of exchange between individuals and organisations.

The dominant influence on Western economic thought for
the last two hundred years has come from the so-called
classical and neo-classical theorists.    Classical economics can be conveniently considered as developing from the
work of Adam Smith (1723-93), and particularly from 'An
Inquiry into the Nature and Causes of the Wealth of
Nations' published in 1776.    Of course, many of Adam
Smith's ideas were derived from the work of other writers
and the classical school which followed him criticised as
well as refining his ideas.    This school also made use of
theories developed by Adam Smith's contemporaries and predecessors.    The most important theorists of the classical
school were Malthus (1766-1834), Ricardo (1772-1823) and
Say (1767-1832).    In the last half of the nineteenth century several theorists more or less simultaneously developed some new concepts and analytical tools which provided
the basis for neo-classical economic theory.    The names
associated with this are Jevons (1835-82), Menger (1840-
1920), Walras (1834-1910), Pareto (1847-1930) and Alfred
Marshall (1840-1920).

Because classical and neo-classical theories are so
widely accepted that they are treated in most textbooks
as received dogma, it is difficult to realise the extent
to which 'The Wealth of Nations' propounded doctrines
which in its day were revolutionary.   'The Wealth of
Nations' was written as a counter-thesis to the prevailing
mercantilist theories, which were primarily concerned with
economic policy as a means of promoting national strength.
In this context state regulation of the economy was regarded as essential.   Adam Smith proposed that national
prosperity, and therefore national power, would be better
served if the government ceased to try to regulate individual economic endeavour.   In this respect 'The Wealth
of Nations' can be seen as part of a much wider movement
questioning established patterns of belief and traditional
views about the social order.   The movement as a whole
was both cause and effect of a major shift of power from a
landed aristocracy to the bourgeoisie which was a crucial
phase in the development of capitalism.   The particular
contribution of 'The Wealth of Nations' was the provision
of a rationale for separating economic decisions from the
province of politics and morality.   For it attempted to
show how the removal of the restraints of centralised control and moral exhortation would enable a natural harmony
to assert itself, producing order combined with liberty in
a situation of economic competition.   However, Adam Smith
and the classical economists were still interested in considering the role of government in certain economic
matters, giving approval, for instance, to the provision
of public education, public health measures and the regulation of conditions in factories.   They described their
discipline as 'political economy'.

Their successors in the neo-classical school were primarily interested in an analysis of the operation of the
economic market.   They were concerned with the process of
distribution through the market rather than with ensuring
economic growth, which they tended to assume.   In consequence they have very little to say about the role of government in the economy except in those situations in which
the market economy manifestly fails.   'Political economy'
had become 'economics'.

The association of classical and neo-classical theory
with capitalism is fundamental to its understanding,
although the theory has relevance to other systems.
Capitalism is here regarded as meaning an economic system
based on the private ownership of the means of production.
Adam Smith was in the first place trying to explain the

existence of order in economic relationships in a system
that lacked a centralised decision-making process.    Such
an explanation was not needed until capitalism had out-
grown its dependence on state control.    Thereafter he
advocated the extension of that decentralisation in a way
that would free capitalism further for independent development.    From that time onwards the mainstream of Western
economic thought has continued to be produced largely from
the study of capitalist economies and therefore is likely
to have greater relevance to such economies.    It has been
influenced by and has in turn influenced the values and
beliefs of such societies and to some extent it has provided a justification for those values, or has been used for
that purpose.


BASIC VALUE ASSUMPTIONS

Neo-classical economic theory is firmly based on the
values of individualism.    This can be seen both in the
assumptions made to provide a simplified model of human
behaviour for the purposes of developing theory and in the
prescriptions for policy that are seen to flow from the
theory.

In order to simplify the model of human behaviour, it
is assumed that people are primarily motivated by the aim
of maximising their satisfactions through seeking pleasure
and avoiding pain.    In doing this they calculate the
advantages of different courses of action in a rational
manner, learning from their experience.    Individuals are
regarded as the best judges of their own welfare.    In
making decisions concerning their welfare, the influence
of purely social factors, such as competition for social
status, are seen as relatively unimportant.

Social welfare is defined as the sum of individual
satisfactions.    Therefore social welfare is increased if
any person is made better off by any transaction without
making any other person worse off.    The condition in
which no transactions can take place without making at
least one person worse off is called 'the Pareto optimum',
after its first formulator, and represents the ideal
objective for neo-classical micro-economics.    As will be
seen, such an optimum takes no account of inequalities in
the distribution of income and wealth.

In prescribing policy, neo-classical theory lays great
emphasis on the importance of individal liberty, in the

sense that people should be given as much freedom as possible to make their own decisions subject only to the condition that they do not harm or infringe the liberty of
others.   This is closely related to the belief that individuals are the best judges of their own welfare and both
views lead to advocating that the government intervenes as
little as possible with economic activity.   An additional
justification for a laisser-faire economic policy is the
view that if people are to learn to act responsibly and to
make 'correct' decisions, they should not be rescued from
the consequences of their own mistakes.   The rewards for
making 'correct' decisions and the punishments for making
'incorrect' decisions should be consistent and unambigu-
ous.

Finally, it should be recognised that neo-classical
economic theory is essentially materialistic in its emphasis.   It does not deny the validity of non-materialistic
values or the importance of people taking into account
non-material satisfactions in their decision-making.   But
by concentrating on economic behaviour, the theories focus
attention on what can be measured and expressed in terms
of money.   The emphasis on the importance of economic
growth is one example of this.   It is not essential to
the theory, but is implicit in much that is written in
support of the theory.

BASIC ELEMENTS OF MICRO-ECONOMIC THEORY

(A)   Supply, demand and the price mechanism

Perhaps the most difficult task in any complex economy is
to co-ordinate satisfactorily the production and distribution of goods and services (commodities) to meet individual requirements without excessive waste.   Neo-classical
economic theory proposes that this can be achieved most
effectively through competition in a free economic market.
The market should be free in the sense that people should
be allowed to buy and sell at whatever price they wish.

The first step in the argument is the hypothesis that
in such a free market economy the quantity of goods which
people will be willing to produce - 'supply' - and the
quantity of goods which people will be willing to buy -
'demand' - will be brought into equilibrium by means of
variations in price.   If at a given price more of a commodity is produced than people are prepared to buy, the
price will tend to fall.   At the lower price more people

will want to purchase the commodity, while some producers
will find production unprofitable.   So consumption will
rise and production will fall.   Similarly, if at a given
price less is produced than people are prepared to buy,
the price will tend to rise, discouraging some consumers
and encouraging increased production.   The price will
continue to vary until supply and demand are equal and the
market is in equilibrium.

This process is seen as being most effective in a situation in which there are many sellers and many buyers, so
that no single seller or buyer so dominates the market
that his decision will be crucial to the determination of
price.   Where competition is restricted among sellers
through monopoly or oligopoly, production will be restricted and the price will be higher than where there is perfect competition, but price will still perform the same
co-ordinating function between supply and demand.

---

*Example*

Let us assume that the demand for butter shows the following response to changes in price:

At an average price of 200p per 1lb 100 thousand tons
is demanded per week.

At an average price of 150p per 1lb 120 thousand tons
is demanded per week.

At an average price of 100p per 1lb 200 thousand tons
is demanded per week

At an average price of  50p per 1lb 400 thousand tons
is demanded per week.

This is shown graphically in Figure 2.1(a), where line D
is the 'demand curve'.

In Figure 2.1(b) is shown the assumed response of the
supply of butter to changes in the price.   Here, the
higher the price the more butter is offered for sale.   In
the short run this will be because the offer of a higher
price for butter will encourage producers to transfer milk
from other uses which were previously seen as more profitable.   In the longer run more milk will be produced by
such measures as improved feeding, increasing the size of
herds, and the movement of resources from other agricultural products to milk production.

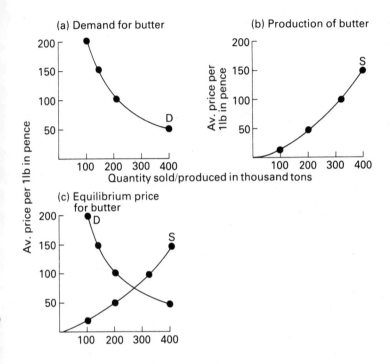

FIGURE 2.1    Supply and demand

In Figure 2.1(c) these two graphs are combined and it can be seen that supply and demand would tend to reach equilibrium and the market cleared at a price of 75p and a production of 250 thousand tons.    If price was less than this, an excess of demand for butter would tend to result in a rise in price, which would encourage greater production, until the equilibrium point was reached.    If the price was higher than 75p, stocks would mount as butter was unsold since at that price more than 250 thousand tons would be offered for sale.    Prices would have to be dropped to enable stocks to be cleared.

Two points need to be noted about the presentation in the example.    First, the curves are intended to show the position at a particular time.    Supply conditions and the preferences represented by demand curves will change over time.    Second, the position of the supply and demand

curves for any particular commodity are affected by
changes in the supply, demand and prices of other commodities.   The result is that in an economy as a whole the
process of adjustment is very complex, involving the integration of many factors which cannot be integrated in such
simple diagrams.

This familiar view of the role of the economic market
can perhaps best be illustrated by the effects of government attempts to control prices.   Governments may try to
keep prices lower than the equilibrium level in the interests of consumers, and more particularly poor consumers.
Having blocked the market processes for rationing by
price, either the government must introduce a formal procedure for rationing the commodities concerned, or informal methods of rationing will develop through, for example,
queueing, limiting the amount sold to a single customer or
restricting supplies to favoured customers.   In either
case a 'black market' is likely to develop, some demand
being met at the controlled price and some at prices much
higher than the equilibrium price.   Alternatively, governments may try to keep prices about the equilibrium
level in the interests of producers.   This results in the
production of a surplus which has to be stored.   Ultimately the surplus must either be destroyed or sold at
much lower prices in a separate market which can be isolated from the market which is being controlled.   An
example is the effect of the EEC's Common Agricultural
Policy (CAP), which is designed to maintain the income of
farmers.   Butter, beef and other 'mountains' of unsold
produce have been sold to poor people in European countries
at special prices, or exported at similar prices to developing or communist countries.


(B)  Marginal analysis and the Pareto optimum

The theory of supply and demand accounts for the existence
of order in a market economy and can be empirically tested
by an examination of actual behaviour.   Examples of this
can be found in many textbooks.   Moreover, logical and
empirical analysis can show how various forms of intervention with the freedom of the market through, for example,
the development of monopoly, the imposition of taxes and
the control of prices can reduce the total benefits to
consumers.   It cannot, however, answer the normative
question whether the allocation of resources produced by a
free economic market will be the most efficient possible.
This question is of considerable importance for decisions

about whether governments should intervene in the economic market.

First of all, as has been indicated earlier, neo-classical theorists take as their criterion of efficiency the Pareto optimum.   This is a situation in which no change in the methods and quantities of the commodities produced (given existing technology) or in their distribu-tion can take place without making at least one person worse off.

In order to show that a free market economy will tend to result in production and distribution approximating to the Pareto optimum, neo-classical theorists use 'marginal analysis'.   This can best be understood by taking an example, in this case from the field of consumption.

The reader will be familiar with the idea that the more a consumer has of any particular commodity, the less value he will attach to additional quantities of it.   The last additional unit of a commodity that a consumer buys, say the last half pound of butter in that week, is known as his 'marginal' purchase.   The value to him of that unit is its 'marginal utility'.   A consumer who wishes to max-imise his satisfaction from purchases of a particular com-modity will go on buying it until the marginal utility of his purchases is equal to the price that he pays for it. This can be seen in the example on p. 34.

For a person with a given income, the marginal utility of a commodity is itself determined by the alternatives that he will miss as a result of buying this particular commodity.   The butter purchaser, for example, is weigh-ing his purchases of butter against the value to him of a range of other foods and other ways of spending his money. The values of these alternatives are known as the opportu-nity costs of this particular purchase.   In choosing between different alternatives, the consumer who is trying to maximise his satisfactions will try to ensure that the marginal utility of all the commodities that he buys is equal.   If it is not, he can improve his satisfaction by transferring his expenditure from commodities with a lower marginal utility to those with a higher.   If all consum-ers proceed in this way a situation will be reached in which, when supply and demand are in equilibrium, the mar-ginal utility for all commodities for all consumers will be equal to the prices paid.   This is an ideal situation, in the sense that no further exchanges can take place between consumers without making at least one of them

*Example*

In Figure 2.2 the line ABC represents the marginal utility
curve of a particular consumer for a product.   The line
OPQ is the market price.   The consumer will purchase the
quantity Y, at which point the marginal utility of the
product will be equal to the price.   At this point his
expenditure is represented by the rectangle OPY, but the
value of his purchases will exceed his expenditure by the
value to him represented by the shaded area AOP.   If he
buys less than Y, say the amount X, he will miss gaining
the excess value in the triangle BRP.   If he purchases
more than Y, say the quantity Z, the loss represented by
the shaded area PQC would have to be deducted from the
gain shown in AOP.   Thus purchasing the quantity Y, where
marginal utility equals price, will ensure that he makes
the greatest gain in utility from his purchases.   It
should be noted that a marginal utility curve can be
derived directly from a demand curve, and the two will
coincide.

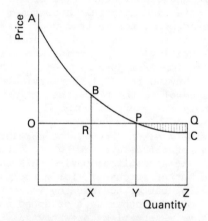

FIGURE 2.2   Marginal utility and price

worse off.   This is one of the conditions for achieving
the Pareto optimum.

It is the contention of neo-classical theory that the
Pareto optimum will be achieved if three conditions are
met:

1   The first condition, as above, is that consumers
maximise their satisfactions by using their income in such
a way that the marginal utility of all commodities pur-
chased is equal to the ratio of their prices.   This is
known as the consumer condition.

2   The second condition is that producers maximise t
their profits by ensuring that the cost of producing the
last unit of the product ('the marginal cost of production'), is equal to the price received for it ('the marginal revenue').   The arguments for this condition are
similar to those that justify the consumer condition.

3   The third condition is that producers maximise their
profits by ensuring that the marginal product of all the
different factors that enter into production - that is,
all the different kinds of land, labour and capital - are
also equal.   For on the same sort of reasoning as before,
it can be shown that if these marginal products are not of
equal value, then it would pay the producer to substitute
one factor with greater marginal productivity for another
with less.   For example he would replace 'expensive'
labour with a new and more 'efficient' machine, or make
more intensive use of land by employing more labour or
more capital on it (e.g. more agricultural machinery or
higher buildings).   These last two conditions are known
as the production conditions.

In this way marginal analysis can show logically how a
free economic market, under certain conditions such as the
existence of perfect competition, consumers successfully
maximising satisfactions and producers successfully maximising profits, will ensure that the Pareto optimum is
achieved.

It should be noted that this analysis explicitly justifies the payment of rent for land, and of profits for
capital as a means of achieving the Pareto optimum.   Thus
a competitive economic market ensures that the opportunity
costs of all the factors of production, land, labour and
capital, are taken into account in determining the distribution of resources in the production of goods.

Criticisms of neo-classical theory have focused first
of all on whether the Pareto optimum is an adequate criterion of efficiency and secondly on whether the model is
a sufficiently accurate picture of modern capitalism to
provide guidance for government policy.   However, before
going on to present these different criticisms of the
theory, it is necessary to discuss certain areas where
neo-classical theorists recognise that provision under a
free competitive economic market cannot achieve a Pareto
optimum.

(C)   Market failure in neo-classical theory

There are certain areas of economic activity where neo-
classical theorists recognise that a free economic market
will not or cannot achieve a Pareto optimum.   One of
these areas is created by the problem of 'externalities'.
A second is the range of commodities described as 'public
goods'.   Third, there are certain commodities described
as 'natural monopolies'.   Finally, there is a whole range
of goods and services about which there is dispute on
whether they come within these categories or not.   Each
of these areas will be discussed in turn.

   'Externalities' are costs and benefits that fall on
someone else other than the person making the decision.
Externalities inevitably tend to occur where there is
delegation of decision-making in the use of resources as
there is in a free economic market.   Examples are the
cost of the pollution of waterways and atmosphere by industrial and domestic processes;   the cost to all users of
transport from delays and inconvenience as more vehicles
are put on the roads;   or the benefits to neighbouring
areas that result from the improvement of a particular
district.   To achieve the Pareto optimum these costs and
benefits should be taken into account in decision-making.
But they will not be included by a consumer maximising
his individual satisfactions or a producer maximising
profits.

   'Public goods' have particular characteristics which
make them unsuitable for provision through the economic
market.   An example is street lighting.   Street lighting
provides benefits for everyone who uses a street and it is
not possible to confine the benefits to those who are
willing to pay for them.   It is not divisible into units
for purchase and sale.   At the same time, the fact that
one person enjoys the benefit of the lighting in no way
lessens the benefits of other people (the marginal cost of
an additional consumer is nil).   These three characteristics - non-excludability, non-divisibility and non-rivalry
- when combined make it almost impossible to make adequate
provision through the economic market.   Other examples
are national defence, police and fire services, sewage disposal and the provision of roads and bridges.   However, it
should be noted that the last three, although generally
recognised as public goods, are not wholly 'non-excludable'.
It is possible to charge a toll to users, but such a toll
could not cover capital costs without being far higher
than is required to meet marginal costs which are very low.

So a private investor would not build sewage systems, roads and bridges unless he could charge a toll that was too high for the Pareto optimum to be achieved.

At this point one is getting very close to what are known as 'natural monopolies'. An example of a natural monopoly is water supply. Here a single system of pipes involving large-scale capital outlay can supply a whole district, and it is wasteful to have competition through the provision of two parallel systems. Other recognised natural monopolies are public utilities like gas and electricity supply, the telephone system, and railways. If these are not provided by government, it is recognised that there must be careful regulation by government of the terms under which the monopoly is granted.

The validity of the neo-classical case for severely limiting government activity in the provision of goods and services, in so far as it depends on arguments about economic efficiency, requires that these areas of market failure are of relatively minor significance. But it can be argued that this is not so. Some economists have made the case for state intervention with regard to particular services. Adam Smith himself, for example, argued for state provision of education. True (1979 but see also Mayes 1980) has argued for government intervention in housing on the grounds that where housing is poor there are major externalities from health and other social costs. In some ways this understates the problem. Whole industries have been made profitable by ignoring the externalities created by irregular employment - for example the British docks based on casual labour up to the end of the Second World War, and the fluctuating building industry today. Similarly, decisions to close factories and other production units create major external costs. This is particularly true where a community depends on a single industry. Since the war the National Coal Board has phased the closing of pits to take this into account in a way that would not be possible if coal mines were operating as individual units in a competitive market economy.

CRITICISMS OF THE PARETO OPTIMUM AND MARGINAL THEORY

The Pareto optimum as a norm

It is not difficult to accept the Pareto optimum as a necessary condition for the maximisation of social welfare. For clearly any position short of that optimum must be capable of improvement in that someone can be made better off without making anyone else worse off.   However, it is clearly not a sufficient condition for satisfactions to be maximised.   There are two main reasons for this.

First the Pareto optimum says nothing about the numerous possible changes that make some people worse off and others better off.   One certainly cannot rule out the possibility that if one could weigh the advantages gained against the advantages lost some of these changes would increase the total of satisfaction.   Second, it can be shown logically that there is a different Pareto optimum for every different distribution of income.   Both these limitations imply the need to make comparisons between the satisfactions enjoyed by different people.

Pigou, in his classic analysis of 'The Economics of Welfare' (1920) faced these issues when he proposed that any change in the distribution of resources that increased the proportion of the national product received by the poor without reducing the national product would increase economic welfare.   He based this proposition on the assumption that the marginal utility of income must be less for the rich than for the poor.   But he also considered that a higher proportion of the satisfaction derived by the rich from their marginal income came from a comparison of their position with that of other rich people so that if all were diminished the lost satisfaction would be minimal.

Other economists (e.g. Bergson, 1966) have denied the validity of Pigou's assumptions and taken the view that the comparison of satisfactions between different people is impossible.   They therefore suggest that if the division of incomes is given by some other, non-economic process, the Pareto optimum will give the most efficient allocation of resources.   Unfortunately, it is impossible to divorce decisions about production from decisions about the distribution of income, least of all in a free market economy.   For in such a market every person's income is determined by the same processes that determine what is produced.   So if cash transfers are used as a means of adjustment, as has been proposed, they have to be continuously adjusted as changes in production and distribution occur.   Such a process would make nonsense of the whole model.

Finally some economists have proposed that one can extend the model to deal with exchanges that make some

people better off and others worse off, by imagining a
system of monetary compensation for loss.   If a particular change makes A better off and B worse off, and if
there is a sum of money that B would accept as compensation for his loss that would still leave a surplus to
benefit A, then the change would increase total satisfactions.   Kaldor (1939), who first put this forward, quoted
the example of the repeal of the Corn Laws, which made
bread cheaper for consumers but reduced the incomes of
landowners.   If landowners could be compensated for the
loss of income by a tax on consumers which was less than
the reduction in the price of bread, then landowners would
be no worse off, and consumers better off than before.
It is difficult to visualise how such payments could be
arranged in practice, so some economists have suggested
that the compensation need not actually be paid.   However, one of the main points about the economic market as
a means of achieving the Pareto optimum is that people are
making real decisions about gains and losses that they
actually experience.   The calculation of a theoretically
appropriate compensation places economic decisions into
the political field.

The relevance of the neo-classical model to modern
capitalism

Neo-classical micro-economic theory purports to justify
the use of the economic market as the primary means for
regulating production and the distribution of resources on
the grounds that it will maximise efficiency.   It can
only be said to do so if the simplifying assumptions of
the model are not too greatly divorced from the real world
of modern capitalism.   Comment has already been made on
the dispute about the extent and importance of externalities in the economic system and the range of commodities
that should be treated as public goods.   This section is
primarily concerned with the reality of the free economic
market.   Something will be said about consumer attitudes,
but the main focus will be on criticisms that relate to
the increase in the power of those who control production.

   The consumption condition for achieving the Pareto
optimum through the economic market depends in particular
on two assumptions being valid:   that consumers are the
best judges of their own welfare and that they make their
decisions independently of purely social factors like
fashion and rivalry.

The first assumption is an attractive one because it demonstrates respect for ourselves and for others as responsible and capable people.    It also contains a large measure of truth in that there is a very wide range of commodities in which the personal preferences of the people concerned are the most crucial factors in achieving satisfaction.    But many decisions require technical knowledge or foresight which is beyond the capacity of individual consumers and often beyond their means to obtain from others.    Moreover, the competitive economic market in which profit is the main goal of producers encourages the provision of inaccurate, or at least biased information.

The influence of social factors on consumer choice is a very obvious phenomenon.    The significance of this factor for the neo-classical model is that fashion, rivalry and conspicuous consumption generally may divert production into channels that make a minimal contribution to total welfare.    For example, a large part of the satisfaction to the individual of his conspicuous consumption may lie in the dissatisfactions of those whose displays are inferior.    If this is so, then the dissatisfactions of the losers must at least partially cancel out the satisfactions of the winners in the competition for display. Moreover, an almost equal satisfaction might be gained if the expenditure of all the rivals was proportionally reduced.    This point was made by Pigou (1920) in justifying an assumption that the marginal utility of expenditure by the rich was lower than that of expenditure by the poor.    Such social factors are particularly open to commercial exploitation in a free economic market.

It is in the assumptions about perfect competition that the neo-classical model is most open to criticism.    A particularly noticeable feature of modern capitalist economies is a tendency for the concentration of production in the hands of a relatively small number of very large firms. For example, Hardie (1979) points out that 'the share of the hundred largest firms in the net output in the UK manufacturing sector ... has gone up from 16 per cent in 1909 to 27 per cent in the early 1950s, and perhaps around 40 per cent now'.    There are a number of possible explanations for this phenomenon.

First, modern technology often results in important economies with increased scale of production.    In the extreme case there may be a constant fall in marginal costs with increasing scale until the whole demand for a

product can most efficiently be met by a single producer.
Natural monopolies are a special case of this situation.
Where this is true, a free market will not achieve the
Pareto optimum, because a monopolist seeking to maximise
his profits will charge a price higher than the marginal
cost of production.

A second reason for the pursuit of size is advanced by
Galbraith (1967).   He holds that in the modern corpora-
tion effective decision-making is in the hands of a
managerial elite.   The primary concern of this elite is
not so much with the maximisation of profits (although
they do have to pay attention to this), but with the maximisation of their personal income.   Managerial income at
the highest levels is more closely related to the size of
the organisation than to the level of its profits.   So
there is constant pressure from managers to enlarge firms
even when this does not result in greater efficiency in
terms of achieving the Pareto optimum.   The validity of
this argument depends on the extent to which judgments of
the success of managers and therefore their security of
employment are based on the rates of profit they achieve.

A third reason for the domination of the market by
large firms may be the pursuit of security.   One of the
difficulties of operating in a competitive market economy
is that constant adaptation is required to a constantly
changing environment.   Failure to adapt is penalised by
loss and perhaps bankruptcy.   Larger firms may be able to
avoid some of the penalties.   Some forms of growth may
enable firms to survive better by increasing their range
of products (horizontal integration) so that decline in
the face of competition in one market may be compensated
by advance in another.   Other forms of growth may enable
a firm to control its environment better by extending its
control over its suppliers and its outlets to consumers
(vertical integration).

Fourth, the costs of innovation and the uncertainties
relating to it are now often so high that only a large and
powerful firm can engage in the process.   An example is
the modern electronics industry in which the setting up of
the manufacture of microchips is very expensive and also
very risky because of the rate of technological change.
A further result of the high costs of initial investment
is that conventional marginal analysis, which is based on
the assumption of relatively smooth supply curves,
becomes largely irrelevant.

It is at this point that a further limitation of the neo-classical model becomes evident.   It is a static rather than a dynamic model in that it ignores problems of time and uncertainty.   First, it assumes relatively rapid and efficient transmission of knowledge and adaptations to change, whereas it is clear that in practice the movement towards equilibrium is often relatively slow and complicated by further independent or consequential changes.   So equilibrium and the Pareto optimum can never be achieved.   Second, the model sees the entrepreneur making the decision that equates marginal cost and marginal revenue at a particular point in time.   But in practice he has to base his decisions on predictions about the future, at least over the short-term and ideally over some longer period.   Achieving the Pareto optimum depends on entrepreneurs making the right forecasts.   The neo-classical economists assume that in these circumstances numerous decision-makers making small marginal decisions are less likely than a 'monolithic' state to make large and wasteful errors.   But this is not necessarily so.   A large number of investors may be over-influenced by an optimistic or pessimistic climate of opinion to produce waste, as witness the railway booms of the nineteenth century and the inter-war depressions.

All these arguments can be used to justify state intervention in the economic market - to limit or control monopolies, to smooth the processes of change and to reduce uncertainty through planning.   The main defence of the neo-classical economists lies in the argument that any state system will tend to perform less well than a free economic market.   For example, there is no system of voting that will ensure that the money spent on any particular good actually maximises satisfactions even in public goods that contribute to the welfare of everyone (Culyer, 1973, pp. 33-6).   Once one gets a situation in which the main gains go to one group and the main costs are paid by another, the tendency to respond to political pressure rather than to an estimate of costs and benefits seems almost insuperable.   At least in the economic market the inequalities in the distribution of power are open to inspection.   In the political system it is impossible to know what pressures are being applied.

The marxist critique

The most radical criticism of the neo-classical paradigm has come from marxists using Marx's critique of classical economic theory.

Marx followed the classical economist Ricardo in
accepting what was called the labour theory of value, and
developed it further.   In this theory the value of commodities is originally determined by their use - 'use-
value'.   But once people begin to produce commodities for
barter, then their 'exchange-value' becomes fundamental.
The exchange-value of commodities is determined by the
value of the labour power involved in their production -
or, more precisely, if one takes account of differences in
the efficiency of labour, the 'socially necessary' labour
power.   This labour power may be applied either directly
in current labour, or indirectly through its incorporation
in machinery and other capital goods or learnt skills.
In essence, one might say that the exchange-value of a
commodity is determined by the opportunity costs of the
labour power employed in its production.

The exchange-value of a commodity is not the same as
its monetary price, but the theory states that there will
be a tendency for prices to be equal to or, in some versions, proportional to exchange-value in the long run.
Exchange-value is the basis for 'natural' prices in this
sense, and such prices will also ensure the most efficient
use of resources.   In this way exchange-value in the
labour theory of value takes the place of marginal utility
as both a positive and a normative concept.   In practice
the theory recognises that in a capitalist market economy
prices will frequently deviate from this ideal.   In the
short run they will oscillate round it because of temporary changes in supply and demand;   in the long run they
may vary because of the effect of monopolies and oligopo-
lies, particularly those associated with  the private
ownership of the means of production.

Labour, like other commodities, has an exchange-value
equal to or proportional to the labour costs of its production.   In the short term this is the cost of the
worker's subsistence, but in the longer term it must cover
the cost of bringing up and training a worker from conception to adulthood as well.   In marxist terms this is the
cost of the 'reproduction' of the labour force.   This
provides a lower limit below which wages cannot remain for
a long period without endangering the system of production.

One of the most important ways in which Marx developed
the labour theory of value was through the concept of
'surplus value'.   The use of tools, machinery and other
capital goods increases the productivity of workers and

enables them to produce far more than is needed just for
the reproduction of labour.   The difference between the
price paid for labour power and the price paid for its
product is 'surplus value'.   It is out of surplus value
that Marx saw all rent, profits and interest being paid
by a process of 'exploitation'.

The labour theory of value as developed by Marx conflicts with neo-classical theory in two main ways.   It
proposes a different relationship between supply, demand
and price, and it takes a different view of the role and
legitimacy of profits and rent.

First then, labour cost is seen as determining price,
price determining demand and demand determining supply.
The logic of this relationship can be seen if one imagines
a manufacturer deciding to produce a commodity.   In calculating price, his prime concern will be to cover his
costs, including his own income.   Having determined a
price that will do this, he will produce as much of the
commodity as he can sell at that price.   However, it
should be recognised that in deciding on a price that will
cover costs, the manufacturer must have some idea of the
demand schedules that will justify investment in the
capital.

Second, Marx denied that 'rent' as the price of the use
of land, or 'profit' as the return on the capitalist's
investment could or should influence the exchange-values
of commodities and therefore their long-run natural price.
The argument is that land is a free gift of nature and it
is only the labour power that is required to produce commodities from land that is actually incorporated in
exchange-value.   Similarly with capital goods, it is the
labour power incorporated in them that determines their
exchange-value, not the interest on the money used to pay
the labour.   Once the capital goods are produced, only
the wear and tear on them enters into the exchange-value
of their products.

In one sense of Marx's formulation, the neo-classical
economists have an easy answer.   If one is looking for a
price that will ensure an efficient use of all resources,
then the opportunity costs of capital goods and land, as
well as those of labour, should be taken into account.
But there is another sense in which Marx's formulation
draws attention to an implicit ideological bias in neo-
classical theory which cannot be so readily argued away.
For neo-classical theory speaks of profits, rent and wages

as the return to the different 'factors of production',
capital, land and labour, and in doing so implies that all
three are equally 'earned'.   But this disguises the fact
that economic relationships are also, and perhaps primarily, social relationships.   Rent and profit are paid not
to 'land' and 'capital' but to landlords and capitalists
whose ownership of these assets is socially determined.
It may be desirable in terms of efficiency in the distribution of resources that the opportunity costs of land and
capital are taken into account in determining price, but
whether and to whom they should be paid is a different
matter.   This can only be determined by social beliefs
about the rights entailed by ownership of property and
money.   Similarly, wages are paid not to 'labour', but to
workers, and the determination of wages by a system that
ignores need may be socially damaging and morally repug-
nant.   The validity of this ideological critique does not
depend on accepting the labour theory of value (Robinson,
1942, p. 18).

## DEVELOPMENTS AND REACTIONS

From the inception of neo-classical theory there were some
economists like Walras who recognised that marginal analysis was ambiguous in its support for capitalism and the
free market economy.   The work of Pigou, a disciple of
Marshall, confirmed this.   In 'The Economics of Welfare'
(1920) he used marginal analysis to examine the effects of
a wide range of economic and taxation policies that fell
well short of a planned economy.   He showed logically
that private gain was not at all an adequate assessment of
social benefits and that the outcome of competition was
not necessarily to the advantage of society.   This result
was not dependent on solving the problem of comparing the
welfare of different individuals.   So although neo-
classical theory has been frequently used to justify a
capitalist system and a free economic market, it does not
actually provide such a justification.

From this point, Western economists have tended to go
in three alternative directions.   A very small number
have examined the implications of the theory for a socialist planned economy.   Others have reaffirmed the basic
value assumptions that make the model congruent with a
capitalist economic system.   A third group have accepted
the existing mixed economy and examined the implications
of the model for marginal changes in the extent and
methods of state provision of services.

An excellent example of the first approach is Maurice
Dobb's 'Welfare Economics and the Economics of Socialism'
(1964).   Dobb, as a Marxist theorist, working in
Cambridge, where Marshall and Keynes remained the dominant
influences, provides an assessment of neo-classical theory
that is probably as fair as one can get.   He analyses the
implications of the theory for pricing in a planned economy and illustrates it from an examination of the Soviet
system.

Dobb considers that the Pareto optimum provides a
necessary but not a sufficient condition for the maximisation of welfare.   It is not a sufficient condition
because the optimum varies with the distribution of
income.   He draws from this two fundamental conclusions.
First there is a prima facie case for providing income in
cash rather than in kind, allowing people to choose for
themselves rather than providing them with what some one
else considers they need.   Second, a system of book-
keeping is required that takes into account marginal
analysis and the opportunity costs of using resources in
one way rather than another for accounting purposes.
However the price calculated by this means may be used as
a 'shadow price' rather than the actual price to the final
consumers.   In that final price other social factors may
influence what is charged, like the desirability of
encouraging or discouraging consumption, or the need to
ensure relative equality of real income.

Numerous economists have responded to the criticisms of
Pigou and others by a restatement of 'liberal' values and
particularly the importance of individual choice.   They
have contrasted the freedom of choice provided by a competitive economic market with the restrictions and ineffi-
ciencies of centralised communist planning.   The most
well-known of these internationally are the Austrian F.A.
Hayek and the American Milton Friedman.   British economists of this persuasion are strongly represented in the
publications of the Institute of Economic Affairs.
Because of their 'anti-collectivist ideology' (George and
Wilding, 1976), these economists generally play down the
importance of those factors that the neo-classical model
cannot take into account, like inequalities in the distribution of income and wealth, and externalities, and advocate measures that will make the capitalist economic system
system closer to the model.   These measures include the
improvement of information systems, legislation to reduce
monopoly and regulate abuse, encouragement of competition,
and sometimes measures to ensure that externalities are

included in costs.   In addition, of course, they also
advocate the return of as many functions as possible from
the state welfare system to the market economy.

Most of these writers implicitly or explicitly accept
the importance of the Pareto optimum as a measure of
efficiency, and base their support for the competitive
market economy on the neo-classical argument that such
an economy will produce results closer to the Pareto
optimum than a centralised state-run economy.   However,
some, like Rowley and Peacock (1975) frankly concede that
the Pareto optimum can often be more effectively achieved
by state action.   But even in these cases they support
the competitive economic market because of its contribution to individual liberty and individual choice.   They
therefore reject the Pareto optimum as a prime value in
favour of liberty and choice.

The third approach is the application of economic
analysis to the appraisal of state services.   The
simplest justification for this is that if rational
choices are to be made about the provision of services,
then the opportunity costs of the services are an important factor to consider.

The earliest attempts at this were 'cost-benefit
analyses'.of major investment projects such as hydro-
electric and transport schemes.   The main focus of these
analyses was on conventional economic criteria, which
could be relatively easily evaluated in monetary terms.
The evaluation of social costs and benefits such as the
effects of noise or increased leisure as a result of reduced travelling time were secondary refinements.   There
are, however, methodological problems at all stages of the
process which limit the value of the conclusions.   Ultimately implementation will depend on a political decision
about the weighting to be given to the economic evaluation.

In services in which social factors are more important
than economic factors, for instance in health or child
care services, a different sort of analysis becomes necessary.   In 'cost-effect analysis' the ends are left clearly to political judgment, and the focus is on the costs
and effects of different methods of implementation.   The
first essential of this type of appraisal is the development of a system of cost-accounting in which the costs are
allocated to specific types of case or treatment, a procedure common in private industry but rare in public service.   This provides the basis for comparing the real

costs and benefits of different forms of care and can lead
to a more efficient use of resources by pinpointing wasteful activities.

More recently efforts have been made to take into
account consumer evaluations of the service they receive.
Davies and Reddin (1978), for example, examined the attitudes of mothers to the various benefits they received
through the provision of school meals, and the implications of this for their pricing and the most efficient
use of school plant.


RELEVANCE TO SOCIAL ADMINISTRATION

By now it should be clear that although neo-classical
micro-economic theory grew up in a capitalist environment,
it has broader relevance to other systems.   It should not
be treated as though its only value was in justifying a
capitalist market economy, although this seems to be the
main pre-occupation of most of those who attack or defend
the theory.   An evaluation must therefore distinguish
between the different elements, varying from the purely
ideological to the simply technical.

To start with the ideological issues, as a theory of
society and a defence of the capitalist market economy,
neo-classical theory takes a particular attitude to freedom and power.   It adopts a liberal interpretation of
freedom as individual liberty, but ignores the contribution of the economic system to other aspects of the distribution of power.   Because control over resources gives
power over the lives of others, the unequal distribution
of income and wealth that results from a free economic
market produces an unequal distribution of power.   This
is particularly true when the resources that are privately
owned include the land and capital that are the means of
production.   Those who are ideologically committed to the
capitalist market economy tend to see it as a primary
defence of individual liberty which in turn makes adaptation to change and economic growth easier to attain.
They tend to ignore the fact that freedom is qualified by
a person's position within the system, those at the bottom
having considerably less freedom than those at the top.
This issue of the distribution of power will be looked at
more closely in several subsequent chapters.

However, it should be recognised that the theory does
stress certain individualistic values that are widely

accepted in our society.   These include the importance of
autonomy and the delegation of decision-making, particularly to consumers;  the acceptance of personal responsibility for the results of one's own decisions;  and the
role of material incentives in individual motivation.
Societies can be built on other principles, although the
larger and more complex the society, the less certain that
this is true.   In most Western democracies most people
have been very soundly conditioned to accepting them.
While it is possible that a determined effort might change
these values, it would take time.   Realistically, most
policy-makers will have to live with the continuance of
present attitudes.   This remains, however, a very debatable issue - the extent to which it is possible to develop
altruistic motivation.   Is the dominance of competitive
over altruistic attitudes in our society the product of
the system or an innate characteristic of human beings?
Some writers on social administration (e.g. Titmuss, 1970)
believe that altruism can and should be fostered;  others
(e.g. Pinker, 1979) stress the importance of recognising
the limits of altruism.   This issue will be discussed
again in the chapter on theories of social justice (chapter 8).

Turning to the Pareto optimum as an ideal of economic
efficiency, it is clear that it is a necessary, but not a
sufficient condition for the maximising of economic welfare.   The most important reason for its insufficiency is
that it provides no standard against which to measure the
distribution of income and wealth.   However, it is also
obvious from the earlier discussion that a competitive
capitalist economic market is not the only way to achieve
a Pareto optimum.   Indeed, the imperfections of existing
markets, and the importance of those areas where an economic market cannot achieve the Pareto optimum has led many
economists using the neo-classical analysis to support the
provision of many state services.

This brings one finally to the value of economic analysis in the assessment of the efficiency of social services
whether they are provided through the economic market or
through the state.   There is, of course, a temptation to
reject the economic assessment of services as valid especially when the contributions of services is so important
to individual welfare and so diffuse in their effects on
society.   However, the fact is that resources are limited
and choices have to be made.   One can leave them to the
hunches of politicians and the pressures of the political
process uninformed about the opportunity costs of different

courses; one can leave them to the professionals and the
administrators who have their own interests and biases;
or one can use some combination of these processes.   But
there is a strong case for feeding into the decision-
making process information about the opportunity costs of
different courses, and an even stronger case for finding
ways of evaluating the preferences of consumers.   Micro-
economic analysis can have a real contribution to make in
this way.


FURTHER READING

What further reading you wish to do will depend on where
you have come from and where you want to get to.

The first problem is that there are very few reliable
critical textbooks.   Almost all conventional textbooks
set out the neo-classical theories as a series of logical
propositions, with or without illustrations from real life
(as opposed to made up examples), and with the dogmatism
of a school book on Euclidian geometry.   There are no
statements of the basic assumptions, no references to the
origins of the theories and concepts (and certainly not to
the social context in which they arose) and no critique of
the ideas presented.   Recently a few critical textbooks
have appeared.   These tend to be written by radical
critics of conventional economic theory and, though better
than the standard textbooks, easily slip into a biased
presentation.   The fact that they have usually declared
their bias does not make it any less real!

If you have already studied economics at school or for
some professional examinations, or even for some degree
courses, there is a fair chance that you will have used
one of the standard texts and were never presented with an
alternative paradigm.   If you used Samuelson's classic
text it will be worthwhile glancing at Linder's (1977)
'Anti-Samuelson' as a reminder of what you may have
swallowed without much question.   A more systematic criticism is provided by Green and Nore (1977).   But perhaps
the best way to start would be from an examination of the
origins of economic ideas, and for this Heimann (1945) is
excellent.   It is true that he gives rather limited attention to Marx, but one can get a real understanding of the
problems that different economists were addressing and
therefore of the solutions they came up with.   This could
usefully be followed by Culyer (1973) which provides a
good introduction to welfare economics.

For the beginner in economics who wants to get a better
grasp of theory, Hunt and Sherman (1978) is clear and
useful, provided you take seriously the authors' declara-
tion of bias, and read something else as well.   Heimann
would also be useful for this, or even a conventional
textbook like McCormick et al. (1974).   Of course most
basic texts cover much more than micro-economic theory and
Stillwell (1975) may be a more useful follow-up to this
chapter because it is focused on the specific topic and is
clear, critical and short.

Alternatively you may want to leave the theory and look
at the ideological issues.   George and Wilding (1976)
summarise these well in the central chapters of their
book, but again watch for the bias (more evident in the
first and last chapters).   Read the originals recommended
by George and Wilding to help you make up your own mind,
and perhaps Heimann again to get it into a broader historical perspective.   Rowley and Peacock (1975) which has
been mentioned in the text presents the liberal view in an
unaggressive way.

Finally you may prefer to go straight on to see how the
concepts are used by economists to examine specific problems.   The books published by the Institute of Economic
Affairs generally present the case for 'radical reaction'
- a return to the economic market.   The philosophy of the
Institute is well presented in the pamphlet 'Towards a
Welfare Society'.   Peters (1966) gives an excellent
account of cost-benefit analysis.   As an example of pre-
judiced reading, when you have finished the book read the
quite contradictory account of its conclusions in the Fore-
word by a member of the Institute of Economic Affairs!
Davies and Reddin (1978), Culyer (1976), Judge (1978), and
Nevitt (1967) provide examples of economic analysis at
work in specific fields.

BIBLIOGRAPHY

* Recommended

Bergson, A. (1966), 'Essays in Normative Economics',
    Cambridge, Mass., Harvard University Press.
Collard, D. (1978), 'Altruism and Economy: a study in non-
    selfish economics', Oxford, Martin Robertson.
* Culyer, A.J. (1973), 'The Economics of Social Policy',
    Oxford, Martin Robertson.
Culyer, A.J. (1976), 'Need and the National Health Service:
    economics and social choice', Oxford, Martin Robertson.

* Davies, B., and Reddin, M. (1978), 'Universality,
  Selectivity and Effectiveness in Social Policy',
  London, Heinemann.
Dobb, M. (1964), 'Welfare Economics and the Economics of
  Socialism: towards a common-sense critique', Cambridge
  University Press.
Galbraith, J.K. (1967), 'The New Industrial State', London,
  Hamish Hamilton.
* George, V., and Wilding, P. (1976), 'Ideology and Social
  Welfare', London, Routledge & Kegan Paul.
* Green, F., and Nore, P. (1977), 'Economics: an anti-
  text', London, Macmillan.
Hardie, C.J.M. (1979), Anti-Trust Policy, in D. Morris
  (ed.), 'The Economic System in the UK', Oxford Univer-
  sity Press.
Hayek, F.A. (1949), 'Individualism and Economic Order',
  London, Routledge & Kegan Paul.
* Heimann, E. (1945, 1972), 'History of Economic Doctrines:
  an introduction to economic theory', Oxford University
  Press.
* Hunt, E.K., and Sherman, H.J. (1978), 'Economics: an
  introduction to traditional and radical views', New
  York, Harper & Row, 3rd edn.
* Institute of Economic Affairs (1967), 'Towards a Welfare
  Society', London, IEA.
* Judge, K. (1978), 'Rationing Social Services: a study of
  resource allocation in the personal social services',
  London, Heinemann.
Kaldor, N. (1939), Welfare propositions of economics and
  interpersonal comparisons of utility, 'Economic Jour-
  nal', vol. 49, pp. 549-52.
Linder, M. (1977), 'Anti-Samuelson: basic problems of the
  capitalist economy: Vol. 2 Micro-economics', London,
  Pluto Press.
* McCormick, B.J., Kitchin, P.D., Marshall, G.P., Sampson,
  A.A., and Sedgwick, R. (1974), 'Introducing Economics',
  Harmondsworth, Penguin.
Mayes, D. (1980), The economic rationale for government
  intervention in housing, 'Social Policy and Administra-
  tion', vol. 14, no. 1, pp. 54-8.
* Nevitt, A. (1967), 'Economic Problems of Housing',
  London, Macmillan.
* Peters, G.H. (1966), 'Cost Benefit Analysis and Public
  Expenditure', Eaton Paper no. 8, London, Institute of
  Economic Affairs.
Pigou, A.C. (1920), 'The Economics of Welfare', London,
  Macmillan, 4th edn, 1960.
Pinker, R. (1979), 'The Idea of Welfare', London, Heine-
  mann.

Robinson, J. (1942), 'An Essay on Marxian Economics',
    London, Macmillan, 2nd edn, 1960.
Rowley, C.K., and Peacock, A.T. (1975), 'Welfare Econo-
    mics: a liberal restatement', Oxford, Martin Robertson.
Samuelson, P.A. (1964) 'Economics: an introductory analy-
    sis', New York, McGraw-Hill, 6th edn.
Smith, A. (1776), 'An Inquiry into the Nature and Causes
    of the Wealth of Nations', London, Dent, 1963.
Stillwell, F.J.B. (1975), 'Normative Economics: an intro-
    duction to micro-economic theory and critiques', Oxford
    Oxford, Pergamon Press.
Titmuss, R.M. (1970), 'The Gift Relationship: from human
    blood to social policy', Harmondsworth, Penguin.
True, C. (1979), The economic rationale for Government
    intervention in housing, 'Social Policy and Administra-
    tion', vol. 13, no. 2, pp. 124-37.

# Chapter 3

# Macro-economic theory
Terry Caslin

The division between micro- and macro-economics is essentially a matter of convenience.  It is expedient to make
this distinction partly because the problems differ and
partly because the method of analysis differs between the
two branches.  Chapter 2 dealt with the workings of individual markets.  The basic problem was seen to be the
determination of the allocation of resources, and the
basic theory that of the determination of relative prices
through supply and demand.  A different line of thinking
begins by asking what determines whether the resources
will in fact be used.  The basic problem in macro-economics is the determination of the flow of income and the
basic theory is the model of the circular flow of income.

The questions which provide the foundation for macro-
economics are:

(i)  What determines the magnitude of the total output
and of the total amount of employment in a country during
some given period of time?

(ii)  What determines the general level of prices?

The relevance of unemployment to the subject matter of
social policy hardly needs to be stressed.  Unemployment
is a key social problem and indeed a growing one with
major ramifications.  The socially damaging effects of
inflation, albeit less widely appreciated, are equally
insidious.  The simultaneous existence of high unemployment and high rates of inflation in western countries
since the early 1970s constitute a crisis for macro-economic theory and policy.  A decade ago there was a strong
consensus that the macro-behaviour of the economy was
fairly well understood and the policy goals could be

achieved by the available instruments.   The consensus no
longer exists.

In the UK at least five main schools of macro-economic
thought can be discerned:  Keynesian (together with modern
interpretors of Keynes);  monetarist;  new Cambridge;
international monetarist;  and marxist.   The discussion
here will attempt, primarily, to highlight the contrasts
between 'Keynesian' and 'monetarist' approaches, though
reference will be made, where appropriate, to the other
approaches.   But first there needs to be some examination
of the 'classical' theory in which both the Keynesian and
monetarist approaches have their roots.


## CLASSICAL MACRO-ECONOMIC THEORY

Prior to the Great Depression of the 1930s, most economists did not consider unemployment to be one of the central problems of the economy.   There were, of course,
dissenters.   Karl Marx believed that economic crises
would become increasingly severe with larger and larger
numbers of workers added to the ranks of the unemployed.
Sooner or later capitalism would collapse because of its
inherent defects.   But Marx was outside the mainstream of
economics.   Most economists believed that there might be
short-term periods of unemployment, but that the market
mechanism would bring about a speedy return to a high
level of employment.   This 'classical theory' was a logical extension of Adam Smith's description of an economy
that would function automatically, as if guided by an
'invisible hand'.

Classical theory predicted that the equilibrium of the
economy would occur only at full employment (i.e. where
the quantity of labour demanded equals that supplied at
the ruling wage rate) since it was assumed that private
markets were perfectly competitive and that prices and
money wages were flexible.   Producers and workers lacked
market power and were thus price-takers and wage-takers
respectively.   Thus if excess supply or excess demand
temporarily existed, money wages and prices would adjust
and eventually return the economy to full-employment
output and unchanged real wage rates.

This conclusion also required the additional assumptions
of perfect information by all economic decision-makers and
perfect mobility of both human and material resources.
Therefore there was no serious friction in the system pre-

venting resources from moving in response to market forces.   Also there were assumed to be no long-run leakages of monies from the circular flow of income between firms and consumers.   All income not spent on consumer goods was lent to be spent on investment goods.

The implications of these assumptions were summarised in 'Say's Law' after the nineteenth-century economist J.B. Say.   Supply was held automatically to create its own sufficient demand.   There could never be a general insufficiency of the demand needed to sell the economy's output.   By the logic of the circular flow, the total value of output produced must equal total factor income generated where that income is just enough to purchase the output produced, since Say's law implied that all income was intended to be spent in one way or another.   Any temporary imbalance between full-employment savings and investment would be automatically corrected by changes in the rate of interest.   The inescapable conclusion, therefore, was that the normal state of a competitive market economy was to have full employment and be in equilibrium. Government participation could not possibly improve on the situation.

In the classical scheme the general price level was held to be determined by the quantity of money.   This was a fairly ancient piece of economic theory, refined over the years and stated with varying degrees of sophistication.   The earlier versions of this Quantity Theory concentrated on the role of money as a medium of exchange, money being demanded purely for transactions purposes. The general price level was determined by the relationship between the quantity of money and the supply of goods and services.   The theory as developed in the USA in the early years of the twentieth century was based on a simple equation of exchange:

$$MV = PQ$$

where M is the quantity of money, V the average velocity at which this money circulates, Q the number of physical transactions in the economy in a year, and P the price at which these transactions take place.   The right-hand side of the equation, PQ, must equal the value of all receipts from the sale of final goods and services over a period of time whilst the left-hand side MV is the total expenditure made in that period.   As it stands, the equation is an identity.   The four terms have been defined in such a way that the equation must hold.   What the quantity theory did

as to assert a particular causal relationship.   Classical economists assumed that the velocity of circulation of
money, V, was a behavioural constant because society has
certain buying habits and relatively consistent spending
behaviour.   Thus the price level would be directly related to the money supply and accordingly the major macro-
economic responsibility of the government would be to provide a stable money supply.   Specifically, the money
supply should be steadily increased at a rate that is adequate to buy the full-employment output of the economy at
stable prices.

## KEYNES'S 'GENERAL THEORY'

We have reviewed the classical theory which dominated economic thinking up to the early 1930s.   The normal condition of a capitalist economy was to have full employment,
and be in equilibrium.   However, confidence in such an
outcome was shattered by the experience of the 1920s and
1930s.   The Great Depression was a worldwide phenomenon,
affecting every major capitalist economy.   Between 1921
and 1940 the unemployment rate in Britain never dropped
below 10 per cent and in 1931 reached 21 per cent.   John
Maynard Keynes's 'General Theory of Employment, Interest
and Money' (1936) was built on that fact.   Keynes
believed himself to be writing a book on economic theory
which would largely revolutionise the way the world
thought about economic problems.   This is in effect what
happened.   Keynes's great achievement was to destroy the
notion of a self-regulating economic system and provide
the theoretical underpinning for a new economics.   He
argued that the inter-war depression was in effect a refu-
tation of Say's law and dismissed the possibility of explaining the persistence of mass unemployment on the basis
of wage-rigidities alone (as the classical theorists had
latterly argued).   Keynes's analysis, added to the idea
that government intervention in the system could help to
effect a cure for unemployment, had obvious implications
for the role of a democratic state in guiding the economy
in the general interest.

    What then were the main characteristics of the Keynesian
approach to the problem of income determination?   It must
be pointed out that it is with a much simplified version
that we are concerned here.   Readers requiring a more
complete version should consult one of the texts recommended at the end of the chapter.   The essence of Keynes's
approach was an attack on the classical assumption of a

tendency towards full employment and the substitution for
it of the possibility of under-employment equilibrium.
His own theory of income determination can initially be
put quite simply as follows:  output and employment are
determined by the demand for output, which comes from two
sources - consumption demand and investment demand.
Investment decisions, which are held to depend on profit
expectations and other factors, are taken for granted at
this stage (i.e. they are autonomously determined).   Consumption demand is held to depend largely on the level of
current disposable income (other influences, including
wealth and the rate of interest are recognised but dismissed from the argument) and when income rises, consumption rises but not as much as income - in other words, as
income rises, saving rises.

On the basis of these assumptions, the level of income
will be determined by the level of investment.   Investment is taken as given by factors lying outside the
theory;  income will attain such a level that saving
equals the given level of investment and income will be
the sum of the consumption from this level of income and
the given level of investment.

These latter points require some further explanation
and we may begin with the ex post equality of saving and
investment.   Ex post simply means after the event or
'realised' in contrast to ex ante, meaning before the
event or 'intended'.   If we divide income receipts into
the amount spent on consumption and the amount saved, and
we divide output into consumption goods and investment,
then it follows from the definitional equality of output
and income that realised saving must always equal realised
investment.   This can be conveniently expressed as

$$Y = C + S$$

where Y stands for income, C for consumption and S for
saving.

$$O = C + I$$

where O stands for output and I for investment.

But   $Y = O$

Thus $S = I.$

Note that consumption goods and spending on consumption

oods must be the same and thus any accumulation of stocks
f consumption goods by firms must be included in invest-
ent.

The ex post equality of saving and investment is of no
nterest until we notice that what happens is not always
hat was intended.   The intended (or ex ante) additions
o saving and the intended level of investment need not
oincide.   As seen above, saving intentions are assumed
o be determined by the level of income while investment
ntentions are quite independent of income.   Savings in-
rease with incomes because higher incomes permit satis-
action of current desires and some provision for the
uture while investment depends largely on entrepreneurial
rofit expectations.   It should be apparent that saving
nd investment intentions will be attainable simultaneous-
y only for a particular level of income.

Furthermore, should there be a change in the level of
investment, saving would have to change equally;   the ex
post equality must be satisfied.   As intended savings are
related to income, to reach a new position where saving
intentions are realised, the level of income will have to
change.   For example, if intended investment is greater
than intended saving this will show as a depletion in
firms' desired levels of stocks.   In order to replenish
stocks, firms will increase output and income.   Income
will rise until intended saving once again equals intended
investment.   As savings are only a fraction of income,
the change in income will have to be greater than the
initial rise in investment.   This is the so-called multiplier principle.   The condition for an equilibrium level
of income (i.e. where there will be no tendency for income
to change) is seen to be that intended saving should equal
intended investment.   Put another way, aggregate demand
must equal production.   The economy will be driven
towards such an equilibrium.

This theory of income determination may be represented
diagrammatically as in Figure 3.1.

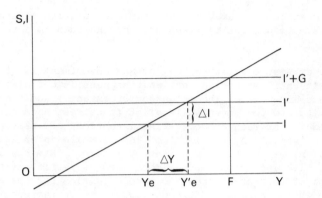

FIGURE 3.1  Determination of equilibrium income by saving
= investment

Here we measure income (Y) along the horizontal axis and
saving and investment along the vertical axis.    Saving
(S) is plotted as a function of the level of income.
Investment (I), being determined autonomously, is represented by a horizontal line.    The equilibrium level of
income (Ye) is that for which intended saving equals the
given level of intended investment.    Figure 3.1 may also
be used to illustrate the affects of economic disturbances and also to clarify the theory of the multiplier, that
is the relation between an initial change in demand for
output and the total change in income to which it gives
rise.    In the traditional Keynesian model most disturbances are held to occur from the real (as opposed to monetary) sector.    If, for example, investment demand is
increased to I', the equality of intended investment and
intended saving can occur only at Y'e.    The increase in
investment is shown by the distance between I and I';  the
increase in income is Y'e - Ye, that is, a multiple of the
initial increase in investment.    The size of the 'multiplier' clearly depends on the slope of the saving function, that is on the marginal propensity to save (MPS).
The MPS represents the fraction of additional saving out
of additional income.    In the simple theory presented
here the multiplier will be equal to the reciprocal of the
MPS ($\frac{1}{MPS}$).    For example, if the MPS = $\frac{1}{5}$ the multiplier
would be equal to 5.    If investment expenditure increased
by, say, £1 million, income would increase by £5 million.

More simply, starting from an equilibrium position, a
rise in investment spending will result in new jobs being
created in the capital goods sector.    Newly employed

labour will spend some of their income on consumer goods
and save the rest.   The increased demand for consumer
goods will lead to increased employment in these industries and cause further rounds of expenditure.   Income
will rise, via the multiplier process, to a new equilibrium level, at which intended saving will equal the new
increased level of intended investment.   Note that the
multiplier process will also run in reverse.   A decrease
in initial spending will lead to a multiple decrease in
income.

The above might appear to be simple mathematical manipulation, but it is sufficient to establish the point that,
given certain conditions about the behaviour of saving and
investment, income may settle at *any* level and there is no
guarantee that it will be at such a level that all of the
available labour force is employed.   Some change of the
original conditions, such as intervention by government to
change the level of intended or planned investment, may be
needed if full employment of labour is an objective of
policy.   This was Keynes's message that was so important
in the 1930s and later.   In Figure 3.1 point F represents
the full employment level of national income.   To reach
full employment, government spending (G) should be added
to investment demand.   The vertical distance between I'
and I' + G represents the amount by which aggregate demand
must rise in order to achieve a full employment equilibrium.

What has been presented here has been a simple version
of the Keynesian theory.   It is incomplete because it
leaves both the rate of investment and the rate of interest undetermined.   For a full version of the Keynesian
theory readers are advised to consult one of the texts
referred to at the end of this chapter.   Therein the
reader will also find the analysis extended to an open
economy (i.e. one that engages in international trade)
with a government sector that spends and levies taxes.
The model becomes more complicated but still predicts the
possibility of the economy settling in an equilibrium
position where unemployment prevails.

Economic policy after the Second World War was dominated, until the 1970s, by 'demand management' based on the
Keynesian analysis.   Successive governments used a series
of tools to maintain the economy at a level of full
employment, though primacy was given to the role of fiscal
policy - government spending and taxation.   Such demand
management was extremely successful in maintaining full

employment in the post-war world but the onset of rapid
inflation in the second half of the 1960s and more especially in the 1970s led to questioning of the Keynesian
orthodoxy.   Could the Keynesian system be applied to
periods of inflation?   If unemployment is a symptom of
inadequate demand, is inflation a sympton of excessive
demand?   Some Keynesians do see inflation in such terms.
Demand-pull implies that the cause of inflation lies in
excess aggregate demand by consumers, firms and the government.   Appropriate 'fine tuning' of demand by fiscal
and monetary policies should keep the economy in balance.
Other Keynesians emphasise autonomous increases in prices
due to increases in wages or other costs.   Such *cost-push*
theorists argue that fine-tuning is inadequate to deal
with excessive wage demands and advocate direct state controls over prices and incomes.   We will return to policy
issues later but must now turn our attention to monetarism, the counter-revolution.


MONETARISM

Throughout the 1960s and 1970s, particularly in the USA
under the academic leadership of Professor Milton Friedman
of the University of Chicago, many economists criticised
the above Keynesian analysis and propounded an alternative
hypothesis.   They derived their ideas from the monetary
theory of the classical economists and argued that a
sophisticated version of the quantity theory of money best
explains the macro-economy.

   A reinterpretation of the historical record by Friedman
and Schwartz (1963) led Friedman to the conclusion that
monetary impulses were the predominant factor explaining
changes in the level of output and prices.   This proposition is the first tenet of the monetarist viewpoint.
There are three other major theoretical propositions:
that the transmissions mechanism is such that monetary
influences affect spending decisions generally;   that the
private sector is inherently stable at an acceptable level
of unemployment;   that allocative detail is unimportant in
explaining short-run changes in money national income.
We will outline each of these propositions in turn.

   Monetarism is essentially a mode of analysis that uses
the equation of exchange (MV = PQ) to organise macro-
economic data.   Monetarists today, however, prefer to
express the quantity theory in terms of the demand for
money.   They add the additional assumptions necessary to

ake predictions about nominal or money national income
real income is regarded as being determined by real
actors such as national resources).   In terms of the
quation of exchange the velocity of circulation of money
V) is believed to be stable because there is a stable
emand to hold on to money.   People hold money (or real
alances) in order to make transactions.   Any speculative
otive (Keynesian) is believed to be of minor importance.
onetarists argue that empirical evidence has shown that
hanges in desired real balances tend to proceed slowly.
elocity, though not a numerical constant, is sufficiently
table to provide a predictable relationship between
hanges in the money supply (M) and changes in nominal
ncome (PQ).   In summary, the monetarist view is that
hanges or, more precisely, changes in the rate of change,
n the quantity of money, induced by the monetary authori-
ies, are the predominant factor explaining instability in
he economy.   This view contrasts with that of Keynesians,
vho, doubting the existence of a stable demand for money,
ave traditionally emphasised the relationship between
ominal income and investment or autonomous expenditure.

Monetarists and Keynesians also disagree on how changes
in the money supply are transmitted to the real sector.
Monetarists argue that the transmission mechanism from the
monetary sector to the real sector is relatively direct.
There is little slack in the linkage from an increase in
the money supply to a rise in nominal income.   There is
no significant leakage caused by a buildup in balances of
cash held.   The transmission mechanism is such that
changes in the money supply change nominal income.   In
shorthand notation.

$$\Delta M \xrightarrow{\text{direct}} \Delta Y$$

($\Delta$, delta, is the conventional symbol for 'the change in')
The demand for money balances is essentially a transactions demand and is relatively insensitive to changes in
the interest rate.   According to Keynesians, the transmission mechanism is less direct since it must pass
through the interest rate variable.   Increases in the
money supply may not directly affect prices or output
because much of the additional money may be absorbed into
speculative balances which are sensitive to changes in the
interest rate.   Thus there may be no direct link, in the
short run, between M and Y because of the slippage caused
by counter-variations in V.   To Keynesians, it is the
effects of changes in taxes and government spending that,
when amplified by the multiplier, provide a more direct,

predictable transmitted effect on Y.   Changes in the
money supply affect interest rates (and money balance
holdings) which affect investment and, via the multiplier,
change income, hence consumption.   In shorthand notation
again

$$\Delta M \rightarrow \Delta i \rightarrow \Delta I^k \rightarrow \Delta Y \text{ and } \Delta C$$

(where i is the rate of interest and k the multiplier)
Money in this transmission mechanism is seen purely as a
substitute for financial assets, as compared with the
direct substitution of money for assets in general, including commodities, envisaged by the monetarist approach.

Closely allied to the view that monetary impulses dominate is the monetarist contention that the economy is
inherently stable at a generally acceptable level of unemployment.   Only erratic monetary growth will disturb this
stability.   The notion of a 'generally acceptable' or
'natural' rate of unemployment does perhaps sound conten-
tious.   In this context it refers to the concept of a
level of unemployment at which inflation will not accelerate.   This natural rate is generally held to be determined by the structure of the real side of the economy and
the institutions of the labour market.   It is thus derived from the concepts of frictional and structural unemployment.   Frictional refers to the normal, usually short-
term, inactivity between jobs and structural to the mis-
matching of applicants' skills or regional location to the
requirements of vacant jobs.   As such, the 'natural rate'
can only be altered by measures which affect the structure
of the job market.   Attempts by the authorities to push
the level of unemployment below its natural rate will only
succeed in the short-run.   In the long-run the inevitable
effect will be an accelerated rate of inflation.

Keynesians do not accept the view that the private
sector is basically stable.   They argue that investment
decisions are highly unstable owing to shifts in profit
expectations and the economy is accordingly oscillatory.
Also, once disturbed, the economy may take a long time to
return to an equilibrium.   Hence their advocacy of short-
run activist stabilisation policies.   Monetarists contend
that so long as the money supply is held on a stable growth
path, real disturbances will be fairly rapidly absorbed
and output will revert to its long-run growth path.

We have seen that the belief that changes in the supply
of money are the predominant factor explaining changes in

nominal income has led monetarists to concentrate on the behaviour of the market for real money balances.   This leads to the fourth basic feature of their approach. Monetarists devote little attention to allocative detail in explaining and predicting short-run changes in income. They hold that expenditures are determined mainly by an excess supply of or demand for real money balances. Knowledge of relative prices, which are determined by particular market circumstances, is not considered to be very useful in predicting short-run changes in income. Keynesians, in contrast, do focus on particular sectors of the economy in trying to predict short-run changes in income.   For example, importance is attached to credit availability and various interest rates as influencing the amount of borrowing and lending and thus expenditure.


THE PHILLIPS CURVE

We must now turn to the controversial question of whether there is a long-run trade-off between inflation and unem- ployment.   The unprecedented juxtaposition of a high rate of inflation and high unemployment in many western indus- trialised countries from the beginning the 1970s presented a crisis for both theory and policy.   'Stagflation' became the economic problem of our time.

In 1958 A.W. Phillips pointed out that for nearly a century in the UK, a stable relationship had existed between the rate of inflation (Phillips actually used the rate of change in money wage rates) and the unemployment rate (Phillips, 1958, pp. 283-99).   He showed that the unemployment rate (U) and the inflation rate (W) moved in opposite directions by specific amounts.   'Phillips curve' estimates in the USA also indicated a stable historical relation - a trade-off - between inflation and unemploy- ment rates.   The average relationship between these two variables was found to be non-linear and followed the general shape shown in Figure 3.2.

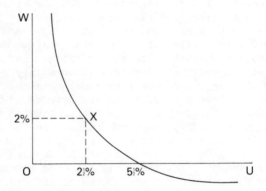

FIGURE 3.2   The Phillips curve

The economic rationale for this relationship was seen in terms of two simple hypotheses:  (i) that the rate of increase of money wages depends on the degree of excess demand for labour, and (ii) that unemployment figures are a good indicator of excess demand for labour.   A combination of these hypotheses produced the Phillips curve shown in Figure 3.2.

The Phillips curve was immediately espoused by many economists who saw it as a new tool for stabilisation, and by policy-makers in government.   The acceptance of a stable Phillips curve presented governments with a policy conflict between output and inflation and the curve dominated inflation-unemployment policy in the 1960s, as governments debated their choice of position on the trade-off curve.   However, towards the end of the 1960s it became increasingly clear that the trade-offs embodied in the curve no longer applied.   Many observations were above existing Phillips curves.   The curve seemed to be shifting upwards everywhere.   Both the unemployment rate and the inflation rate moved in the same direction - up.   How could this happen?   One explanation was that the Phillips curve had shifted upwards and was associated with a wider acceptance of cost-push theories of inflation.   If trade-unions have the power to set wages independently of the state of demand in the economy, and if they exercise it, the price level becomes union-determined.   Import-cost rises, particularly oil prices, was another facet of this theme.

The other explanation was in terms of an expectations-augmented version of the demand-pull theory of inflation.

In 1968, working independently, Milton Friedman and Edmund
Phelps developed a new hypothesis about unemployment and
inflation.   By the mid-1970s their view that there was
no unique stable Phillips curve had been widely accepted,
while the theory they advanced had gained substantial
acceptance and empirical support in some countries but
little or none in others.   It denied the existence of the
traditional Phillips curve trade-off in the long run.   To
them its biggest weakness was that it gave no place to
people's expectations of inflation in determining actual
inflationary experience.   According to the Phillips
curve, if the economy were to be held constant at some
such position as X in Figure 3.2, the rate of inflation
would also remain constant.   Friedman and Phelps argued,
however, that people would come to realise that inflation
was permanent, they would 'expect' it and would build this
expectation into their demands for wage and other price
increases.   This would lead to an acceleration of the
rate of inflation.   According to the Friedman-Phelps
hypothesis (hereafter F-P) the actual rate of inflation is
given by a demand-pull element, due to decsion-makers
raising their prices in response to excess demand, plus
the expected rate of inflation.   There will be a separate
short-run Phillips curve relating actual inflation to
national income for each expected rate of inflation.

An important implication of the F-P hypothesis is that
if the authorities try to maintain the level of unemployment below the natural rate of unemployment (or, what is
the same thing, try to maintain the level of national
income above full-employment income), the actual rate of
inflation will eventually accelerate on account of adaptive inflationary expectations.

Another implication of the hypothesis is that the long-
run Phillips curve is vertical.   If national income is
just at the full-employment (natural rate of unemployment)
level, there is, by definition, no excess demand pressure
on inflation.   Any inflation that occurs can only be
expectational inflation.   If, for example, everyone
expects 4 per cent inflation, then all prices and wage
rates will be raised by 4 per cent and an actual inflation
rate of 4 per cent will occur.   So long as the monetary
authorities pursue a permissive monetary policy, that is,
they allow the money supply to rise by 4 per cent, the
inflation will be 'validated'.   Full-employment income
and the natural rate of unemployment can be maintained
indefinitely with a 4 per cent expected and 4 per cent
actual inflation.   The same argument could be repeated

for *any* rate of inflation and thus the full-employment
national income together with the natural rate of unemployment is compatible with any actual rate of inflation.
The long-run Phillips curve becomes vertical at full-
employment income.   Note the point about a 'permissive
monetary policy'.   In the absence of an increase in the
money supply the inflation will lower the real purchasing
power of the country's money stock.   The aggregate demand
function will shift downwards and the inflationary pressure will be removed.

The implications of the F-P hypothesis for economic
policy should be obvious.   Any attempt by the government
to reduce unemployment below its natural rate, by expansionary policies, will merely cause the rate of inflation
to accelerate.   A corollary of this is that the government must accurately determine the natural rate of unemployment because it is the only acceptable target for
long-run stabilisation policy.   A further implication is
that once a period of excess demand inflation is under
way, inflationary expectations will accelerate the inflation.   An attempt to control such accelerating inflation
by contracting national income may see rising unemployment
associated with still rising rates of inflation as expectations may dominate the effect of declining demand and
output.   A long period with unemployment above the
natural rate may be required before inflationary expectations are revised downward sufficiently to permit the
actual inflation rate to fall.

The F-P hypothesis is based on adaptive price expectations.   Namely, past behaviour is extrapolated into the
future.   Some monetarists have added a new twist to price-
formation behaviour expressed in the rational expectations
hypothesis.   This denies the existence of a Phillips
curve trade-off even in the short period.   The public
reacts immediately because it knows what the effects of
economic policy will be.   Thus traditional policies
cannot reduce unemployment even in the short run.


AN ASSESSMENT OF KEYNESIAN AND MONETARIST VIEWS

Much of the debate in economics today is presented to the
public as an argument between Keynesians and monetarists.
The debate has been very emotional partly because of the
personalities involved, many of whom are well-recognised
polemicists.   Some of the emotionalism has certainly
arisen because of the political issues involved.   Despite

disclaimers, there was a strong connection between monetarism and the upsurge in right-wing strength in both the
UK and the USA in the 1960s and 1970s.   However, to
classify economists as Keynesians or monetarists, though
it might have its uses in media reporting, can cloud the
underlying substance of the issues.   It might be argued
that today the Keynesian and monetarist positions are, in
the Hegelian sense, in the synthesis stage of development.
Already the conventional wisdom in macro-economic theory
accepts the better parts of both Keynesian and monetarist
viewpoints.   In a number of theoretical areas (e.g. the
transmission mechanism) the difference between Keynesian
and monetarist schools is one of degree rather than of
principle.   Many of the divisive issues can be reduced to
a set of empirically testable propositions.   Admittedly,
testing so far has at best produced somewhat ambiguous
results, but as more empirical evidence becomes available
it should be possible to settle certain areas of controversy.   But while there may be a synthesis in theory,
there is still disagreement over answers to the normative
question, what should stabilisation policy be like?

We have seen in this chapter that there are two main
differences between Keynesian and monetarist schools of
thought.   There is disagreement over the major source of
serious fluctuations in national income and disagreement
over the issue as to whether there is a long-run trade-off
between inflation and unemployment.   These differences
are reflected in the stabilisation policy measures advocated.

Monetarists hold that monetary causes are the major
source of disturbances that affect the economy.   They
also hold that the money supply is exogenous, meaning that
the supply is determined by the central bank and neither
expands nor contracts with changes in the level of business activity unless the central bank decides to allow it
to do so.   Unless disturbed by erratic growth of the
money supply, the economy is inherently stable at the
natural level of unemployment.   Accordingly, monetarists
argue that the rate of growth of the money supply should
be controlled.   They oppose an active, discretionary
policy, arguing that time lags between recognition, action
and effect could make such policy destabilising.   The
best results, they believe, would be obtained by following
a monetary rule whereby the money supply would be expanded
at a constant rate, year by year.   An expansion equal to
the growth rate of real national income will put monetary
policy in a neutral stance that will allow the economy's
own self-regulatory powers to work.

Fiscal policy is, according to the monetarists, by itself largely ineffective in influencing the level of activity.   Changes in government expenditure will, by the way it is financed, induce large changes in interest rates which in turn cause large offsetting changes in private interest - sensitive expenditure.   For example, increases in government expenditure will crowd out an equivalent amount of private expenditure.   Monetarists would confine fiscal policy to the role of influencing resource alloca- tion and income distribution.

We have seen that monetarists believe that there is no long-run trade-off between inflation and unemployment. On the contrary, their belief that the long-run Phillips curve is vertical implies that any attempt by the govern- ment to maintain unemployment below the natural rate will result in an accelerating rate of inflation.   Lack of precise knowledge of the natural rate of unemployment implies that governments should not aim at a target unem- ployment rate.   Rather they should try, by micro-economic measures, to improve the structure of the labour market and the structure of industry.   The 'natural rate' is not an 'inevitable' rate.   Measures which improve the occupa- tioaal and geographical mobility of labour will reduce the natural rate.

In contrast to these monetarist views, Keynesians argue that most of the disturbances in the economy originate in the real sector.   Variations in investment are emphasised and non-monetary causes of these variations are stressed. The money supply is endogenous, meaning that it is deter- mined (at least in so far as relatively mild cyclical fluctuations are concerned) by forces such as the level of business activity and rates of interest.   The central bank merely responds, for example, by increasing the money supply in an attempt to stabilise interest rates, once an expansion of national income gets under way.

Keynesians in the UK are, in fact, quite a wide group with many views that differ among themselves, but they are, for the most part, not the same as so-called neo- Keynesians, in the USA.   Many British Keynesians deny the importance of money more or less completely and many hold a wage-cost-push theory of inflation.   In the USA most Keynesians are demand-pull theorists and the differences they have with the monetarists are largely with respect to quantitative magnitudes.   That having been said, Keynes- ians in both countries doubt the economy's ability to pro- duce a high and stable level of employment unaided and

they thus advocate active demand management.  Discretionary fiscal policy is the tool they commend to offset the
fluctuations in the level of economic activity. . It is
recommended as being more predictable, less uneven in
impact and faster acting on economic activity than discretionary monetary policy which would be confined to a supporting role.  It is further argued that, at most, there
is only a partial crowding out of private expenditure by
government expenditure and, as a result, fiscal policy is
capable of altering the level of income independent of any
change in the money supply.

Most Keynesians also hold that there is a long-run
trade-off between inflation and unemployment.  Thus the
government should aim at an unemployment target via discretionary demand management policies.  Though such policies will involve inflation, Keynesians believe that the
long-run Phillips curve can be shifted downwards by the
adoption of prices and incomes policies or, more broadly,
by reforming the structure of collective bargaining.
Then there will be a lower 'traded-off' level of inflation
for any given level of unemployment.

## THEORETICAL DEVELOPMENTS

Controversies will no doubt continue in macro-economics
and indeed must continue if progress is to be made in
understanding how the macro-economy works.  We will round
off this overview of macro-economic theory by indicating
briefly some of the ways in which the theory is developing.

### The modern interpretation of Keynes

It may be no coincidence that decline in the acceptance of
the simple Keynesian model has been accompanied by a
theoretical reappraisal of 'what Keynes really meant'.
Various authors, especially Leijonhufvud (1968), have
argued that the sort of non-monetarist position outlined
above does great injustice to Keynes.  They distinguish
between the 'Economics of Keynes' and 'Keynesian Economics', implying that later economists, perhaps uncon-
sciously, replaced Keynes's views by their own.  Keynesianism in practice became fiscalism despite the fact that
before writing the 'General Theory' Keynes had published a
major two-volume work called 'A Treatise on Money'.
Leijonhufvud argues that the 'liquidity trap' position

grossly misinterprets Keynes's own views.   Keynes, he
contends, believed that changes in interest rates would
have a profound effect on the economy.   Investment decisions would be responsive to changes in the rate of interest and the central bank could control interest rates.

Perhaps the special circumstances of the 1930s explain
why Keynesianism became fiscalism.   Feelings at that time
that it would be impossible to persuade the Bank of
England to pursue a strong expansionary policy, coupled
with some empirical evidence suggesting that in the conditions of the 1930s businessmen were not much influenced in
their investment decisions by changes in the rate of
interest, might explain the emphasis on fiscal policy as a
'pump-priming' device.   In normal conditions, however,
Keynes would have placed primary emphasis on the use of
monetary policy.

The multiplier, which lies at the heart of the Keynesian model, is seen by Leijonhufvud (1969) as an 'illiquid-
ity phenomenon'.   His argument concerns the reason for
the downward spiral in output during a depression.   This
is normally presented as a dynamic multiplier process;
sacked workers spend less and thus cut effective demand,
etc.   Leijonhufvud argues that money balances will provide an initial buffer stock of liquidity which insulates
the economy, cutting the multiplier process short in its
tracks.   The multiplier will only operate when the unemployed are unable to borrow or sell assets on a sufficient
scale to maintain their previous lifetime consumption plan
but they would like to.   Thus the emphasis is on missing
or imperfect markets, not on any fundamental psychological
law, to explain a relationship between current income and
consumption.   Leijonhufvud concludes that quantity theorists and Keynesians should be able to agree on one thing
at least and that is how great disasters are fashioned.
'On one view or the other, the system becomes prone to
them, only when it has first been squeezed dry of "liquidity"' (Leijonhufvud, 1969).

The reappraisal of Keynes has led in two related directions.   First, there is temporary equilibrium literature
and, second, a growing literature on constrained equilibrium macro-economic models.   Both are beyond our scope to
discuss here, but certainly the debate has helped to popu-
larise a number of new ideas and has led many to re-read
the 'General Theory'.

The new Cambridge school

The 'new Cambridge' view encompasses a wide range of ideas emanating from the members of the Cambridge Economic Policy Group of the Department of Applied Economics at the University of Cambridge, under the directorship of Wynne Godley.   New Cambridge ideas came to prominence in the United Kingdom in the 1970s but they have received comparatively little attention elsewhere.   The new Cambridge (NC) school of thought developed as a critique of orthodox Keynesianism.   The analyses and policy conclusions deal almost exclusively with the long-run behaviour of the economy.   In this respect, and in fact in respect of a number of policy conclusions, the NC view is similar to that of the monetarists.   However, the underlying model is closer to the Keynesian model than to the monetarist model.   It is basically an income-expenditure flow model with no explicit financial sector or supply side.

In accord with UK Keynesians, the NC theorists hold that inflation is largely determined by trade union power. Exogenous factors, such as a rise in import prices, are also recognised as likely to give rise to inflation.   The NC theorists argue that under free collective bargaining the effect of a devaluation on the balance of payments is probably minimal, whilst its effect on the rate of domestic inflation is large.   Trade union militancy, in the face of reduced real incomes, sets off a wage-price spiral which erodes any initial competitive price advantage conferred by the devaluation.   The exchange rate should be primarily directed towards achieving the government's inflation target.

It is perhaps with respect to their views on long-term import controls that the NC school has been most controversial.   Arguing for an expansionary fiscal policy to reduce unemployment, raise output and simultaneously lower the rate of inflation (via reduced workers' frustration), they come up against a balance of payments constraint. Belief in a continued decline in the UK's share of world trade and in the likelihood that import penetration will increase leads them to expect that at full employment output there will be a large balance of payments deficit. Given their views on devaluation, they believe that it will be necessary to introduce permanent controls in order to restrict the rate of growth of imports.   In summary, the NC school favour expansionary fiscal policy to achieve full employment and import controls to deal with any consequent balance of payments deficit, whilst the exchange rate is adjusted to achieve the government's inflation target.   Incomes policies are not seen as practicable.

The new Cambridge approach remains controversial. Doubt has been fairly widely expressed as to the value of their contribution to macro-economic model-building and the validity and interpretation of their estimates have been questioned.   Perhaps the main value of the group to date has been in its informed observations on current economic issues.

## Marxist theory

A marxist analysis of the macro-economy is largely neglected in economics textbooks.   Where presented at all it tends to be subsumed under 'structuralist' approaches or even under 'sociological' approaches.   There it tends to be confused with 'cost-push' and with a collection of somewhat ad hoc explanations of the macro-economy arising out of structural imperfections.   It is admitted that a fully adequate marxist analysis still has to be constructed, but there have been attempts.

Marxists stress the need to relate recent experience of inflation, unemployment and policy developments to an analysis of post-Second World War experience as a whole. It is argued that inflation has ceased to be primarily an economic problem and has become a major socio-political problem.   Unemployment has always been so.   The effect of qualitatively changed conditions in the labour market and the consequential movement in money wages has been to substitute chronic inflation for periodic depression as the major problem facing the capitalist system in the post-war world.   For reasons which may be summarised as a change in the balance of class strength in favour of the working class, resulting from the course and outcome of the war, the period has been characterised, at least until quite recently, by relatively full employment.   One result of this has been that money wages have risen continuously.   Faced with rising money wages, capitalists have sought to contain the increase in real wages and fend off pressure on profits by raising prices.

Further socio-political changes have intensified these pressures.   In all forms of employment and strata of society there has been a continuous rise in the level of real income regarded as normal and furthermore expectations of continuously increasing living standards have

also become normal.   Educational and psychological implications of the mass-produced economy together with international demonstration effects are suggested as reasons
why discontent is endemic.   The most direct way in which
workers can strive to realise their aspirations is to seek
higher real wages.   As capitalists have been unable to
prevent workers from obtaining money wage increases in
excess of productivity growth and workers have been unable
to prevent capitalists from raising prices the result has
been chronic inflation.   Variations in the rate of inflation, both between countries and at different times are
explained in terms of the international character of the
capitalist system and in the role of the state.   State
intervention and expenditure has grown relentlessly
throughout the post-war period, mainly due to increases in
the provision of collective services by the public sector
and in the proportion of household expenditure financed by
transfer payments.   Whilst this might appear to represent
beneficent capitalism with the neutral state looking after
the interests of all, marxists would consider it as an
aspect of the rising historical and moral element in the
value of labour power and as an attempt to ensure a supply
of labour power with characteristics appropriate to the
changing production process.

Inflationary pressure is thus seen as having socio-
political origins.   The competing claims of private consumption, investment, public provision, defence expenditure and the balance of payments have exceeded the availability of resources.   Efforts to commandeer resources
for one use, if not acquiesced in by those from whom the
resources are to be taken, call forth responses designed
to frustrate them which show themselves in higher prices.
There is insufficient social control (not that there have
not also been some technical problems).   The situation
cannot be adequately defined in terms of the economic concept of excess demand.

In the marxist view, attributing the cause of inflation
to social abstractions like the money supply or excess
demand obscures the social conflicts underlying the
chronic inflation of modern capitalism.   The expansion of
the money supply is seen essentially as a symptom rather
than a cause of inflation.   It is the result of the state
accommodating to socio-political pressures.   To suggest
that inflation can be 'cured' by controlling the rate of
increase in the money supply is just another way of saying
that state expenditure on social welfare services should
be cut or that private consumption should be restrained by

increasing taxes, or that unemployment should be allowed
to increase until the workers respond sensibly.   If these
things were possible there would be no problem of inflation to cure in the first place.   Technical cures for
inflation which depend for their implementation on the
absence of the very socio-political pressures which cause
the inflation make no sense.   Long-run control of inflation is impossible without fundamental changes in the
nature of social reality.   The apparent current success
of monetarist policies in the UK in reducing inflation is
viewed as likely to be short-lived, given the inevitable
socio-political implications of their huge cost in terms
of unemployment.   It might be added that it is a misinter-
pretation of the marxist position to suggest, as some
monetarists do, that monetarism is compatible with marxism.
There is no room for a monetary theory which postulates a
direct causal link from money to prices, for this would
provide a second and independent explanation of inflation,
in addition to conflict theory.

The marxist approach is as yet underdeveloped.   What
seems certain, however, is that a convincing marxist
analysis of inflation would play an important part in
determining the context in which struggles over policy
take place.


Other theoretical developments

Finally, a brief note on the main characteristics of the
international monetarist school and of the so-called
supply-side economics.

International monetarism has principally developed as
an extension of orthodox monetarism and became increasingly popular with the advent of flexible exchange rates in
the early 1970s.   This extension particularly stresses
the influence monetary factors exert on the balance of
payments or the exchange rate, the direct domestic influence of monetary factors being de-emphasised.   If monetary growth in the UK is faster than elsewhere there will
be an outflow of money across the exchanges.   The exchange
rate will fall pushing up the price of imported goods
which will in turn lead to pressure for pay rises.   These
will eventually offset most or all of the gains in competitiveness won by falling exchange rates.   The end result
will be faster inflation not faster growth.

Supply-side economics found its way into the literature

in the late 1970s.   Touted by some as the new revolutionary school of thought destined to replace the thinking of
Keynes and his followers, it has been the source of heated
debate within the economics profession, particularly in
the USA.   The basic thrust of supply-side economics is to
stop rising inflation that results from an excess of
aggregate demand over aggregate supply.   Since reducing
aggregate demand to slow inflation causes unemployment, it
is preferable to stimulate the supply side that will
result in lower costs of production and lower product
prices.   Lower prices and improved productivity will
encourage more output while solving unemployment and in--
flation.   Supply-side economics proposes to achieve these
goals by designing tax cuts to encourage individuals to
work more and households to save more.   Stimulation of
business capital investment, reducing the number of regu-
lations and cutting government spending on public services
will likewise raise productivity.

In the UK the policy has been couched in the more traditional language of incentives and markets but many economists who support such supply-side concepts in principle
believe that its successes can only be modest.

SOCIAL WELFARE ASPECTS OF MACRO-ECONOMIC POLICY

In this final section we shall examine what has since the
mid-1970s been called the UK's economic crisis.   There is
some question as to whether it has been a uniquely UK or
economic phenomenon.   This is beyond our scope here but
Habermas (1975) has provided a forceful analysis of crisis
within a holistic view of modern capitalist society.   We
shall confine our attentions to the symptoms and causes of
the UK's problems and consider the implications for social
policy of macro-economic policy.

A distinguishing feature of the 1970s was the decline
in growth of output in the UK.   Related to this decline
was the high level of inflation triggered by the oil
crisis of the mid-1970s.   Between 1975 and 1980 the rate
of increase of retail prices fell below 10 per cent only
in one year, 1978 (it peaked at 27 per cent in 1975).
Between these same years the number of registered unemployed doubled.   By December 1980, 2.8 million, over 10
per cent of the working population, were so registered,
and the figure was still rising.   In some regions unemployment was over 20 per cent.

A key dimension to an understanding of the crisis is
the role of state expenditures.  Although different definitions of public expenditure lead to significantly different impressions of the growth and importance of the
public sector in the UK, there can be no doubt that public
expenditure has grown as a proportion of national income,
from 35 per cent of GDP in 1950 to 42 per cent in 1980.
This growth has been common to all western industrial
societies and explanations have been advanced on both
macro and micro fronts.   The explanations vary from
natural laws (Wagner and Weber, 1977) through displacement
of taxation (Peacock and Wiseman, 1967) and the impact of
Keynesian policies (Buchanan and Wagner, 1977) to the
state's contribution to the reproduction of capital
(O'Connor, 1973).

Finally, in respect of the symptoms of the crisis, a
combination of the previous factors had important implications for government borrowing.   Since charges on services generate only very small amounts of revenue and
resistance to taxation appears to be increasing, the only
other source of revenue is borrowing.   Thus the Public
Sector Borrowing Requirement (PSBR), which is broadly the
difference between what the government spends, or lends to
others, and what it collects in revenue, grew as a proportion of GDP from a negative value in 1970 (following a
peak in the 1960s of 5.3 per cent in 1967-8) to 11 per
cent in 1975.   The movements of the PSBR in the 1970s,
compared with the 1950s and 1960s, are unusual and partly
explain why the PSBR is at the centre of the debate about
economic policy, particularly with respect to its impact
on interest rates and the money supply.

Here, then, are the main crisis symptoms.   Theorists
differ radically, however, in their understanding of the
cause of the economic crisis and its relation to the
growth in the role of the state.   We shall now review
these different theories and the proposals which emanate
from them.


Keynesians

Keynesian policies of demand management dominated macro-
economic policy from after the Second World War until the
1970s.   The state was seen to have a central role in
managing aggregate demand such as to maintain the economy
in balance at a level of full employment.   Concern over
inflation largely centred on the problem of wage claims

and whether a moderate amount of unemployment might have
to be accepted as the price of wage stability (the
Phillips trade-off).   However the emerging twin problems
of low investment by industry and high wage demands by increasingly powerful trade unions found Keynesians needing
to move far beyond Keynes.   The 1960s saw both Conservative and Labour governments introducing incomes policies
and tinkering with the notion of economic planning.   A
number of writers have argued that this constituted a move
towards a form of corporatism albeit within a liberal
democracy (e.g. Winkler, 1977;  Crouch, 1979;  see pp.
149-53 for a fuller discussion).   The essential features
of this form of corporatism are an economy still based on
private ownership but where there is considerable state
control over investment decisions and over prices and
incomes together with a political structure which involves
the trade unions and business organisations in national
planning.   Now that the Conservative Party has returned
to a philosophy of minimal state interference, corporatism
has been abandoned to the Labour Party and particularly to
its left wing.   There it forms part of the Alternative
Economic Strategy which would seek to expand the economy
and assist such expansion with controls on the growth of
imports.


Marxists and socialist transformation

Marxist analysis of the crisis begins with social conflict.
The crisis of UK capitalism is seen as essentially an
interruption in the process of capital accumulation, leading to stagnating output and employment.   The interruption is due to the declining rate of profit.   Explanations
for the declining rate of profit vary in their emphasis.
Some argue that class conflict has led to workers obtaining a greater share of what is produced than is compatible
with high profit rates.   Others argue that the key problem lies in the over-supply of goods relative to the
available demand, particularly in the context of the competition from new international industrial powers.   Still
others point to the substitution of capital for labour in
the production process and the consequent reduction in the
rate at which surplus value is produced.   Whatever the
explanation proffered, the state's attempts to counteract
the slump have made the situation worse:   inflation in the
1970s, massive increases in unemployment in the 1980s.
Marxists see the capitalist class faced with an inescapable conflict between policies which would be required to
restore accumulation and the requirement that the govern-

ment rules by consent.   The stark alternatives under capitalism are continuing economic recession or the surrender of liberal democracy to the restoration of profitability.   Only the transformation of society to a planned economy geared to the satisfaction of need can overcome the dilemma.   Marxists hold that central government planning is compatible both with efficiency and democracy. It is a form of planning that can best serve the interests of society.

Monetarism and public expenditure cuts

Just as the crises of the 1920s and 1930s were instrumental in the acceptance of Keynesian techniques of demand management, so the crisis of the mid-1970s contributed to the ascendency gained by monetarism.   We have seen earlier in this chapter that to monetarists the key problem is inflation;   a higher rate of unemployment may be a necessary price to be paid in order to achieve monetary stability.   The central tenet of monetarism is that inflation is caused by the money supply increasing more rapidly than the level of output.   Monetarists reject the view that trade unions using their monopoly power to pursue excessive wage demands cause inflation.   Wage demands are simply the mechanism by which excess demand is transformed into price rises, though clearly wage claims will have impact on the level of unemployment.   Public expenditure and its impact on the rate of growth of the money supply are seen at the root of the crisis.

What then does monetarism imply for social policy? The priority is seen to be firm control of the money supply.   The money supply is generally defined as 'sterling M3' and includes all sterling deposits held by UK residents:   that is, it includes bank deposit accounts and sterling certificates of deposit as well as notes, coins and bank current accounts ('M1').   The government can influence the money supply through its power to print money, and its impact on the level of bank deposits.   The latter is affected by government borrowing from banks who can expand their credit and thus create money.   The policy implication is obviously the need to reduce the PSBR. Large tax increases being untenable, the solution must be to cut public expenditure.

This was demonstrated clearly in the opening sentence of the first public expenditure White Paper produced by the Conservative government elected in 1979 which stated that 'public expenditure is at the heart of Britain's economic difficulties' (Cmnd 7746, 1979, p. 1).  Mrs Thatcher had two stated objectives, to reduce the rate of inflation - the aim which was given over-riding priority - and to improve the rate of growth of the economy via supply-side policies.  She claimed that success in reducing inflation was a precondition for improving the rate of growth of the economy and the control of the money supply was seen as the main instrument for controlling inflation.  Hence the need for public expenditure cuts such as to control the PSBR and the money supply.

The centrepiece of the monetarist experiment was the Medium Term Financial Strategy (MTFS), unveiled in the 1980 budget.  It specified targets for the rate of growth of the money supply (taking £M3 as the most reliable indicator) and targets for the PSBR over a four year period, during which both were intended to be reduced gradually. The commitment to control the money supply, to bring down inflation, to set monetary targets and to control public expenditure by cash limits were all policies which had emerged under the Labour government in 1976 in order to retain the confidence of the financial markets.  But whereas the Labour government stumbled into monetarism as a pragmatic necessity, the Conservative Party became ideologically committed to it.

This is not the place to judge the effectiveness of the monetarist experiment.  Enough to say that many commentators believe that the experiment was indeed limited and that the moderation in the rate of inflation owed little to the monetary targets and a great deal to the depth of the recession and the numbers employed (see Wickens, 1981; Pratten, 1982).  Indeed, in its first four years in office the government increased public expenditure overall.

In so far as our immediate concern is with the implications of macro-economic policy for social welfare we must clear up some of the confusion that attends the discussion on public expenditure 'cuts'.  Such 'cuts' rarely take the form of simple cash deductions from a department's expenditure.  In the first place cuts may be selective, entailing the reduction of some programmes while others are increased.  Thus the net effect of a round of 'cuts' may well be an increase in overall expenditure.  This is in effect what happened in 1980-1 when defence expenditure rose by 3 per cent and law and order by 3½ per cent, while education and housing were cut by 4 and 6 per cent respectively.  'Cuts' may be in relation to previously planned

levels of expenditure.   'Cash limits' may be used to cut
the volume of expenditure, as has been the case with the
three main services which dominate local government -
education, housing and social welfare.   Alternatively,
expenditure may be 'cut' by failing to increase resources
in line with needs, by increasing charges for services and
by shifting part of a programme into the private sector.

The nature of the 'cuts' outlined here suggests that
perhaps what we are witnessing is not so much a cut in
total state spending (at least not yet) but a restructuring in specific directions;   the continuation of a trend
begun in the late 1960s.   The government sees such cuts
and restructuring as helping to combat inflation by reducing the PSBR and permitting a reduction in taxation.
Likewise, it sees resources being released to the private
sector to generate employment and exports.   An alternative hypothesis is that the restructuring constitutes the
state's attempt to alter and adapt social policies in the
interests of capital at a time of economic crisis.

Whatever the interpretation there is no doubt that
social expenditure will be further cut back in the near
future.   The predominant economic and political approach
to public expenditure in the early 1980s is based on the
assumption that the market is a superior system of distribution and the most efficient mechanism for the allocation
of goods.   Accordingly, we may expect to see pressure
develop for reprivatisation of parts of the welfare state,
more specifically for expenditure to switch from direct
state provision of services to public subsidisation and
purchase of privately produced services.   Policies
designed to improve efficiency in the social services can
also be expected.   There are already portents that education and social security policies will be adjusted to
adapt the labour force more effectively to the needs of
the labour market.   Nowhere do we see long-term planning
in relation to explicit social objectives in the distribution of resources for welfare.

The public expenditure policies of the late 1970s and
the early 1980s have exposed the crucial relationship
between social and economic policy.   They reveal the
heavy dependence of social spending on economic considera-
tions.   Social policy has been subordinated to economic
policy.   Obviously economic magnitudes underpin public
expenditure on social services, but the presumption of
dominance does not necessarily follow from this interdependence.   It is the precedence afforded to 'market

values' that has undervalued expenditure on social services and led to the emphasis on economic policy.   In fact,
the simple distinction made between economic policy and
social policy is a false one.   It is impossible to have
a macro-economic policy which is not also a social policy.
Responsibility for the management of the economy cannot be
separated from responsibility for the social effects of
such management.   Economic policies contain implicit and
sometimes explicit assumptions about the sort of society
the government is attempting to create.


FURTHER READING

Many of the comments with respect to further reading made
at the end of chapter 2 apply here equally.   No textbook
on macro-economic theory and policy provides an analysis
of the issues that anyone should simply read and accept as
definitive.   Economists do disagree.   There is a conflict between theories and it is a conflict which mirrors
the wider struggle between interest groups in society at
large.   The view taken here is that the understanding of
one theory is aided by a knowledge of the others.   The
sensible way to an understanding and assessment of the
issues regarding the conduct of macro-economic policy in
the UK is to look at a variety of authors and perspectives.

There are presentations of Keynesian economics in every
general or macro-economics textbook.   To the standard
type, Lipsey (1979) and Samuelson (1980), we would add two
relatively new introductory texts:   Baumol and Blinder
(1982) and Scott and Nigro (1982), both of which provide
concise and up-to-date treatments.   A highly readable
study of Keynes's work and ideas is provided by Stewart
(1972).

Much of the literature on monetarism is couched in
technical terms, but in addition to the treatment in the
standard texts the following should be accessible;   Friedman (1968) and (1970), Anderson (1973) and Johnson (1971).
Kaldor (1970) offers a dissenting voice.   Vane and
Thompson (1979), present an analysis of the main aspects
of the monetarist/Keynesian controversy and three collec-
tions published by the Institute of Economic Affairs
(A. Seldon ed. (1972);   (1974;   and (1975)) contain
articles covering the whole range of orthodox opinion.

An excellent and brief summary of the competing

approaches to the problem of inflation is provided by
Trevithick (1980).   The more advanced reader is advised
to consult Trevithick and Mulvey (1975).   Attempts at
analysing macro-economic issues from a marxist perspective
include Glyn and Sutcliffe (1972);  Yaffe (1973);  Devine
(1974);  and Mandel (1975), especially chapter 13.

On the reinterpretation of Keynes, Leijonhufvud (1978)
and (1969) are the standard references, but an easier read
is provided by Coddington (1974).   A neat summary of the
new Cambridge position is provided in Cross (1982) chapter
7.   More advanced readers will find Cross to provide a
stimulating appraisal of the whole area under review.

Mrs Thatcher's 'Economic Experiment' is assessed by
Wickens (1981).   Pratten (1982) also discusses this and
a number of other current economic issues in simple language, understandable to those without a training in economics.   Aaronovitch (1981) puts forward the idea of an
Alternative Economic Strategy.

The current recession and possible radical reconstruction of social welfare in the UK has been accompanied by
the publication of quite a number of pertinent books.
Recommended are George and Wilding (1976), Gough (1979)
and particularly Taylor-Gooby and Dale (1981).   Walker
(1982), specifically explores the usually neglected relationship between social and economic policies.   Cole,
Cameron and Edwards (1983) provide a lively, though rigor-
ous, analysis of the competing theoretical perspectives
and show the links between economic theory and political
practice.

BIBLIOGRAPHY

* Recommended.
** Recommended for easier reading.

Aaronovitch, S. (1981), 'The Road from Thatcherism',
    London, Lawrence & Wishart.
* Anderson, L. (1973), The State of the Monetarist Debate,
    'Federal Reserve Bank of St. Louis Review', vol. 56.
* Baumol, W.J., and Blinder, A.S. (1982), 'Economics', New
    York, Harcourt Brace Jovanovich.
Buchanan, J.M., and Wagner, R.E. (1977), 'Democracy in
    Deficit: The Political Legacy of Lord Keynes', New
    York, Academic Press.
Cairncross, F., and Keeley, P. (1981), 'The Guardian Guide
    to the Economy', London and New York, Methuen.

** Coddington, A. (1974), What Did Keynes Really Mean?, 'Challenge', November-December, pp. 13-19.
* Cole, K., Cameron, J., and Edwards, C. (1983), 'Why Economists Disagree', London, Longman.
* Cross, R. (1982), 'Economic Theory and Policy in the UK', Oxford, Martin Robertson.
Crouch, C. (ed.) (1979), 'State and Economy in Contemporary Capitalism', London, Croom Helm.
* Devine, P. (1974), Inflation and Marxist Theory, 'Marxism Today', March.
Friedman, M., and Schwartz, A.J. (1963), 'A Monetary History of the United States, 1867-1960', Princeton University Press.
Friedman, M. (1968), Money: Quantity Theory, 'International Encyclopedia of the Social Sciences', vol. 10, New York, Macmillan.
* Friedman, M. (1970), 'The Counter-Revolution in Monetary Theory', London, Institute of Economic Affairs.
* George, V., and Wilding, P. (1976), 'Ideology and Social Welfare', London, Routledge & Kegan Paul.
* Glyn, A.J., and Sutcliffe, R.B. (1972), 'British Capitalism, Workers and the Profits Squeeze', Harmondsworth, Penguin.
** Gough, I. (1979), 'The Political Economy of the Welfare State', London, Macmillan.
Green, F., and Nore, P. (1977), 'Economics, An Anti-Text', London, Macmillan.
Habermas, J. (1975), 'Legitimation Crisis', Boston, Beacon Press.
Huhne, C. (1983), 'Guardian', 10 March.
* Johnson, H.G. (1971), The Keynesian Revolution and the Monetarist Counter-revolution, 'American Economic Review', vol. 61.
* Kaldor, N. (1970), The New Monetarism, 'Lloyds Bank Review', May.
Keynes, J.M. (1936), 'The General Theory of Employment, Interest and Money', London, Macmillan.
* Leijonhufvud, A. (1968), 'On Keynesian Economics and the Economics of Keynes', London, Oxford University Press.
* Leijonhufvud, A. (1969), 'Keynes and the Classics', London, Institute of Economic Affairs.
Lipsey, R.G. (1983), 'An Introduction to Positive Economics' (6th edn), London, Weidenfeld & Nicolson.
* Mandel, E. (1975), 'Late Capitalism', London, New Left Books.
O'Connor, J. (1973), 'The Fiscal Crisis of the State', London, St James Press.
Peacock, A.T., and Wiseman, J. (1967), 'The Growth of

Public Expenditure in the UK' (2nd edn), London, Allen & Unwin.

Phillips, A.W. (1958), The Relation between Unemployment and the Rate of Change of Money Wage Rates in the United Kingdom, 1861-1957, 'Economica', vol. 25, November.

** Pratten, C.F. (1982), Mrs Thatcher's Economic Experiment, 'Lloyds Bank Review', January, no. 143.

Samuelson, P. (1980), 'Economics' (11th edn), New York, McGraw-Hill.

* Scott, R.H., and Nigro, N. (1982), 'Principles of Economics', New York, Macmillan.

* Seldon, A. (ed.) (1972), 'Inflation, Economy and Society', London, Institute of Economic Affairs.

* Seldon, A. (ed.) (1974), 'Inflation, Causes, Consequences and Cures', London, Institute of Economic Affairs.

* Seldon, A. (ed.) (1975), 'Crisis', London, Institute of Economic Affairs.

** Stewart, M. (1972), 'Keynes and After' (2nd edn), Harmondsworth, Penguin.

** Taylor-Gooby, P., and Dale, J. (1981), 'Social Theory and Social Welfare', London, Edward Arnold.

** Trevithick, J.A. (1980), 'Inflation, A Guide to the Crisis in Economics' (2nd end), Harmondsworth, Penguin.

* Trevithick, J.A., and Mulvey, C. (1975), 'The Economics of Inflation', Oxford, Martin Robertson.

* Vane, H.R., and Thompson, J.L. (1979), 'Monetarism', Oxford, Martin Robertson.

Wagner, R.E., and Weber, W.E. (1977), Wagner's Law, fiscal institutions and the growth of government, 'National Tax Journal', vol. 30.

* Walker, A. (ed.) (1982), 'Public Expenditure and Social Policy', London, Heinemann.

* Wickens, M.R. (1981), The New Conservative Macroeconomics, 'University of Southampton Discussion Papers in Economics', no. 8114.

Winkler, J. (1977), The Coming Corporatism, in R. Skidelsky (ed.), 'The End of the Keynesian Era', London, Macmillan.

* Yaffe, D. (1973), The Crisis and Profitability, 'New Left Review', July-August.

# Chapter 4

# Marx and marxism
## Sandra Walklate

Marx is one of the great figures of nineteenth-century
scholarship whose work spans most of the separate social
science disciplines. His work and the work of his followers provided a radical alternative view to other
theories of social analysis until the 1960s. More
recently its influence has been more significant, particularly in sociological analysis. It is impossible to
cover in such a short space as is available here all the
intricacies of debate and controversy surrounding Marx's
work in all its breadth. This chapter will therefore be
focusing on the key sociological elements of his work and
the work of his followers which have most keenly influenced writers on social administration. Even so, this
should be recognised as no more than an introduction, to
be followed by further reading.

## KARL MARX (1818-83)

Karl Marx was born on 5 May 1818 in Trier, Germany.
Little appears to be recorded about his early life; of
significance, however, is his time spent at the University
of Bonn and then subsequently Berlin. There he joined
the Young Hegelians and was influenced not only by the
ideas of Hegel but also by those of Feuerbach in the
writing of his doctoral thesis. His marriage, and move
to Paris in 1843, saw him influenced by socialist ideas,
and saw the formation of his friendship with Engels.
Marx was expelled from Paris in 1845, and after some time
in Brussels, where the 'Communist Manifesto' was written,
he arrived in London. It was Engels who introduced him
to the working conditions of those involved in textile
manufacture and it was in the reading room of the British
Museum where Marx did most of his work. He died in his
study in 1883.

THE INTELLECTUAL CONTEXT OF HIS WORK

There were essentially three major influences on Marx's
writings;  the work of the German philosophers, the
writings of the French historians;  and his own study of
the British economists Smith and Ricardo.   This intellectual background in which Marx's ideas were formulated contributes to the key themes which hold his work together,
namely the concepts of progress, alienation, perfectability, and the totality of history.

The idea of progress refers to the successive stages of
development in which the writings of Hegel presume the
true spirit of human beings unfolded.   For Marx this unfolding was seen to emerge out of conflict.   This constituted a marriage of Hegel's ideas with the French historians' view of history as a process of class struggle.
Hence, the true spirit of humankind unfolded through successive stages of history as a result of conflict and
struggle.

The notion of alienation, reflected in its early form
in the work of Rousseau, refers to the distortion of the
natural state of human beings as a result of their involvement in society.   The Hegelian interpretation of this was
again an important influence on Marx's thinking.   Hegel
was concerned with the way in which the construction of
social systems by people led to their alienation from
their own spirit.   Marx deals with this issue more socio-
logically in that he is concerned with the way in which
individuality is lost in collectively organised activity.
The most significant form of this alienation for Marx was
economic alienation;  the domination of living individuals
by an organised economic system focused on goods and
machinery.

Perfectability refers to the extent to which the capabilities of human beings are formed and realised as a
result of their relationship with the environment and circumstances within it.   The possibility is raised here of
changing the environment to produce a more complete development of human capabilities.   In other words, change the
conditions in which people live and their nature as people
will change.

The final theme, the totality of history, draws the
rest together.   The essence of this idea is again reflected in Hegel's work, in the doctrine of historical materialism to be discussed more fully shortly.   However, this

suggests that the understanding of one particular historical moment requires an understanding of it by reference to
the total history and structure of a particular societal
form.   For Marx, 'the (written) history of all hitherto
existing society is the history of class struggle' ('The
Communist Manifesto', opening line).   Thus Marx is concerned with the total historical structure of a society as
it is characterised by its constraints on and alienation
of the true spirit of humankind.

The synthesis of these philosophical themes ultimately
led Marx to concern himself with the processes of capitalism in which people suffered alienation, and to an expectation that post-capitalist society would see the fulfilment of their individuality or true spirit.

In looking at capitalism Marx was further influenced by
his reading of the British political economists, particularly Smith and Ricardo.   He rejected Adam Smith's view
that men are naturally motivated by self-interest and that
competition is the most effective way of reconciling self-
interest and social control in the creation of a harmoni-
ous state.   On the other hand, he found in Ricardo's
labour theory of value the basis for a new understanding
of class conflict in society.   In integrating these ideas
into his philosophical ideas Marx regarded the economic
structure as the root of those influences which defined the
individual's view of himself and his relationship to the
social world.   To grasp the essence of Marx's development
of these ideas attention will be focused in the following
pages on the concepts of historical materialism, surplus
value, alienation and class and class struggle.

Historical materialism

In Marx's view, to understand the nature of human beings
one must understand their relationship to the material
environment and the historical nature of this relationship
in creating and satisfying individual needs.   This material environment may, in the first instance, be the constraints of the physical environment.   However, as societies develop and become more complicated, the environment
itself will become more complicated and comprise more
socio-cultural constraints.   Hence, for Marx, experience
comes before ideas, or more specifically, society determines the nature of human consciousness.   Consequently,
this is one of the factors which distinguishes human beings
from other species.   The relationship between people,

their work and their environment is to be related to the
socio-economic structure and organisation of society.   So
an understanding of historical processes makes possible an
understanding of human nature and the social relationships
which exist at any particular point in time.

Marx, like Durkheim, associates social change with increasing social differentiation as a result of the division
of labour.   In tribal societies, or pre-class systems, he
argues, the division of labour occurred mainly on sex
lines - men providing food and women rearing children - as
a consequence of that particular relationship to the physical environment.   Such a society is communal in emphasis.
Private property and individuality do not exist.   More
complicated societal forms, he suggests, emerge as a
result of the production of surplus wealth and the consequent acquisition of private property.   These material
conditions enable one group in that society to separate
itself from others and take a dominant position.   Marx
saw this as the essence of the class-divided societies of
the ancient world, such as those of classical Greece and
Rome.

Marx sketches out the further stages of historical
development through the feudal to the bourgeois capitalist
systems, emphasising throughout that the changes from one
stage to another need to be understood in terms of changes
in the dominant mode of production, which forms the
essence of the material environment.   Thus the structure
of the economic system - the infrastructure - is seen to
be the base of other relationships such as the legal and
political systems - the superstructure.   Social change
occurs as a result of conflict produced by the antagonistic relationships characteristic of a class society based
on capitalist production, as opposed to the older class-
divided societies since their relationship to the means of
production is qualitatively different, as discussed in the
following sections.   Social changes are eventually precip-
itated by a shift in power resulting from a change in the
mode of production.   Marx considered bourgeois capitalism
to be the last stage before socialism.   This would emerge
as a consequence of revolutionary change allowing people
to express their true nature.


Surplus value

In chapter 2 (pp. 42-5) the concept of surplus value was
introduced in the context of a critique of micro-economic

heory.   Here it is necessary to enlarge on the social
mplications of surplus value by showing its relationship
.o capital accumulation and so to the concepts of class
:onflict and alienation which are discussed in the next
;ections.

   In chapter 2 surplus value was defined as the differ-
:nce between the price fetched by a product and the cost
›f the labour employed in its production.   Surplus value
rises in the specific historical context of private
›wnership of land and capital.   In these circumstances
:he non-owners are forced to sell their labour power to
:he owners of land and capital in order to earn their
.ivelihood.   The owners are thereby enabled to extract
:he surplus value by a process of 'exploitation', paying
.he workers less than the value of their production.
This process leads to the 'alienation' of the workers in
:he various senses discussed in the next section.

   Surplus value is used by the owners of the means of
›roduction partly to maintain themselves and to maintain
:he mechanisms of the state that protect their interests.
3ut part of the surplus value has to be used to ensure the
:eproduction of capital and the maintenance of future
›rofits.

   Marx divided capital into two categories:   'constant
:apital', the cost of machinery, etc., and 'variable
:apital', the cost of raw materials and wages.   The main-
:enance of profits in a situation of competition between
:apitalists requires the steady expansion of constant
:apital both absolutely and in relation to variable capi-
:al.   In this way the accumulation of capital becomes the
organising principle of the economic and social system.
This results in the development of a contradiction within
the system.   On the one hand, there is a higher rate of
exploitation because the workers receive a lower proportion of the value of their product.   On the other hand,
Marx argued, there would be a tendency for the long-term
rate of profit to decline.   These contradictory tendencies towards a higher rate of exploitation and a lower
rate of profit in the process of capital accumulation
would result in an increasing polarisation between the
classes, and increased class-consciousness among the
workers, leading eventually to the workers' revolution.

Alienation

Marx observed that the advance of capitalism, characterised by the division of labour intrinsic to the manufacturing process, resulted in workers becoming equated with
the product of their work.   This process he referred to
as 'objectification';  that is workers become like
objects, servants to the product of their work, whilst
simultaneously having little power over the product of
their work or the work process.   In this way workers are
alienated from a labour process which has been socially
constructed.

Alienation, as a consequence, occurs in a number of
distinct ways.   People are alienated from the product of
their labour.   They have no control over what happens to
their work, and their labour power is a commodity to be
bought and sold in the market system.   They are also
alienated from the work process itself. Since the mechani-
sation and rationalisation of the factory process is
geared towards mass production, each worker is only involved in a small compartmentalised part of the production
process.   This provides no satisfaction for the worker.
Finally, people are seen to be alienated from themselves
and their fellow workers.   Here it is suggested that the
capitalist process diverts human beings from their true
nature since they are subordinated to the economic system
and are simultaneously isolated from others by the
demands of that system.   This labour process is central
to the production and reproduction of class relationships.

In this way a particular social and economic structure
is seen to have considerable impact on the true nature of
individuals.   This true nature, Marx suggests, can only
be realised by overcoming the problem of alienation.
This can be achieved through the abolition of private
property and its control over wage labour.   The fundamental sociability of human beings would be reconstituted by
this process.   Communism, in Marx's view, will provide
the context in which this sociability will ultimately be
achieved.   Thus collectivised resources and products are
the way to fulfilling true individuality;   that is, change
the material environment and individual consciousness will
also change.

Class and class conflict

The capitalist system, resulting in the alienation of workers, is seen to be rooted in class relationships which are characterised by a conflict of interests.  These relationships, for Marx, need to be understood in their historical context.

Marx does not offer a systematic and coherent definition of class but this does not mean that an understanding of the concept cannot be inferred from his writings on the subject.  Primarily, classes are constituted around the patterns of property ownership within any economic system. In some societies, as in ancient Greece or Rome, such class divisions resulted in one class being dominant over another.  However, only in the class societies of capitalism do such relationships produce active conflict as a consequence of the productive process.  Under the capitalist mode of production the division of labour results in the owners of the productive process having power over the non-owners, i.e. the workers.  But the centralisation of work and production in factories and similar workplaces has the effect of providing the conditions in which workers can develop common interests.  Hence the emergence of conflict since their interests do not necessarily coincide with those of the owners.  Marx suggests that ultimately the working class will recognise its common interests and act upon them.  This will result in a 'class in itself' becoming a 'class for itself'.  The emergence of such class consciousness is seen as crucial to paving the way for any new or revolutionary social relationships.

The ruling class, however, using the surplus value derived from alienated labour as a source, achieves not only economic domination, but also political domination. It is the intertwining of these two which poses a barrier to the emergence of class consciousness.  Thus, on the one hand the productive process extracts a surplus from the workers so that the owners themselves might live, that is, effects a relationship of exploitation.  On the other hand this economic control is the means by which it is also possible for the ruling economic class to become the ruling political class;  that is, to effect a relationship of oppression.  Economic power results in control over the propagation of those attitudes and values considered appropriate to ensure a continued commitment to the nature of the workplace.  Whilst the workers continue to be alienated, this situation is perpetuated.  The systematic and continued accumulation of capital by the ruling class allows such continued power.

Marx's use of this simplified model of class relations
does not prevent him from recognising that not all groups
in society fit into such homogeneous divisions.   There
are marginal and transitional groups who may not be wholly
integrated into the class system.   The 'Lumpenproletariat
of 'thieves' and 'vagabonds' would fit into this category.
More recently, writers have been concerned to locate
gender and ethnic divisions within Marx's analytical model
Nevertheless, he suggests that the contradictions which
emerge from class conflict are the key mechanism through
which class consciousness will emerge.


DEVELOPMENTS FROM MARX

The foregoing analysis provides some insight into the main
influences on Marx's thought and the nature of his
theories.   However, there are many difficulties which
arise from his work.   These are reflected in the various
attempts made to develop his overall theoretical schema.
Such attempts explore what Marx actually meant by his
theory, whether it can be considered scientific, and how
it can be related to political action.   These developments can only be briefly sketched here.

During the first years after Marx's death, his writings
were influential in two main arenas;   in the academic
social sciences and in the emerging socialist political
parties.   It was in this latter field that the debate
arose about the scientific status of Marx's work, known as
the 'revisionist controversy'.   This occurred within the
German Social Democratic Party between Bernstein (1909)
and Kautsky (1899) and Luxemburg (1899).   In a series of
articles in 'Die Neue Zeit', a newspaper founded in 1883
and edited by Kautsky, Bernstein and Kautsky debated
Marx's predictions concerning the future of capitalism and
their scientific status.   Bernstein argued that Marx's
work did not stand the test of empirical evidence since
his predictions were not being confirmed by events.
Kautsky and Luxemburg responded to this by reiterating the
orthodox marxist view that the capitalist system would
ultimately break down.

In the academic arena Marx's work provoked a response
in both the work of Max Weber (1904) and the work of
Durkheim (1894).   Weber's writings reflect a concern with
the economic determinism implied by Marx.   Weber regarded
this stance as simplistic, since it was a view from a particular value position and consequently could not be con-

sidered to be universally applicable.   He was also unhappy with the idea that socialism would result in the
'dictatorship of the proletariat'.   Weber felt that the
result of socialism would more probably be rule by bureauc-
racy increasingly reflected in the trends of the time.
Durkheim was influenced by Marx partly in his teaching and
partly in his own consideration of class conflict, although
he was hesitant about accepting Marx's view of the fundamental importance of the economic system.

The academic debate on marxist theory was overtaken by
the Russian Revolution of 1917, when Lenin attempted to
put the theory into practice.   The ground for debate then
moved from elucidating the theory and considering the evidence for it, to the relationship between marxist theory
and political action.

The writings of Lukács (1971) and Gramsci (1971) were
particularly concerned with Marx's theory as a guide to
political action.   Both were concerned to identify Marx
as presenting a 'philosophy of praxis' rather than a science of society.   In other words, they argued that Marx
was presenting a particular view of the working class, its
historical location, and the action necessary to change
its position.   Lukács suggested that marxism could only
be an 'objective science in practice'.   Since social
theories in general tended to support the interests of particular groups or classes, Lukács argued that marxism
could be regarded as objective since it aligned itself
with the working class on whom the social system ultimately depended.   Commitment and objectivity were not seen to
be inconsistent since the philosophy of praxis was the
central concern.   More recently, Lukács has criticised
his own views and suggested that present-day capitalism
required an 'objective analysis' rather than an 'objective
practice'.

Similarly, Gramsci wrote of the importance of marxism
as a philosophy guiding the proletariat in its struggle.
Gramsci spent most of his life in prison as a consequence
of the rise of fascism in Italy in the 1920s and saw the
importance of understanding the power that one group
exerts over another, not as physical coercive power but as
intellectual and moral power, giving wide-ranging consent
to the system.   Such relationships he labelled hegemonic
relationships, which he necessarily saw as pedagogical;
that is, as teaching relationships.   Thus, he argued, the
control of the workers was subtly exercised through the
church, the school, the press and workers' associations.

This was the means by which the bourgeoisie perpetuated
'false consciousness' in the workers.   In order for the
working class to achieve power, it was necessary to legitimate its potential to rule through wide-ranging cultural
acceptance;   that is, it needed to achieve hegemonic
power.   This, Gramsci argued, was the task of education
in the broadest sense of that term.   This, for him, was
the means by which the workers would free themselves from
the dominance of the ruling class.

This emphasis on political activity by marxist writers
can be partly explained by the events of the 1920s and
1930s and the Second World War.   The same events discour-
aged other forms of marxist debate until its re-emergence
as an intellectual and political force in a wide range of
disciplines in the 1950s.   At this time two main strands
of theory emerged within sociology - structural marxism
and critical theory.

Structural marxism

Structural marxism has its origins in the work of Louis
Althusser and some modern anthropological thought.
Althusser is concerned to establish marxism as a science
in so far as it is a theory which provides an understanding of the inner logic of societies.   He was concerned
with that which occurs without individuals in society
either being aware or having knowledge of its occurrence.
Thus, Althusser argues, the object of study is the mode of
production and how this relates to the social structure -
the political, social and cultural systems.   The key
concern is how one mode of production is changed to
another.   Structural marxism focuses attention, then, on
'structural causality';   how and why contradictions emerge
within a social formation, or set of social relationships.
The ultimately determining factor of such contradictions
is seen as the nature of the economic system, hence the
concern with the mode of production.   Althusser suggests
that contradictions may occur at different times between
different parts of the system and spends some time discussing how an ultimate breakdown of the system is avoided,
through the operation of the 'ideological state apparatuses' and the 'repressive state apparatuses' (Althusser,
1971).   The connections between this and a functionalist
view are dealt with elsewhere in this book (pp. 125-6).

The extent to which structural marxists have advanced
in terms of the notion of 'structural causality' is open

to question;  the structuralist approach itself being very
diverse.   The work of Goldmann (1964) and Poulantzas
(1978) illustrates its development and diversity.   Goldmann focuses on the processes by which social classes
create cultural 'structures of meaning'.   Poulantzas
focuses attention on political structures and their connections with social classes and social change.   However,
the ultimate goal of structural marxism is to show how
these various parts of a total social structure are inter-
related, in an attempt to modify the sharp distinction
made by Marx between the infrastructure and the superstructure discussed earlier.   In the last analysis, however, the economic infrastructure is still regarded as
being determinate.

Critical theory

Critical theory, latterly associated with the writings of
Habermas and Offe, is derived from ideas originally formulated within the Frankfurt Institute for Social Research.
This approach is 'critical' in two ways.   It rejects the
view that societies are governed by law-like patterns of
inter-relationships (a criticism of positivism) and, in
contrast to structural marxism, it rejects the ultimate
determining nature of the economic base.   Critical theory
focuses attention on the shaping power of ideology.

Habermas (1976) expresses the view that the process of
capital accumulation, the organising principle of capitalism with which modern industrial societies operate, has
resulted in the economic system surrendering some of its
autonomy to the state.   He suggests that the contradictions or 'crises' experienced by the capitalist system
have resulted in an increasing interdependence of the different parts of the system.   The main difficulty is to
maintain a continued 'legitimation' or acceptance of a
particular social order.   Concern is therefore directed
towards how motivations and rewards are produced for the
maintenance and reproduction of the existing society;
that is how the 'communicative behaviour' of individuals
is created in the shared symbols of society (Habermas,
1979).   Thus consciousness, or class consciousness, is
not just the outcome of material production, but is also
the outcome of the shaping power of ideologies, which
legitimate the social order.

Those associated with this school of thought do not

necessarily totally overlook the role of the political and
economic processes in overcoming the crises of capitalism.
The work of Offe (1972b, 1975) looks at the intermarriage
of these parts.  He emphasises the role of the state not
as a neutral entity, but as a bureaucratic system with
knowledge and expertise specifically geared towards the
maintenance of social harmony, ensuring a continued commitment to it.

Some would argue that critical theory, given the nature
of its emphasis, has strayed from the spirit of Marx's
thought.   Indeed it focuses attention on issues which are
not peculiar to marxist writers but can also be found in
non-marxist thought.   In particular, some useful parallels can be made between the ideas suggested here and
those of Bell (1976), a non-marxist social commentator,
who discusses the importance of understanding the shaping
power of value-systems.

Theories of the state

Drawing attention to the role of the state in modern
capitalist society and the notion of the state in 'crisis',
is a significant point of convergence for many marxist
writers, particularly in the context of the welfare state.
Before presenting an overall critical assessment of the
marxist perspective a brief introduction will be presented
to the various approaches taken by marxists in understanding the role of the state in modern capitalist society.

In 'The Communist Manifesto' Marx and Engels state
that:  'the executive of the modern state is but a committee for managing the common affairs of the whole bourgeoisie'.   Modern marxist theories of the state share the
same basic premise.   There are, however, differences in
emphasis.   E.O. Wright (1975) has identified three main
approaches to analysing the role of the state:  the instrumentalist, the structuralist and the Hegelian marxist.
Instrumentalist theories suggest that the state serves
the interests of the bourgeoisie because it is controlled
by the capitalist class.   Structuralist theories are concerned with the way in which state activity is determined
by contradictions in the economic structure, which neutra-
lises its power.   Hegelian marxist theories emphasise the
state's positive role in perpetuating the ideology and the
processes of legitimation necessary for the continuance of
a capitalist society.   In terms of constructing a theoretical framework for understanding the nature and operation

of the welfare state, it is considered here that this last
category seems to offer the most sophisticated level of
analysis.

This needs to be understood alongside another main concern of marxism, that is, understanding how the state
deals with crises.   O'Connor (1973) usefully introduces
this concept.   He suggests that the capitalist state is
required to fulfil two functions which are often contradictory, accumulation and legitimation.   To achieve both
these goals the state must maintain the condition of
social harmony.   These goals are served by 'social capital' expenditure, a category he suggests covers nearly
every form of state expenditure.   In the context of welfare expenditure, for example, some education expenditure
increases productivity, some insurance schemes facilitate
the reproduction of the workforce, some social security
benefits pacify the reserve workforce.   Such expenditure,
when added together serves both the goals of legitimation
and accumulation.

Why particular lines of action and particular policies
are adopted depends upon the route chosen by the state
thought to be in the general interests of capital.   Offe
(1975) suggests there are four 'mechanisms of selection'
available.   Such choices need to be understood in terms
of the structure of the state itself setting the para-
meters of possible action;   the ideological system defining some events as problems and others not;   decision-
making procedures which normally operate to lessen the
impact of reform;   and, if all other mechanisms fail, re-
pression.   It is necessary then, not only to understand
public spending as a means of accumulation and legitimation, but also to understand the structure and procedures
of the state which make this possible.   The relevance in
the context of social administration for offering an insight into these concepts will be returned to shortly.


OVERVIEW AND CRITICAL ASSESSMENT

The foregoing discussion provides an insight into the many
and varied strands of marxist thought.   It is convenient
to compare marxism with functionalism at this point since
the two theories have much in common, but also have significant differences.

In the first instance marxism, like functionalism,
adopts a holistic level of explanation.   Social processes

and social formations are to be understood by reference to
the ongoing totality of society which exists within a particular historical framework.   However, unlike functionalism, marxism sees this whole within a view of history
which demands a dynamic rather than a static analysis.
Thus, at any particular historical moment, relationships
within society are to be seen as a product of past historical relationships and those relationships which are continuing.   The emphasis is not only one of ongoing process
but of an ongoing antagonistic process.   Society is then
seen as being rooted in conflict rather than the consensus
envisaged by functionalism.

However, like functionalism, marxism is also concerned
to identify the different elements of a social whole and
how they are related.   Marxism sees the economic system
as being, if not ultimately determinant, then at least
very significant in forming such relationships.   Functionalism lays no such stress on a particular feature of
society, providing that the functional prerequisites of
that society are met, and social order maintained.   More
recently, however, marxists have addressed themselves to
understanding the maintenance of social order, given that
revolutionary circumstances do not appear to be materiali-
sing in developed capitalist economies.

A consequence of emphasising the holistic level of analysis is that it reduces to a minimum the role accorded to
understanding interpersonal relationships and individual
choices in the social process.   This is a more accurate
comment on some strands of marxism than of others.
Habermas for example, as a critical theorist, lays great
stress on understanding the communicative processes
between individuals particularly in his more recent writings (1979).   This may be seen as a development of understanding how particular social formations permeate even
the interactive processes and does not necessarily accord
the individual purposive control over his actions.   It is
possible to argue that Habermas is unfolding here the para-
meters to social action within which individuals exert a
limited choice and sense of purpose but which nevertheless
constrain their capacities.   There is obviously a degree
of tension between the levels of analysis postulated here,
in the attempt to avoid a deterministic image of human
beings - a tension which exists between all macro-sociological analyses and their micro-sociological counterparts.
Meanwhile the control exerted by society over the consciousness of human beings and their potential to act
independently of that control remains problematic.

A second level of critical analysis emerges from considering the extent to which Marx or marxism constitutes a
scientific enterprise.  The problems surrounding this
sort of evaluation are dealt with in chapter 1, however
one of the main figures in that debate, Popper, also constitutes an outspoken critic of marxism and therefore
requires consideration here.  As has been pointed out
earlier in this book, Popper was keen to propose a way of
distinguishing scientific from non-scientific enterprise
by introducing and developing the notion of falsifiability.
This notion suggests that a scientific process comprises a
testing procedure, in which evidence is uncovered to
either corroborate or discorroborate an initial hypothesis.
Thus, a hypothesis may be shown to be at fault but may not
be shown to be true.  As far as Marx's writings are concerned then, events suggest that his theory and predictions
have not stood the test of time, that is:  the ultimate
breakdown of the capitalist system has not materialised.
Similarly, other occurrences, for example, the 'embour-
geoisement' of the working class, the failure of communism
in the Soviet Union, are processes which it is suggested
bring the marxist model under serious question.  Here the
criticism is not so much directed against Marx but against
marxism.  Marxists, in Popper's view, have responded to
such events by reshaping the evidence to fit the theory
instead of amending the theory in the light of the evidence.  Thus marxism becomes rather like a religion, not
without meaning, but without scientific status since it
renders no publicly testable objective knowledge.  This
is an issue which has provoked considerable debate - see
Suchting (1972) in particular, for a more sophisticated
analysis.

The extent to which this is a valid point may depend
upon the strand of marxism under discussion.  Althusser,
for example, is concerned with the process of refining the
theory rather than the production of testable hypotheses,
but this may not be true of other marxist writers.  In
contrast the works of Westergaard and Resler (1975) and
Miliband (1969) are both studies rooted in empirical evidence.  Once that evidence has been interpreted then it
is open to critical evaluation from the academic community
to make a decision on the adequacy and accuracy of the
interpretation of the data.  Here the problem becomes one
not so much for marxism but for social science in general,
given the variety of theoretical perspectives available to
analyse the same data, as the contents of this book alone
indicate.

More recent criticisms of marxism have emerged as a
consequence of increasing social awareness of divisions in
society other than those of class.   The extent to which
Marx or marxism encompasses an understanding of ethnic and
gender divisions and their relationship to class divisions
in society is a considerable area of debate provoked by
the growth in feminist and black consciousness movements
of the 1960s.   Again, within sociology, marxism was not
alone in its lack of analysis of such social divisions,
and attempts have been made to rectify this (see Giddens
and Held, 1982).   A further area yet to be developed
within marxist theory is to offer an understanding of the
emergence of nationalism and the nation state which has
played such an important part in more recent world history.

A final general comment concerns the basis of the divergences and consequent debates within marxism as to the
interpretation to be placed on events in society.   These
divergences are as much a reflection of the extent to
which marxists themselves are optimistic or pessimistic
about the likelihood of a revolutionary outcome from the
capitalist mode of production, as they are differences in
analysis.   Such divergences are possibly one of the consequences of a model that tries to predict the long-term
future.


RELEVANCE FOR SOCIAL ADMINISTRATION

In adopting a marxist perspective in this context, the
welfare in question becomes the welfare of the capitalist
system.   Consequently, a marxist perspective has considerable value in providing an alternative explanation of
many of the phenomena of the welfare state.   It opposes
the conventional view that the state provision of social
services is a humanistic reaction against the more extreme
negative consequences for the individual of *laisser-faire*
capitalism.   It also opposes the view of those like
Marshall (1965, pp. 28-30, 96) that the welfare state represented an alternative form of society to both socialism
and capitalism.   Rather it suggests that in general the
welfare state and the social services provide the conditions necessary for the continuance of the capitalist
system.   It also draws attention to some of the contradictions in the capitalist system that the welfare state
may not be able to resolve.

If the welfare of the capitalist system is the focus of

concern then attention is drawn to understanding not only
the operation of the social services or the post-Second
World War package of legislation, but also government aid
to private capital, the control and operation of national-
ised industries, etc.   In this wider context government
action as a response to economic crises becomes more
easily understood.   The welfare state is seen as a stage
in the historical process contributing to the negation of
human nature.   It is a controlling force, helping to
keep people motivated to serve the capitalist system and
inhibiting the raising of class consciousness.   The
effectiveness of this process can be highlighted by considering the use of different marxist concepts in analysing the welfare state at different levels of operation.
The first is to re-consider the notion of political
economy.

There are several alternative ways of analysing the
growth and development of the welfare state employing the
notion of political economy, some of which are dealt with
elsewhere in this book (see chapter 3).   In the context
of a marxist analysis of the political economy of the welfare state, Gough (1979) offers this definition of the
welfare state:   'the use of state power to modify the
reproduction of labour power and to maintain the non-working population in capitalist societies' (p. 44).   Gough
suggests the state employs such power in a number of different ways.   First, it controls and regulates people's
spending power and habits.   This occurs most obviously by
controlling taxation and the levels of social security
benefits, but also by subsidising some goods, by providing
some services free, and by controlling what there is to
purchase.   Second, certain practices of child-rearing are
perpetuated - hence the importance of the nuclear family
reflected in social policy and the role accorded to women
in such policy (see Wilson, 1977).   Third, the non-working population is supported in different ways to ensure
that the elderly, the sick, and the disabled still have
some purchasing power.   In the same way, the working
population who may at any time become non-working, have
benefits made available to them.   This focus ultimately
leads Gough to consider the growth of state expenditure in
these areas of social concern, and to offer an analysis of
why such activities of the state are the first to be cur-
tailed in times of recession.   Drawing attention to the
welfare state as operating in this way poses an alternative
image of the practices associated with the welfare state.

First, attention can be drawn to the role and function

of social work and similar social services.  Gough expresses this as follows:  'However useful are the social
services, however crucial is the welfare state to "civilised life", it constitutes an unproductive burden on the
productive marketed sector of the economy' (Gough, 1979,
p. 108).

This distinction between productive and unproductive
workers is a useful one.  Historically, social workers
have been understood to have grown out of the various
charitable organisations of the nineteenth and early twentieth centuries.  Such organisations operated within a
particular system of motivations and rewards in which the
poor and unfortunate were not seen to be the responsibility of the state.  The growth of capitalism places social
workers in a system where the state has taken responsibility for the poor and needy.  As a consequence, whilst
caring for their clients, social workers serve the needs
of the capitalist system.  This argument is pursued in
further detail by Corrigan and Leonard (1978), who suggest
that, given the contradictory role in which social workers
operate under capitalism, it is possible to reinterpret
the nature of that work.  Thus, the personal service professionals of Halmos (1978) may become the radical social
workers of Corrigan and Leonard.

A further implication of the work of Gough is developed
in the notion of crisis.  That the capitalist process has
to deal with crises is not in dispute.  Monetarists,
Keynesians and economists of various schools, would seem
to concur with the marxists on this point, though obviously they all vary on prognosis (see chapter 3).  Marxists
would attribute the recession of the 1970s and early
1980s to the strategies of an advanced capitalist society
in attempting to maintain the processes of accumulation
and legitimation (O'Connor, 1973).  That one of these
strategies involves cutbacks in public expenditure would
again seem reasonable to monetarist and marxist alike;
however the ultimate effects of such cutbacks is disputed.
O'Connor (1973) argues that the subsequent unionisation of
public sector workers which occurred during the 1970s is a
result of the threat which such cuts pose to the professionalisation of public service workers.  Social workers
themselves were seen to respond to this in the winter of
1978-9.

So far attention has been paid to the relevance of
marxism to social administration in the general framework
of the welfare state, dealing with contradictions it may

not be able to solve.   However, it is possible to consider more specific aspects of the welfare state employing
such concepts.   Navarro (1978), for example, has made
use of the notion of class struggle for understanding the
current structure of the health service.   He suggests
that the historically determined class base of the different political parties alongside the particular social
structure reflected in British capitalism has resulted in
the National Health Service being structured in such a way
as to maintain state control over the reproduction of the
workforce.   Similarly, the operation of the education
system, particularly the sociological observation concerning the failure of the 1944 Education Act to achieve
equality of opportunity, is explained by marxists    a
number of different ways.   Bowles and Gintis (1976) suggest there are 'rules of correspondence' between the education system and the economic system which prevail
against equality being realised since this would fail to
provide the range of skills and attitudes necessary for
the economic system to maintain itself.   Althusser (1970)
identifies the school as part of the 'ideological state
apparatus' whose 'crushing' influences ensure the reproduction of the labour force, ensuring that the notion of
equality of opportunity remains part of the ideology but
not of the practice.

   Marxist analysis may also be useful for understanding
the relationship between different sectors of the welfare
state.   Mishra (1977) suggests that marxism is unable to
explain the work of the voluntary organisations, because
these organisations operate outside of the state sector
and are not subject to the same motivational and reward
system.   Such a view seems to misunderstand the highly
interdependent relationship which exists between the state
and voluntary sectors, not only in terms of financial
backing but also in terms of day-to-day practices (Clayton
and Walklate, 1979).   Why this inter-relationship occurs
may not be as a result of the needs of a pluralistic
society as suggested by the Wolfenden Committee (1978), but
may be seen as a part of a legitimating tradition.   Voluntary organisations exist alongside state services to
perpetuate the individualistic ethos necessary for the
survival of capitalism whilst simultaneously allowing the
welfare state to adjust to any potential crisis situations
through the mechanisms available to it;   that is, by
greater dependency between these sectors (Walklate, 1980).

   The final area in which marxist analysis has been used
pursues the role of ideology further.   George and Wilding

(1978) have made a significant contribution to understanding the formation of social policy by emphasising the ideo ideological motivations behind it.    They adopt a class conflict perspective;  that is, that social policy needs to be seen in terms of the outcome of conflicting forces in society, particularly conflict between the ruling class and the working class.    They identify within this framework different groups of thinkers concerning social policy;  the anti-collectivists, the reluctant collectivists, the Fabian socialists and the marxists.    George and Wilding offer a critique of the understanding of social justice implied by each of these positions.    This is a useful connection with issues discussed in chapter 8. They make explicit the marxist ideal of a collectivised economic system as the means by which the ultimate welfare of the individual is achieved.    This would allow individuals to express their true spirit, reflecting the marxist conception of a socially just society.

CONCLUSION

As can be seen from the foregoing discussion, marxist concepts have been utilised in the context of social administration in a number of different ways;  to understand the nature and structure of the welfare state in its inter internal and external relations, to offer an understanding of the 'contradictions' faced by its workers, and to understand the value-system which supports it.    Its relevance depends on the extent to which these contributions outweigh the shortcomings of a holistic level of analysis which gives pre-eminence to the economic relations of society.    Its limitations are similar to some of those of functionalism.    However, one of the major differences between functionalism and marxism lies in the latter's implied recipe for social change through revolutionary activity.    Functionalism's inherent conservatism inhibits the emergence of such recommendations.    Marxism's implied reworking of the notion of social justice suggests a way whereby the removal of poverty or the goal of equality of opportunity might become realities.    The decision remains as to whether such a radical reorganisation of resources through revolution is socially acceptable to all.    It is interesting to note, however, that similar conclusions concerning capitalism are reached by Bell.    As a non-marxist, he addresses himself to the crises facing modern capitalist societies and expresses the problem as follows:

Irony apart, there are real crises ahead for the public

household in all societies.    But they do not derive
primarily from the 'iron laws' of economics;   they are
the recurrent dilemmas of private vices and public
interests now writ large.    The resolution essentially
can come only from a consensual agreement on the normative issues of distributive justice;   in the balance to
be struck between growth and social consumption.    But
can there be growth? (D. Bell, 1976, p. 236).

The necessary value-judgments implied by this statement
and by marxism are ultimately a matter for personal commitment and the political arena.


FURTHER READING

For those students interested in developing an understanding of Marx, then Giddens (1971), Bottomore and Rubel
(1963), and Swingewood (1975) are useful starting points.
For those more inclined towards an economic analysis,
Gamble and Walton (1972) may prove worthwhile.    As indicated in the chapter, Marx's thoughts have been developed
in several different directions.    Giddens and Held (1982,
particularly section 2) is recommended as a sociological
introduction to such developments.    However, students
might also find Habermas (1976 and 1979), Offe (1976),
Althusser (1971), Poulantzas (1978), and Wright (1978)
worth pursuing in their own right.    For an introduction
to marxist concepts as applied to the welfare state, Gough
(1979) and Taylor-Gooby and Dale (1981) provide differing
but interesting analyses.    The more specific operations
of the welfare state have also been explored employing
marxist frameworks;   on education, see Bowles and Gintis
(1976);   on medicine, see Navarro (1978);   on social
security and housing, see Ginsburg (1977);   on women, see
Wilson (1977).    George and Wilding (1978) offer an interesting analysis of the ideological background to the formation of social policy.

   The foregoing references are useful beginnings to pursuing an indepth analysis of the welfare state from the
marxist viewpoint.    Of interest, however, is the work of
Bell (1976, particularly chapter 6).    Though a non-
marxist, he provides some provocative social comment on
the nature of capitalist societies and the problems faced
by them.    Clearly written, this may provide students with
a helpful balance to some of the more general marxist
texts available.

BIBLIOGRAPHY

 *  Recommended.
 ** Recommended for easier reading.

Althusser, L. (1970), 'Reading Capital', London, New Left
    Books.
* Althusser, L. (1971), 'Lenin and Philosophy and Other
    Essays', London, New Left Books.
* Bell, D. (1976), 'The Cultural Contradictions of Capital-
    ism', London, Heinemann.
Bernstein, E. (1909), 'Evolutionary Socialism', New York,
    Huebsch.
* Bottomore, T., and Rubel, M. (1963), 'Karl Marx: Selected
    Writings', Harmondsworth, Penguin.
* Bowles, S., and Gintis, H. (1976), 'Schooling in Capital-
    ist America', London, Routledge & Kegan Paul.
Clayton, P., and Walklate, S.(1979), What did you do in the
    Strike, Volunteer?, 'Community Care', 7 June.
Corrigan, P., and Leonard, P. (1978), 'Social Work Practice
    under Capitalism: a Marxist Approach', London, Mac-
    millan.
Durkheim, E. (1894), 'The Division of Labour in Society',
    Chicago, Free Press, 1960.
* Gamble, A., and Walton, P. (1972), 'From Alienation to
    Surplus Value', London, Sheed & Ward.
Gay, P. (1962), 'The Dilemma of Democratic Socialism', New
    York, Collier-Macmillan.
George, V., and Wilding, P. (1978), 'Ideology and Social
    Welfare', London, Routledge & Kegan Paul.
* Giddens, A. (1971), 'Capitalism and Modern Social
    Theory', Cambridge University Press.
Giddens, A. (1981), 'A Contemporary Critique of Historical
    Materialism', London, Macmillan.
* Giddens, A., and Held, D. (1982), 'Classes, Power and
    Conflict: Classical and Contemporary Debates', London,
    Macmillan.
* Ginsberg, N. (1977), 'Class, Capital and Social Policy',
    London, Macmillan.
* Goldmann, L. (1964), 'The Hidden God', London, Routledge
    & Kegan Paul.
**Gough, I. (1979), 'The Political Economy of the Welfare
    State', London, Macmillan.
Gramsci, A. (1971), 'Selections from the Prison Notebooks',
    London, Lawrence & Wishart.
* Habermas, J. (1976), 'Legitimation Crisis', London,
    Heinemann.
* Habermas, J. (1979), 'Communication and the Evolution of
    Society', London, Heinemann.

109 Chapter 4

Halmos, P. (1978), 'The Personal and the Political: Social
Work and Political Action', London, Hutchinson.
Kautsky, K. (1899), 'Neue Zeit', XVII, 2.
Lukacs, G. (1971), 'History and Class Consciousness',
London, Merlin.
Luxemburg, R. (1899), 'Sozialreform oder Revolution?',
Berlin.
Marshall, T.H. (1965), 'Social Policy', London, Hutchinson.
McLellan, D.(ed.) (1983), 'Marx: The First Hundred Years',
Glasgow, Fontana.
Miliband, R. (1969), 'The State in Capitalist Society',
London, Weidenfeld & Nicolson.
Mishra, R. (1977), 'Society and Social Policy: Theoretical
Perspectives on Welfare', London, Macmillan.
Navarro, V. (1976), 'Medicine under Capitalism', Neale,
Watson Academic Publications Inc.
Navarro, N. (1978), 'Class Struggle, the State and Medi-
cine', Oxford, Martin Robertson.
O'Connor, J. (1973), 'The Fiscal Crisis of the State',
London, St James Press.
Offe, C. (1972a), Advanced Capitalism and the Welfare
State, 'Politics and Society', vol. 2.
Offe, C. (1972b), Political Authority and Class Structures
- An Analysis of Late Capitalist Societies, 'Inter-
national Journal of Sociology', vol. 2, no. 1, pp.
73-108.
Offe, C. (1975), The Theory of the Capitalist State and
the Problem of Policy Formation, in Lindberg et al.
(eds), 'Stress and Contradiction in Modern Capitalism',
Lexington, MA, Lexington Books.
Offe, C. (1976), 'Industry and Inequality: the Achievement
Principle in Work and Social Status', London, Edward
Arnold.
Offe, C. (1982), Some Contradictions of the Modern Welfare
State, 'Critical Social Policy', vol. 2, no. 2.
Offe, C., and Ronge, V. (1975), Theses on the Theory of
the State, 'New German Critique', vol. 6.
Poulantzas, N. (1978), 'Political Power and Social
Classes', London, Verso.
Suchting, W.A. (1972), Marx, Popper and Historicism,
'Inquiry', vol. 15, pp. 235-66.
Swingewood, A. (1975), 'Marx and Modern Social Theory',
London, Macmillan.
**Taylor-Gooby, P., and Dale, J. (1981), 'Social Theory
and Social Welfare', London, Edward Arnold.
Walklate, S. (1980), The Role of Voluntary Organisations
in the Welfare State: Implications for theories of the
State, unpublished paper presented to the BSA State
and Economy Study Group.

Weber, M. (1904), 'The Protestant Ethic and the Spirit of
    Capitalism', English edn, London, Allen & Unwin, 1976.
Westergaard, J., and Resler, H. (1975), 'Class in Capital-
    ist Society', London, Heinemann.
Wolfenden Committe (1978), 'Wolfenden Committee Report on
    Voluntary Organisations', London, Croom Helm.
Wilson, E. (1977), 'Women and the Welfare State', London,
    Tavistock.
Wright, E.O. (1975), Some Recent Developments in the
    Marxist Theory of the State, Bay Area Kapitalistate
    Group, February.
Wright, E.O. (1978), 'Class Crisis and the State', London,
    New Left Books.

Chapter 5

# Functionalism
## Sandra Walklate

Functionalism, the theory to be discussed in this chapter, like marxism, is concerned with society as a whole; its structure, its processes, and the means by which social order is maintained. It assumes that such processes cannot be explained by reference to individual attitudes and behaviour alone but focuses on those aspects of society that help shape individuals. Unlike marxism, it is more concerned to explain the features of society that support its stability rather than those that promote radical change. In this way it represented in its origins a conservative reaction against individualism as indicated in chapter 1. Functionalism, again unlike marxism, integrates the explanations of economists and political scientists into the general view of society that it presents rather than attempting to explain such phenomena.

Functionalism has been given its name because its explanation of social structure and social processes relies on the way in which different functions are performed by different sub-systems within society. Although similar conceptual frameworks can be found amongst social anthropologists, particularly in the work of Radcliffe-Brown (1881-1955) and Malinowski (1884-1942), the earliest forerunners of functionalism were the French sociologist Comte (1798-1857) and the British sociologist Spencer (1820-1903). Comte declared the subject matter of sociology to be 'social statics', the study of whole societies, and 'social dynamics', the study of the processes by which whole societies change. Spencer added to this the view that society was like a biological organism which requires its parts to function interdependently for its continued survival. However, for the purposes of this book it is appropriate to start the more detailed discussion of functionalism by looking at the work of the French sociologist Durkheim.

111

EMILE DURKHEIM (1858-1917)

Durkheim, like his predecessors, saw society as an interdependent social whole.   He was particularly interested
in identifying what he termed the 'social facts'.   Such
facts had a reality above and beyond the individuals who
made up a society and were to be explained by the pattern
of interdependence existing between them.   This view is
best understood by reference to specific works.   Here
reference will be made to Durkheim's 'Division of Labour
in Society' (1893), 'The Rules of Sociological Method'
(1895) and 'Suicide' (1897).

In 'The Division of Labour in Society' Durkheim outlines his view of society as a moral entity in the first
instance.   It is moral, in that the agreements made
between men carry with them moral obligations, rights and
duties.   Social order emerges from these moral relationships since they require a consensus to exist between
individuals, and the agreements made constrain individuals
to behave in the interests of the consensus.   'The Division of Labour in Society' introduces this view of social
relationships through the concepts of 'mechanical' and
'organic solidarity'.   Mechanical solidarity exists in
primitive societies.   Here, the family and the tribe may
be one and the same.   Consequently, people are held
together by their common relationships, values and beliefs,
which are binding upon them.   As populations increase,
complicating the processes of interaction and creating
competition for the available roles to be played, social
order is maintained through organic solidarity.   Organic
solidarity is based on social differentiation, that is the
necessity for individuals to fill and perform different
roles in society which are differentially evaluated.   The
division of labour, then, is seen not just as an aspect of
change in the workplace but is also a process of moral
change, that is, change in the nature of the consensus
supporting the social order.   It is a change in the
pattern of expectations between individuals.   Thus in
moving from a simple to a more complicated society, stability is maintained by adjustments in the nature of the consensus supporting the social order.   Durkheim thus emphasises consensus and implies the importance of function
and interdependence.

'The Rules of Sociological Method' stresses the importance of these concepts and the task of the sociologists
in uncovering the nature of the inter-relationships between
the various component parts of society.   The sociological

method is seen as an objective search for 'social facts'.
These facts are real and possess object-like qualities
which the sociologist can identify and relate to other
social facts.   Durkheim's work 'Suicide' serves as an
illustration of this sociological method.   Durkheim
observed that the suicide rates for different countries
varied between countries but remained steady for any one
particular country year by year.   For Durkheim, the explanation for such variation and consistency lay, not in
the individual motivation for suicide, but in understanding the comparative structures of these societies.   The
suicide rate acted as an indicator of the stability of
the structure.   The explanation of the rate lay in a
second social fact, the comparative role played by religion in these societies.   There is observed, then, a
relationship between the declining importance of religion
in any particular society and its suicide rate.   The
cause of suicide is located in its interdependence with
religion and the relationship both have in supporting the
moral consensus of society.

## KEY CONCEPTS

This discussion of the work of Durkheim identifies certain
key concepts underpinning a functionalist view of society.
A preliminary review of these will be given before pursuing further developments of functionalist thought.

In the first instance it is important to stress the
analogy used by functionalists of society as an organism.
It is not intended that direct biological parallels be
made but that the model be used to highlight the importance of understanding the nature of the interdependence
and co-operation required for any system, biological or
social, to function efficiently.   Functionalists are consequently concerned with identifying two key features of
any social system;   the nature of the component parts, and
how they work together.

Two further concepts, structure and function, continue
the biological analogy.   'Structure' refers to the location of the component parts of a system and the nature of
their inter-relationships.   'Function' refers to the role
played by the component parts in enabling the system as a
whole to work efficiently.   For example, just as in human
beings the digestive system, the circulation of the blood,
and the limbs, are differently located, have particular
relationships with each other, and perform different roles

in providing an efficiently working and integrated body,
so a social system is viewed as having a particular structure with particular functional components allowing for an
integrated social whole.  The problems inherent in using
such an analogy will be discussed later.

A further functionalist concept is the notion of social
differentiation.  Through this concept functionalist
analysis attempts to incorporate an understanding of the
processes of social change into the theory.  It emphasises the way in which population growth, for Durkheim in
particular, results in increasingly complicated relationships requiring an increasingly complicated social system
to maintain the integration and equilibrium of the whole
system.  Thus modern societies are socially differentia-
ted, have a wide range and variety of roles to be filled
which have different functions and are differently evaluated.  The fullest development of these concepts is to be
found in the first instance in the work of Talcott
Parsons.

## TALCOTT PARSONS (1903-79)

The work of Talcott Parsons is so important in functionalist analysis that it is difficult to encapsulate its
impact on modern sociological thought in the space available here.  The reader is therefore particularly directed
to the further reading for a fuller grasp of Parsons's
work.  Parsons is concerned with understanding the nature
of social systems.  He suggests they share the same basic
characteristics which are controlled by the same requirements whether such systems are seen as the interaction
between individuals or between organisations or societies.
For example, when interaction occurs between two individuals, they are concerned to fulfil their individual goals
and consequently create between them patterns of expectations concerning each other's behaviour.  For interaction
to continue, then, it needs to be both mutually satisfying
and fulfilling;  that is, it must function internally, for
their individual satisfaction and externally, for their
relationship with each other as well as their relationship
with the outside world.  Parsons suggests that all relationships whether individual or societal operate to fulfil
functional purposes in this way, and hence share the same
basic characteristics as social systems.  He identifies
four basic functions which must be performed if a system
is to operate effectively;  adaptation, goal attainment,
latency (or pattern maintenance) and integration.  The

relationship between these four functions can be represented diagrammatically (as in Table 5.1).

TABLE 5.1   Parsons's categorisation of functional pre-
requisites for a social system

|          |          | Instrumental (Means) | Consummatory (Ends) |          |
| -------- | -------- | -------------------- | ------------------- | -------- |
|          | A        |                      |                     | G        |
| External |          | Adaptation           | Goal Attainment     |          |
| Internal |          | Latency (alias pattern maintenance and tension management) | Integration |          |
|          | L        |                      |                     | I        |

(Rocher, 1974, p. 45;   see also Parsons et al., 1953.
AGIL is a mnemonic intended to facilitate remembering
these functions.)

These functions require fuller explanation:

1  Adaptation.   Any social system must be able to adapt
to changes in its environment if it is to survive and meet
the basic needs of its members.

2  Goal attainment.   Any system, Parsons argues, requires
a common agreement concerning the goals of the system, how
these goals are to be achieved and the mechanisms of their
successful pursuit.

3  Latency.   This requisite, more commonly referred to as
pattern maintenance, is concerned with the extent to which
any system relies upon the continued maintenance of the
values of that system.   This is to ensure the continued
adequacy of motivational levels designed to promote commitment to the values and roles of the system concerned.

4  Integration.   This final function, as its name implies,
exists to ensure coherence and solidarity.   Co-ordination
between the component parts of the system is maintained
and deviant activity inhibited.

This model is intended to apply to any social system.
Having identified these universal functional pre-requisites, Parsons further elaborated the model to identify the

'pattern variables' in a range of social systems and the
relationships of the sub-systems within them.   In this
elaboration Parsons reflects his concern with the maintenance of social order to prevent 'a war of all against all'
which leads him to be primarily concerned with consensus,
equilibrium and integration.

However, having stressed these notions, Parsons, like
Durkheim, is equally concerned with understanding the
nature of social processes, or, as mentioned earlier the
processes of social differentiation.   Durkheim saw the
move from a simple to a more complicated social organisation in terms of a change in the moral base of the system,
that is in terms of a move from mechanical to organic
solidarity.   In a similar way, Parsons looks at the
changes from a non-industrial to an industrialised society
by emphasising the importance of understanding the changes
in the values of that society.   One dimension of this
process can be seen in changes in the role of the family.

For Parsons the change from a non-industrial to an
industrialised society is characterised by a move from the
extended family to the nuclear family.   In the extended
family there is inter-generational involvement in child-
rearing.   Skills and roles are passed from parent to
child, and there is no separation of home and work.   In
contrast, the nuclear family, consisting of parents and
children, makes possible, Parsons argues, geographical
mobility for work, investment in the child for developing
individual skills, and appropriate sex-role stereotyping
behaviour.   Thus the family provides the child not only
with biological care but with the personality, the attitudes and values subsequently needed to survive in a particular societal organisation.   The school, in an industrialised society endorses these attitudes and values and
adds to them by providing children with the means by which
they are emancipated from the emotional ties of the family
and acquire an understanding of rather more universalistic
values concerning achievement and its evaluation in subsequent adult roles.   In school, then, the child learns not
only the skills associated with work, but also the attitudes and values considered appropriate to a responsible
adult and the kind of relationship this implies with
others.   Relating this to the model of functional pre-
requisites discussed earlier, Parsons is here discussing a
sub-system of the more general system.   The child adapts
to a particular environment in which the pursuit of certain
goals is considered worthwhile.   The family and the school
together provide the child with the cultural values and

attitudes to maintain the pursuit of these goals (latency).
The education system, in its mass impact, ensures the continued integration of the social system.   Thus, despite
becoming increasingly more complicated, integration and
equilibrium are maintained in the process of change as
mechanisms are evolved by which to ensure this.

This particular example draws attention to the way in
which Parons intends the notion of equilibrium to be
understood.   Equilibrium, it appears, is an ideal state
towards which any system, whether biological or societal,
is directed.   This does not mean that the system is constantly in equilibrium, but suggests that every change
produces reactions which in turn are responded to.   Hence
at any one time, as in the move from a non-industrial to
an industrial society, the system may be in a state of
disequilibrium.   However, the overall direction of movement is to remove such strains from the system.

## MORE RECENT FUNCTIONALIST DEVELOPMENTS

The work of Parsons, briefly presented here, served to
influence much sociological theorising, particularly
during the 1950s.   Several writers developed specific
aspects of functionalist analysis and its concern with the
establishment of consensus and the maintenance of equilibrium.   The writers discussed here are Merton, Davis and
Moore, and Smelser, each of whom is concerned with very
different aspects of functionalist analysis.

### Merton

The work of Merton is important to functionalist analysis
for two reasons.   He is in the first instance critical of
the functionalism presented by Parsons, and, second, presents his own series of functionalist propositions.

Merton's dissatisfaction with functionalism stemmed
from two concerns.   First he considers it inadequate in
providing an understanding of the mechanisms of social
interaction.   Second, he considered that sociology needed
to be an empirical as well as a theoretical discipline,
that is concerned with theories of the 'middle range'.
He felt the concepts introduced by Parons were too vague
for this purpose.

For Merton, the biological analogy and its application

as a means of understanding the functional unity of society, is misleading, for it is possible to observe that not all institutions in society are so well integrated that changes in the functioning of one institution produces consequences in all others.   Merton suggests it is important to specify the relationships which are necessarily interdependent.   For example, changes in the Football Association are not necessarily going to produce repercussions in the Anglican church, though changes in the Anglican church might have repercussions for other religious groups.

The biological analogy produces a further problem for Merton in that it has been used to suggest that all units function together to provide for the stability or equilibrium of the whole.   Merton again suggests that this may not necessarily be the case.   The functioning of some units may in fact have disruptive or disturbing consequences for the stability of others, for example the effect of the introduction of cable television on the established television companies.   Such effects Merton labelled 'dysfunctional', not necessarily to be interpreted as 'bad', but intended to clarify the kind of functioning which is under consideration.

Finally, Merton was dissatisfied with the assumption that certain institutions were indispensable to the system because they served to fulfil needs that were functional pre-requisites of society - the need for food, shelter, procreation, etc.   Merton suggests that this overlooks the extent to which 'structural constraints' influence how these requirements are met.   For example, a modern industrial society requires an education system of a qualitatively different kind from that of a tribal society, but within the constraints set by the demands of the system there are 'functional equivalents' or 'alternatives' which will serve the same purpose.   That is, the actual type of education system in any modern industrial society can vary within that society and between societies, and still fulfil the functional pre-requisites proposed by Parsons.

In modifying the basic assumptions of functionalism in this way, Merton is suggesting that attention be focused on understanding functions in terms of the consequences which events or actions have.   In doing this, Merton introduces a further distinction between what he refers to as 'manifest' and 'latent' functions.   'Manifest' refers to those functions which are recognised and intended; 'latent' refers to those aspects of an institution's or

component of society's functioning which are unrecognised
and unintended.   The performance of these latent functions may be functional or dysfunctional for the institution or society concerned.   The main purpose of introducing the distinction was to make possible a modification of
functionalism's emphasis on purposive action by drawing
attention to the importance of understanding the unintended consequences of action.

Despite having introduced these conceptual modifications of functionalist theory in order to produce a more
meaningful understanding of the nature of action in any
social system, Merton still assumes that the norm of any
system is stability, achievable by maintaining a consensus
supportive of the system.   This is reflected quite clearly in Merton's development of the relationship between the
social structure and Durkheim's notion of 'anomie', that
is normlessness.   Merton, in offering an understanding of
deviant behaviour, assumes that the consensual values of
American society are material success achievable by hard
work.   The social structure, he argues, exerts pressure
on individuals to strive towards such success, even though
the system is organised in such a way that it is not possible for everyone to succeed to the same degree.   People
react to these pressures in different ways.   They may
accept or reject the cultural goals of society, and they
may accept or reject the recognised means to achieve these
goals.   Using these concepts, Merton identifies five
modes of adaptation:

TABLE 5.2  A typology of individual adaptation (Merton,
1968, ch. 4)

| Modes of adaptation | Culture goals | Institutionalized means |
|---|---|---|
| Conformity | + | + |
| Innovation | + | - |
| Ritualism | - | + |
| Retreatism | - | - |
| Rebellion | ∓ | ∓ |

(+ = acceptance;   - = rejection;   ∓ = rejection of prevailing values, acceptance of new values.)

In this way Merton offers a means by which different
responses to the demands of the social system can be iden-

tified at an individual level.   The typology has been
influential in promoting further research into different
types of deviant responses to the social system.    In
this, and other ways, Merton's clarification of Parsons's
concepts furthered his aim of giving functionalism an
empirical base.


Davis and Moore

The way in which the social structure operates to exert
such pressure on individuals, that is, how the system of
stratification operates, is discussed more fully in the
work of Davis and Moore.   Within the functionalist perspective stratification is seen to be common to all societies;   that is, all societies are divided into strata or
layers with each layer possessing differential power and
access to differential material rewards.    Marx, as indicated elsewhere, was also concerned with the distribution
of power and rewards within society.    But whereas Marx's
attention was focused on the inevitable conflict that such
distribution produced, functionalists are concerned with
the way in which stratification operates or functions to
produce consensus within the social system.    Thus social
inequality through stratification is assumed to be functionally necessary for the smooth running of any society
since it ensures that the most important positions in
society are filled by the most qualified persons.

   Davis and Moore express this in terms of two problems
faced by any society;   to instil in the right individuals
the desire to fill certain positions, and, once these
positions are filled, to instil the desire to perform the
duties attached to them.   Societies ensure that these two
problems are dealt with by attaching different rewards to
different positions so that inequality becomes institution-
alised.   The ranking of the various positions is determined by their importance to society and the amount of
training or talent required to fill them.   So, by offering differential rewards in terms of material gain and
power, a society can ensure the necessary motivational
inducements to strive for those positions better rewarded,
and also ensures that only those with the talent will gain
such positions.

   Davis and Moore's understanding of social stratification can be seen to rest on a number of assumptions.
First, talents are differentially distributed in any
society.   Second, the division of labour inevitably pro-

duces different rewards for different roles which in turn
induce the motivation to fill and perform adequately the
roles available.   Third, such a process is not only functionally necessary for every society to ensure that all
the needs of society are met, but also that such inequality is seen to be empirically present in all societies
and is therefore universal and inevitable.

This explanation of stratification produced a considerable response.   Gans (1971), for example, accepts this
analysis and uses it to identify the various functions of
poverty ranging from the performance of cultural functions
to creating jobs, to allowing the interests of others to
become dominant (see chapter 9, pp. 220-1).      Others rejected the analysis to varying degrees since it does contain some serious difficulties.   Assessing the relative
functional importance of different positions in society
would seem problematic.   For example, the possibility of
comparing objectively the functional importance and differential rewards to be allocated to the refuse collector
and the doctor with respect to health care would seem to
be a difficult task.   The way in which the system of
stratification may fail to uncover the full range of tale
talents available, that is, may operate dysfunctionally,
would also appear problematic.   This is an illustration
of what is considered to be one of the major limitations
of functionalism in general, which will be considered
shortly.   Davis and Moore also fail to analyse the processes of change as they affect stratification, an issue
dealt with by Smelser.

Smelser

The writings of Smelser, particularly his 'Social Change
in the Industrial Revolution' (1959), indicates how a
functionalist analysis might be employed to understand the
processes of social change by utilising the notion of
structural differentiation.   In essence, Smelser suggests
that when a system, institution, or organisation becomes
outmoded and can no longer fulfil adequately the demands
put upon it, it differentiates itself or divides itself
into two or more units as a means of adapting to the new
circumstances and simultaneously continuing to perform its
functions.   Smelser considers that this process of adaptation has seven definite and specific stages.   He illustrates these with an analysis of the changing structure of
Lancashire society, showing how different elements can be
seen to be adapting to each other and to the changing

industrial scene.   For example, he suggests that the
early trade union organisations and friendly societies
were one of the means by which the gap created by the
division of labour between work and home was mediated and
equilibrium maintained.

Such a view of social change is not peculiar to the
work of Smelser, but is implied by others concerned with
the processes of modernisation.   Smelser's initial writing led to further understanding of the processes of
social differentiation.   This is reflected in the later
writings of Parsons in which he focuses attention on the
evolution of societies (for example, 1977) and the work
that is referred to as 'convergence theory'.   Here concern is with  the transformation of primitive societies to
modern societies;  identifying the characteristics of a
modern society;  and viewing such processes of change in
global, universal terms.   It is argued that the processes
involved are inevitable and that the differences between
societies will diminish as they become more complex.
There is, it is suggested, one ultimate societal type
towards which all societies converge once industrialisation has begun.


OVERVIEW AND CRITICAL ASSESSMENT

In this brief account of functionalist analysis it is possible to identify three themes which have subsequently
been developed by different writers.   In the systems
theme societies are viewed as integrated social systems.
In the structural-functional theme, attention is focused
on the nature and operation of the social structure in
terms of social stratification or differential institutions.   Finally, the evolutionary theme, reflected in the
later writings of Parsons, focuses attention on the processes of social differentiation.   All of these themes
are underpinned by a coherent approach, which has both
advantages and limitations as an explanatory tool.

In adopting a holistic approach, that is the analysis
of social wholes, functionalism draws attention to the
nature of societies and their operations as they exist
over and above the individuals who make up that society.
This involves recognising the importance to be attached to
the patterns of social, economic, and political structures
whose existence and inter-relationships, it is presumed,
have a life of their own.   This is a similar level of
analysis to that adopted by marxism (chapter 4), but

stands in contrast to that adopted by symbolic interactionism (chapter 7).  Thus functionalism draws an important distinction between explanations in terms of individual motivation and explanations in terms of the needs of
society as a whole.  Merton was unhappy with this distinction, but nevertheless it has led functionalists to
offer explanations of the maintenance of social order in
terms of the interdependence of the component parts of the
system, change in one part producing change in another.
It has also led to the identification of certain characteristics and processes pertinent to all societies.  It
can be argued that this is one of the advantages of functionalism since it enables attention to be paid to the
longer-term consequences of social activity rather than
those immediate to the event or action concerned.  This
may be particularly useful if, for example, concern is
with understanding the nature and development of different
welfare systems.  However, such explanations are produced
by a teleological argument, that is, one inferring cause
from effect.  To suggest that systems operate interdependently to maintain equilibrium or social order and that
such equilibrium is maintained because change in one
dimension provides change in another does not provide an
adequate understanding of how and why such mechanisms
operate in the way that they do.  This failing derives
from the way in which functionalists view the processes of
social change, not from the holistic level of explanation.

As has been seen, social or structural differentiation
is the process by which social change is seen to occur.
Such a view implies that in situations of rapid technological change there must be a pluralistic distribution of
and access to power (see chapter 6).  To maintain social
equilibrium the system must have means which enable it to
respond to any strains or tensions that are revealed.
Thus power to influence the system must be, potentially,
available to all;  adequate mobilisation will then be all
that is required to ensure a positive response to the tension that such pressure produces.

The accuracy and adequacy of such a view of the processes of social change and the implied pluralistic view of
society is questioned by those who, like the elitists discussed in chapter 6, view power as being more unevenly
distributed in society (pp. 142-5).  It is also questioned by those, like marxists, who see the conflict produced by such an uneven distribution as the primary means
by which social change occurs.  It is possible to over-
draw a criticism such as this.  Goulder, for example,

posits a more sophisticated functionalist analysis of
social change than that implied by the notion of dysfunc-
tion by discussing such processes in terms of 'reciprocity'
and 'autonomy'.   Gouldner (1967) states that: 'In so far
as a system is composed of some parts which have a degree
of functional autonomy, it possesses potentialities for
certain types of changes or responses to tensions which
would not exist if it had no functionally autonomous
parts.'   However, even here, change is necessarily of a
gradual and minimally disruptive nature.   The potential
for radical or revolutionary social change is limited
within the functionalist framework.

This limitation may be closely associated with the
analogy used when functionalists view social systems as
having similar properties to biological systems.   Tensions between the parts of a biological organism do not
necessarily lead the organism to adapt successfully to
such tensions, but may result in the destruction of the
organism as a whole.   The circumstances in which this may
occur in social systems, or how such eventualities are
dealt with, are not fully catered for within the theory.
It may be that this has yet to be considered.   There is
growing concern with the processes of modernisation, the
complexities involved in this, and the conscious guiding
of underdeveloped societies to acquire the trappings of
modern societies by the strategies and planning of governments.   This may be the level at which functionalism
needs to devise its propositions, that is, in global societal terms.

Such a justification does little to rectify the assumptions made by functionalism about the nature of the individuals and their relationship with society.   These
assumptions are the natural result of adopting a holistic
approach.   Parsons does concern himself with social
interaction, but this is still very much in terms of a
systems approach.   Consequently functionalism, rather
like marxism, has a somewhat passive and plastic image of
the individual.   Human beings are seen to be manipulated
and manipulable by forces external to their own intentions or desires.   Thus models of man which afford attention to the subjective formulation of individual action
are generally excluded from consideration.   This was one
of the concerns expressed by Merton about functionalist
analysis.   However, the extent to which his own propositions allow for such an alternative view of the individual
is debatable since his model ultimately implies that the
choices made available for individual modes of adaptation
to the system are made available by the system itself.

It is argued by some sociologists that functionalist
analysis is free from the problems of subjectivity which
accrue in other types of analysis, because it is concerned
with the needs of social systems which are, at a fundamental level, seen to be universal.   This would establish
functionalism as scientific in the traditional sense of
this term discussed in chapter 1.   Functionalists feel
able to make such claims because they have identified the
core needs for any social system to survive and operate.
This is consistent with Durkheim's view that the identification of 'social facts' was the concern of the sociologist.   These facts are not a part of individuals, but a
part of the pattern of the interdependence within and
between systems and are thus objective.   There are, however, two difficulties associated with making such claims.
In the first instance, this stance means that functionalists are locked into describing a particular system and
its functions at a particular point in time.   Their
desire to be objective and value-free limits the theory's
potential for explaining why a particular structure exists
in a particular form.   For comparisons would inevitably
involve the expression of value-judgments, unless such
explanations are to remain teleological, and circular.
Second, this stance has the consequence of rendering functionalist explanations supportive of the status quo at any
particular point in time.   Again, the desire to be objective and value-free has often resulted in a lack of critical concern for any tensions observed within a particular
society.   For policy recommendations can never be made
without commitment to values.   As has been discussed
elsewhere, such inhibitions are not the prerogative of
functionalist analysis.


RELATIONSHIP WITH OTHER THEORIES

As may now be clear, some of the problems and limitations
of functionalism, as well as its advantages, are not the
prerogative of the particular set of propositions per se,
but are derived from the level of analysis which functionalism adopts.   This issue is worth pursuing further
before discussing the relevance of functionalism to social
administration.   The work of Althusser is particularly
relevant here.

Althusser's writings, discussed in the chapter on 'Marx
and marxism', belong to that branch of marxist though referred to as 'structural marxism', and have many parallels
with the work of Parsons.   These parallels emerge in their

most concrete form in 'Ideology and Ideological State Apparatuses' (in Althusser, 1971).   Briefly, Althusser presents an analysis of the role of ideology as the 'social cement', indispensable to 'social cohesion', which, he argues, is a 'functionally necessary' for the existence of every type of society.   Ideology is a part of the process by which society ensures the continued dominance of the ruling class and the competence within the populace to fulfil the roles and complete the tasks available.   This process occurs through the 'repressive state apparatuses', the police, armed forces, etc., and the 'ideological state apparatuses', schools, the church, etc.   In schools, in particular, children learn the various skills, the 'know-how' for modern industrial society and: 'the attitude that should be observed by every agent in the division of labour according to the job he is destined for' (p. 180).   Teachers, then, become, unwittingly, 'agents of the state', and pupils 'passive receptacles'.   The similarities between this view of the process of schooling and that identified by Parsons discussed earlier are remarkable.   Not only does Althusser make difficult an understanding of the processes of social change if ideological processes have such an effect, but also, like functionalism, he denudes the individual of any role, intention or constructive purpose in the process. Mennell (1980, p. 90) expresses it thus:   'He sees people as mere *Trager*, supports or carriers of the social formation whose actions and motives are determined by their location in the formation.   The notion of human subjectivity is dismissed as a consequence of human subjection.'

Although the subjective nature of human activities is not a proclaimed concern of either functionalism or Althusserian marxism, the importance which is attached to such aspects of human behaviour cannot be dealt with adequately by mere supposition.   A useful link between the study of the behaviour of individuals making conscious decisions and the study of whole societies can be made by using the symbolic interactionist perspective discussed in chapter 7.   A particular example making the link with functionalism is Erikson's (1966) 'Wayward Puritans', discussed more fully in that chapter.

Functionalism also has links with classical microeconomic theory (chapter 2) and pluralism (chapter 6). It will be readily apparent to those familiar with the neo-classical paradigm that Davis and Moore's explanation of stratification owes much to the neo-classical theory of wages.   This is discussed further in chapter 9 on theories

of poverty.   The significance of pluralist political
theory has also been mentioned earlier.   The relationship
of both these theories to functionalism is commented on
further at the end of chapter 6 and in chapter 10.

## RELEVANCE FOR SOCIAL ADMINISTRATION

In assessing the relevance of functionalist theory for the
study of social administration, it is important to recognise that in the formative period for the discipline, from
1945 to 1970, much of the writing on the subject assumes
an implicit functionalist framework.   The literature is
replete with quotations which suggest that changes in service provision can be adequately explained by the recognition of a need or generalised social forces (Carrier and
Kendall, 1973).   Even Titmuss, according to Riesman's
analysis of the theoretical basis of his work, may be best
understood within a functionalist framework, although
Carrier and Kendall specifically exempt him from some of
their general criticism.

   The acceptance of such a framework was partly due to an
optimism during the period about the potential for piecemeal change but also owed something to the nature of the
theory itself which echoed some of the ideals of the welfare state.   Although Durkheim was concerned with the
processes of maintaining moral welfare, not through state
intervention but by a revival of the occupational guild
system, he commented that the worker needs to feel:   'he
is serving something.   For that he need not embrace vast
portions of the social horizon, it is sufficient that he
perceives enough of it to understand that his actions have
an aim beyond themselves' (Durkheim, 1960, p. 76).   Durkheim would probably have considered collectivist welfare
systems as over-generous, leading individuals into a self-
indulgent lifestyle.   It may be argued that such views
are a product of Durkheim's historical moment.   However,
they serve to indicate the limits to the policy implications of functionalism, as will become clearer.   But
within these limits the contribution of functionalism to
understanding policy is not negligible.

   First of all, in looking at broad trends in social
policy, functionalism shows that the development of the
social services cannot be explained just as a result of
pioneering philanthropy or innovation, but also of a gradual adaptation of the system to meet the needs of a changing society.   For example, it has often been pointed out

that the 'welfare state' in Britain in 1945 was closer to
the proposals put forward by the Webbs in the Minority
Report of the Royal Commission on the Poor Law in 1908
than the proposals of the majority Report.   This does
not mean that the Webbs were ultimately more influential,
but rather that their proposals proved more acceptable as
a solution to the stresses of society within the developing power structure.   In one respect at least the Webbs
proved very much out of step with the pressures of the
time, and that was in the rejection of state insurance
against unemployment and sickness.   Here the majority
Report proved more realistic.

Second, functionalism can provide a framework for the
analysis of stresses and strains in society both at a
national level and between and within organisations.   For
example, functionalism has always drawn attention to the
functions undertaken by the family and how these and its
structure have changed as society has developed.   A
proper analysis of these functions may enable more coherent policy development.   British policy tends to treat
each aspect of policy that affects the family independently - taxation, social security, housing, nursery school
provision and so on.   Functionalist analysis draws attention to the ways in which changes in one system affect
another.

Merton's emphasis on manifest and latent functions and
on the possibility of conflicting interests within a
social system is also relevant at different levels of
policy-making.   At a national level, for example, it can
throw light on the role of the social security system.
This is manifestly designed to alleviate poverty.   But it
also serves the needs of industry by making it easier to
hire and fire workers according to the demand for particular products.   Conflict between these two functions
appears in the determination of levels of benefit and of
contributions.   A higher rate of benefit designed to
alleviate poverty may be financed by higher contributions
which increase poverty, while both rates may discourage
some people from accepting employment at the wages which
employers are prepared to offer.   Similarly, within
social service organisations, Merton's concepts draw
attention to the fact that one of their latent functions
is to provide satisfying employment to staff and this may
conflict with their manifest functions of meeting the
needs of clients, pupils or patients.   An interesting
example of this is Calnan's (1982) study of hospital
casualty departments in the British National Health Ser-

vice.   He shows that the desire of the professional
interests to develop a specialist, career-oriented service
conflicted with the expectation of many members of the
public of an alternative to general practice for many
purposes.   Merton's analysis of types of adaptation to
pressure also provides a reminder that deviance often has
a positive function for those who reject society's expectations.   This is one reason why punishment is so often
ineffective.   Attention is therefore drawn to wider problems in society which fuel the deviance.   Cloward and
Ohlin (1961) refined Merton's theory to provide an explanation of delinquency based on the inability of working-
class youngsters to achieve legitimate material goals by
legitimate means.   This theory was the basis for the
American 'Mobilisation for Youth' programme (discussed in
Downes and Rock, 1982, pp. 232-6).

All of the examples cited, which stem from applying the
functionalist frame of analysis, reflect the piecemeal
social engineering approach which is associated with it.
Functionalism's static approach to understanding social
change inhibits the analysis of policy-formation in a historical or radical manner.   The implicit conservatism
within the theory, from Durkheim onwards (with the possible exception of Gouldner) has this result.   This, combined with the overall focus on consensus, stability, and
the desire to remain value-free, constitutes a major limitation to its critical insight into social processes,
particularly those concerned with the formation and practice of social policy.


FURTHER READING

The student wishing to obtain a clear overview of functionalism will find Rex (1961) and Cohen (1968) useful
starting points;   perhaps moving on to Bottomore and
Nisbet (1979) for a more detailed analysis.   For those
wishing to take their knowledge of functionalism further,
the works of Durkheim (1938 and 1951) are interesting and
stimulating.   Further developments of functionalism are
to be found in Parsons (1951) and the evolutionary theme
can be particularly pursued in Parsons (1977).   Much of
Parsons's writing is difficult;   the less adventurous may
find Rocher (1974) helpful.   Given the relevance of the
work of Merton (1968) and Davis and Moore (1945) to the
ideas discussed here and elsewhere in this book, it may be
useful to read these in the original.   Demerath and
Peterson (1967), Giddens (1977 and 1982) and Mennell (1980)

give a good overview of the problems raised by functionalism.   Particularly recommended is the article by
Gouldner in Demerath and Peterson as a critical development of functionalist ideas.   Students will find Mishra
(1977) and Downes and Rock (1982) good general introduc-
tions on the relevance of functionalism to social administration.   Cloward and Ohlin (1961), Carrier and Kendall
(1973), and Calnan (1982) are more specific in their
implications.


BIBLIOGRAPHY

  *  Recommended.
**  Recommended for easier reading.

Althusser, L. (1971), 'Lenin and Philosophy and Other
    Essays', London, New Left Books.
* Bottomore, T., and Nisbet, R. (1979), 'A History of
    Sociological Analysis', London, Heinemann.
* Calnan, M. (1982), The Hospital Accident and Emergency
    Department. What is its Role?, 'Journal of Social
    Policy', vol. II, pt 4, pp. 483-483.
* Carrier, J., and Kendall, I. (1973), Social Policy and
    Social Change, 'Journal of Social Policy', vol. 2,
    pt 3, pp. 204-24.
* Cloward, R.A., and Ohlin, L.E. (1961), 'Delinquency and
    Opportunity: a Theory of Delinquent Gangs', London,
    Routledge & Kegan Paul.
**Cohen, P.S. (1968), 'Modern Social Theory', London,
    Heinemann.
* Davis, K., and Moore, W.E. (1945), Some Principles of
    Stratification, 'American Sociological Review', vol. 10,
    no, 2, pp. 292-9.
* Demerath, M.J., and Peterson, R.A. (1967), 'System,
    Change and Conflict', New York, Free Press.
* Downes, D., and Rock, P. (1982), 'Understanding Deviance:
    a Guide to the Sociology of Crime and Rule Breaking',
    Oxford University Press.
* Durkheim, E. (1938), 'The Rules of Sociological Method',
    Chicago, Free Press.
* Durkheim, E. (1951), 'Suicide: a Study in Sociology',
    Chicago, Free Press.
Durkheim, E.(1960), 'The Division of Labour in Society',
    Chicago, Free Press.
Erikson, K.T. (1966), 'Wayward Puritans', London, John
    Wiley.
Gans, H. (1971), The Uses of Poverty: the Poor Pay All,
    'Social Policy', vol. 2, no. 2.

Giddens, A. (1976), 'New Rules of Sociological Method', London, Hutchinson.
* Giddens, A. (1977), 'Studies in Social and Political Theory', London, Hutchinson.
* Giddens, A. (1982), 'Profiles and Critiques in Social Theory', London, Macmillan.
Gouldner, A.W. (1967), Reciprocity and Autonomy in Functional Theory, in Demerath and Peterson (1967).
* Mennell, S. (1980), 'Sociological Theory: Uses and Unities', Nashville, Thomas Nelson.
* Merton, R.K. (1968), 'Social Theory and Social Structure', New York, Free Press.
* Mishra, R. (1977), 'Society and Social Policy: Theoretical Perspectives on Welfare ', London, Macmillan.
* Parsons, T. (1951), 'The Social System', Chicago, Free Press.
Parsons, T., Bales, R.F., and Shils, E.A. (1953), 'Working Papers in the Theory of Action', Chicago, Free Press.
* Parsons, T. (1977), 'The Evolution of Societies', Englewood Cliffs, NJ, Prentice-Hall.
Radcliffe-Brown, A.R. (1952), 'Structure and Function in Primitive Society', London, Cohen & West.
**Rex, J. (1961), 'Key Problems in Sociological Theory', London, Routledge & Kegan Paul.
**Rocher, G. (1974), 'Talcott Parsons and American Sociology', Nashville, Thomas Nelson.
Riesman, D. (1977), 'Richard Titmuss: Welfare and Society', London, Heinemann.
Smelser, N.J. (1959), 'Social Change in the Industrial Revolution', London, Routledge & Kegan Paul.

# Chapter 6

# Pluralist and elitist theories of political processes
Geoffrey Ponton

The theories considered in this chapter have been developed within the discipline of political science, although they have also been influenced, especially in the theory of elitism, by political sociologists - that is to say, people brought up in the sociological tradition who have turned their attention to political institutions. Political science began to develop a separate identity within the social sciences towards the end of the nineteenth century. It was first concerned primarily with 'political theory', a combination of political philosophy and the study of constitutions and constitutional procedures. From the beginning of the twentieth century, when the firs first studies of voting behaviour were made, political science has become increasingly concerned with the study of political behaviour, how decisions are actually made and the influences brought to bear on decision-making, but ideological issues remain close to the surface.

The origins of pluralism lie in a dual challenge to existing ideas which was recognised by some political thinkers in the nineteenth and early twentieth centuries. At the philosophical level, a movement grew up in Britain in the nineteenth century to counter what was seen as the excessive statism of some German thinkers on the one hand and, on the other, the extreme notion of those who understood society to be simply a collection of individuals, 'a pile of sand', with the state and other organisations having no corporate identity. At an empirical level in the United States a theory of political pluralism arose out of the perceived need to recognise and incorporate into political analysis the reality of group politics in the modernised, industrial state of the twentieth century. This essentially descriptive theory was later to develop elements of prescription in the hands of some theorists.

Elitism as a theory came about more out of a desire to
provide an alternative explanation of social dynamics to
the class theory of Marx.   Later, elitism was to be presented as a harsher but more realistic model of industrialised society than the pluralist 'orthodoxy'.   Elements
of these two theories have recently been brought together
in a new synthesis known as corporatism.

THE PHILOSOPHICAL ORIGINS OF PLURALISM

The philosophical school of English pluralists arose
mainly out of a reaction to the elevation of the entity of
the state to almost mystical levels of significance among
mainly German thinkers like Treitschke.   This elevation
was accompanied by a growth of nationalism associated with
new ideas of race based on irremovable physiological characteristics.   A group of writers emerged with the intention of countering such ideas and also of providing an
alternative to the excessively narrow individualism of
English liberal theories of society.   The problem was
basically the relationship between state and individual.
They saw the organised group within the state both as a
link between individual and the state and also, as Maitland
argued from a background of legal theory, as a 'living
organism and a real person with body and members and a
will of its own'.   Thus the group had a dynamic role to
play in society.

One of the leading pluralist thinkers of this time,
John Neville Figgis, saw the key to freedom in the modern
state as based on the right of groups to organise and to
conduct their operations freely within the state.
Society, then, should not be seen merely as a collection
of individuals, nor the state as an all-embracing, monolithic, overweening power.   Society was composed of a
collection of groups not necessarily large in size, whose
membership was limited but overlapped with that of other
groups.   Tastes, prejudices, moral ideals and so on were
not acquired only from the national orthodoxy, but from
family and community, the educational system and numerous
other 'collective organisms'.   Therefore a state which is
properly concerned for its citizens will find a recognised
place for the groups which express their 'social nature'
(Barker, 1978, pp. 94, 95).

David Nicholls (1975) has identified three main principles underpinning this pluralist theory.   The first
principle is the notion of group personality, a legal

term but based in a social reality just as real in its way
as the component individuals which make it up.   This idea
is derived from the manner in which groups act in a uni-
fied way, entitling us to describe them in a fashion which
would normally be used of individuals.   In addition, the
action of a group is not simply the collectivity of
actions of its component individuals - it is something
more.   As a group, new ideas can arise and new directions
be taken.   The law should recognise this social reality
and accord freedom for groups to live and grow.

Nicholls's second principle of pluralism is the denial
of the sovereignty of the state.   Sovereignty implies a
monopoly of rights and degrades the function and contribution of both individuals and groups.   For the philosophical pluralists, the aim of state activity is the maximisation of liberty based on the division and disperson of
power.   This aim is not absolute because some limitation
on liberty is necessary for order, but it does require
social justice and economic equality in order that freedom
to do something can be practised.

Third, pluralists considered that the disperson of
power and the freedom of groups was the only basis upon
which liberty could be sustained.   The long-standing
principle of toleration would become inevitable because
of the inability of any single group to become dominant.
This avoidance of the domination of one group would, para-
doxically, need to be maintained by a strong state.   However, this pluralist school had no fully agreed theory of
the state.   They did recognise the real possibility of
conflict between groups and the state and that in some
cases the groups might be in the right - which implies the
right to civil disobedience.   But they did not really
face up to the threat to the freedom of the individual
which might come from the group itself.   They also neglected the possibility of an alliance between the state and
the most powerful groups to control society.   In sum,
although a decentralisation of authority and diffusion of
power was seen as desirable to and within groups, they
considered that the state should not normally interfere
to secure this.

The philosophical pluralist movement was part of a
change in thinking which came to see that state action,
rather than inhibiting the development of capitalism,
could be harnassed to preserve it.   But this positive
role of the state, intervening for the general benefit of
the whole people (by providing a better material standard

of living, for example) could develop into an authoritarian paternalism.   To avoid this the state should merely provide the social order in which groups can flourish and, if necessary, adjudicate between them.   They were opposed to state policies pursued on the basis of some common or 'national' interest.   They accepted that there would be some conflict or tension between groups but this could be a positive thing, in which true freedom was more likely to survive.   Their firm belief was that the biggest threat to society in their time was the increasingly powerful state.

## THE AMERICAN SCHOOL OF PLURALISM

The descriptive school of pluralism is usually traced back to a book called 'The Process of Government' by Arthur F. Bentley, published in 1908.   It systematised a growing school of thought which analysed American government not in terms of great men and abstract ideals, but as the creation of groups with essentially economic interests. The individual is understood as the product of group conditioning and the relationship between government and groups as a dynamic one - very much a process.   Not only is the whole of the social process one of interaction of individuals and groups within their environment, but the governmental structure itself is one of groups interacting with other groups.

The basic strength of a group depends on its inner cohesion of shared interests.   Shared interest may be challenged and decline under the pressure and tensions of the multiple group loyalties in modern society.   Cohesion of groups may be intensified or undermined by hostile pressure from rival groups.   The role of 'official' or government groups is to impose agreements on groups in conflict in order to maintain an acceptable level of social stability.   Constitutional rules and conventions and other social principles accepted throughout society will reduce conflict and enhance consensus and therefore stability.   Bentley did not underestimate the importance of ideas and ideals but he argued that such concepts as leadership or public opinion could only be understood in group terms.   The symbolic expression of value gives meaning and direction to group action.   He was a strong believer in the quantitative method, although he recognised that further interpretation was needed in order to take account of feelings and ideas.

Although Bentley's work went unnoticed for many years,
in time it became very influential, particularly after the
Second World War among a group of scholars who were coming
to maturity in the United States at that time.    The
analysis of the mass politics of the twentieth century was
founded upon this dynamic, complex structure of interlock-
ing voluntary groups, based on economic, ethnic, religious
and many other interests.    They operate within a system
of principles, rules and policies designed to co-ordinate,
regulate, guide and encourage their activities - the
system called liberal or representative democracy.    The
groups are intermediaries between individual and government, and instead of one man, one vote as the guiding
principle, it is 'a fair share to every legitimate group'.
This, incidentally, concentrates attention on economic and
material interests.

In studying the expression of group interests in the
context of a liberal democratic structure of government,
attention was increasingly paid to the stability of the
political system in the face of apparently massive social
change.    This led to a model which explained that stability in terms of a self-regulating equilibrium.    This can
be most clearly seen in Easton's 'systems' model (Easton,
1965).    According to this model, the governmental policy-
making structure is subject to 'inputs' consisting of
demands and supports largely derived from interest group
pressure, reflecting dissatisfaction and tensions within
the system.    The government responds to these pressures
with policy initiatives designed to assuage the demands,
reduce tensions and increase support, particularly in the
form of votes.    Thus policy implementation (output) modi-
fies the social circumstances which gave rise to the original demands but in so doing gives rise to new demands
which, in their turn, have to be processed.    In this way
the equilibrium is maintained by incremental adjustments.
Collapse can occur if the demands on the system become too
heavy for it to process them effectively.

This model, though primarily intended to be descriptive,
quickly acquired normative overtones.    There was an
assumption that a pluralist system would be morally neutral in its group arrangements, giving all those with
interests and the will to pursue them the opportunity to
do so untrammelled by ideological limitations.    The politician was seen as a 'middleman', the arbitrator between
conflicting interests.    At the same time, the model also
emphasised the virtue of toleration, not only because it
was considered that differences in society could only be

suppressed at too high a cost, but also because the toleration of differences, far from promoting divisiveness,
would contribute to social cohesion and unity by inducing
an awareness of the importance of freedom of action and
fair treatment in the policy.   As a logical consequence
of this kind of reasoning, the attainment of a genuinely
pluralist society becomes a natural good to be sought for
its own sake.   It is the optimum social and political
organisation;   a balanced, tolerant, humane society giving
each man the maximum opportunity for self-fulfilment based
on a variety of groups.   This analysis, even more than
elite theory, was presented as an alternative superior in
every way to the marxist model (at least as seen in practice) which it saw as its main rival.

## CRITICISMS OF PLURALISM

Since the 1950s the descriptive model has been subject to
increasing criticism, stimulated particularly by the
social unrest of the 1960s, which the model could not
easily explain.   The 1960s protesters were different and
unexpected, utilising as they did unorthodox, unofficial
channels of protest and dissent based on ideals rather
than materialist values.   Moreover, they were not the
underprivileged and needy but often the comparatively
affluent.   It was pointed out that if toleration was a
major characteristic of pluralist society, another was inequality.   Some groups, by virtue of superior status or
resources, or because of greater opportunities for social
disruption, had better access to the decision-makers than
groups who lacked some or all of these qualities.   In
particular, new groups, or those with unorthodox political
or moral views, would have great difficulty in acquiring
influential status even when, like the blacks in the
United States, they represented a sizeable segment of the
population.   So, far from the government being a neutral
referee, it really acts as the enforcer of the preferences
of the predominant social interests.   Pluralism was also
accused of bias towards questions concerning the distribution of resources between groups rather than the general
good.   So various groups could compete for government
aid, while questions of general concern like health services or urban renewal were neglected.   The general good
is a preoccupation of socialism.   Pluralism recognises
the possibility of incremental reform only, not of general
social transformation.

Critics soon attacked the claim that pluralist theories

were not ideological.    Even if the prescriptive use of
the theory was discounted, the model focused on these elements of Western political processes that provided the
most favourable evidence for its arguments.    In addition,
it played down the impact of ideas to an excessive degree.
Its belief that significant changes were only achieved
incrementally and concerned material reward left little
room for a dynamic role for ideas, beliefs and principles.
Yet human history seemed to give the lie to this view as
one contemplated great mass movements based on nationalis-
tic, religious or philosophical beliefs.    The case
against the down-grading of ideas and the incremental
change view of political movement is contained in Bernard
Crick's notable polemic against Michael Oakeshott (Crick,
1972).

The restoration of ideas and values to a more prominent
place in pluralist thinking was signified by Easton's 1969
address to the American Political Science Association on
the post-behavioural revolution in political science.    He
recognised that the events of the 1960s in the United
States and elsewhere had called the pluralist model seriously into question, especially in its failure to find a
primary role for values in political action.    He drew
attention to the fact that many aspects of the protest
movements of the 1960s could not be easily explained
except in terms of a revision of moral values especially
on the part of the young.    Moreover, in the forefront of
the protests were often not the economically deprived and
underprivileged, but college students, a group comparatively well off in their opportunities and expectations
and usually members of the economically and socially
advantaged middle class.

Some pluralist assumptions have come to be recognised
as culture-based, the analysis being little more than a
rationalisation of the American and British types of political systems.    Indeed, it also has analogous resemblan-
ces to the market theory of economics - a free competition
of interests operating within consensual agreements concerning such matters as majority rule, effective communications, and incremental gains.    Many have recognised in
the model not only an assumption of equilibrium as the
norm but a strong bias in favour of the status quo - it is
a conservative model.

Of the various detailed criticisms of pluralism, I have
selected three for discussion.    These are Dahrendorf's
criticism of the emphasis on equilibrium;  Olson's ques-

tioning of the motivation towards group activity, and
Beer's view that pluralist processes lead to 'a paralysis
of choice'.

Dahrendorf is concerned to refute the assumption that
the natural state of society is one of equilibrium and
that the 'proper' function of the political system is to
correct any temporary, marginal disturbance of that
equilibrium.   On the contrary, he argues, the natural
state of the political system is one of disequilibrium and
the dynamism of social change is fuelled by conflict.
Thus the comparatively static nature of the equilibrium
model based on consensus is replaced by a model of social
change based on conflict.   The question then arises:   if
the social dynamic is based on conflict, how can the
system sustain itself in workable existence over time with
sufficient coherence and stability?   The answer, according to Dahrendorf, is not consensus on principles and
rules of the game, but constraint.   Social order is maintained by the coercive powers of the state.   Of course,
the model is the extreme case.   In the real world consensus and conflict, agreement and constraint go together in
various combinations but the coercive characteristics of
the state - not necessarily invoked but whose potential is
known - should be given their proper due.   Associated with
constraint is the concept of power and the combination of
certain interests to maintain themselves in power or to
try to acquire power.   Thus it is that he finds the pluralist equilibrium model a partial and inadequate explanation of the working of the social and political system.
It encourages the classification of some behaviour as
'deviance' and there is no place for deviance.   But
Dahrendorf sees the positive side of power as providing
men with protection against the badness of their fellow
men.   The lack of agreement and the existence of uncertainty in the affairs of men means that we require a
'plurality of decision patterns' or variety and competition;   in other words, there is a necessity for conflict
(Dahrendorf, 1968, pp. 140-9).

Olson looks at two pluralist principles:   that society
needs to be free and open in order that any of those who
wish to form interest groups may do so, and that those who
have a political interest to pursue will have sufficient
motivation to do so.   The underlying assumption here is
that, at least in economic groups, self-interest and group
interest coincide sufficiently to justify joint action.

Olson questions this assumption.   His argument is that

a group is 'a number of individuals with a common interest', but at the same time members of the group have
individual interests.   A large number of individuals are
in a position analogous to that of persons in a competitive economic market.   For any individual to sacrifice
time and money to support a group organisation would not
be in his interests because his individual efforts would
have no significant effect, and if the group gained benefits without his support he would still receive those
benefits.   Therefore rational, self-interested individuals would not support group efforts even if all were
convinced that the group policies were in their interest.
Some people may object that more altruistic behaviour may
be expected even where economic interests are at stake.
But most writers, including Marx, assume rational behaviour in pursuit of economic interests and Olson notes that
even the state with all the emotional patriotism which
attaches to it and its ideological forces cannot finance
its most basic and essential activities without compulsion.

From this argument as he elaborates it, Olson draws
three conclusions:

(a)   the larger the group, the more it will be in the
individual's self-interest not to bear the cost to him of
supporting group interests;

(b)   small groups are more likely to organise and will
have distinct advantages;

(c)   large political interest groups will only form if
coerced into it or they have already formed for other
purposes.

Olson's model goes some way to explain why large groups,
like consumers, or for that matter economic classes, have
great difficulty in organising to pursue their interests.
Nevertheless, the fact that some such groups do exist
suggests that Olson's model accounts for many of the limitations of the pluralist model without completely invali-
dating it.

Finally, I look at what Samuel Beer (1982) describes as
'the paralysis of public choice'.   He points out that
group politics is intrinsic to the collectivism now a
major characteristic of British politics.   This has resulted in a fragmentation of the decision-making system which
the steady debilitation of the major political parties can
do little to correct, while all this has been exacerbated

by the rise of 'populist' dissenting group activity.
Another of Beer's terms, 'pluralistic stagnation', was
originally used to describe the inability to muster a
majority for any coherent policy in the irreconcilable
conflicts of the Weimar Republic.   But it can also be
used to refer to the defence of an established status quo.
Some groups may be so strong strategically vis-à-vis the
government that they can veto government action, while
others will be able to influence votes sufficiently to
prevent change.   A third explanation for stagnation is
when there exists a large number of organised interests.
We can envisage a situation where, by all following some
common rules and procedures, all gain considerable benefits.   But this depends on all following the common
rules.   If only one group follows them it will lose out.
The result is that no groups adhere to the beneficial
rules.   This is, of course, an application of Olson's
arguments to the interaction of groups.   The results of
the operation of these factors are 'immobility and inco-
herence - in brief a paralysis of choice'.   Beer sees
this as characteristic of contemporary British collectivist and welfare politics.   Because there is a large
number of groups competing for government resources, no
one group will make much differenct to the level of government expenditure.   So there is no reason why they
should exercise restraint in their demands.   Such restraint would bring no immediate benefit to them or any
other group, but it would immediately penalise the group
showing self-restraint.   The problem is the working
structure of numerous groups which cannot be fully aware
of what others are doing or enter into agreements with
them.   The unhappy result is that all agree that moderation of demands is necessary but the structure of the
situation defeats this very moderation.

Pluralist theory, then, has arisen to try to explain
the twentieth-century phenomenon of group politics, and
also to give a rationalised justification of the liberal
democratic state especially in its American and British
manifestations or their derivatives.   The model could
only hold up in a period of economic prosperity which
masked the deeper conflicts in the structure of society.
Faced with steadily growing economic difficulties on a
world scale and with the emergence of new types of social
and political protest, the model has come to seem increasingly inadequate both as an explanation and as a justification of the political system.   We now find that, increasingly, new models which involve substantial modifications
of conventional pluralism are being developed.   They are

based on various interpretations of what is described as
post-industrial society, and involve such conceptual
schemes as the management of conflict and corporatism.
These will be considered after looking at the development
alongside pluralism of elitist theories which, in their
turn, have developed contemporary variations and have also
been affected by the ramifications of pluralist analysis.


## ELITISM

The theory of elitism was originally developed in the
nineteenth century primarily as an attempt to counter the
marxist economic class theory of society, with its emphasis on inevitability and Utopianism.    Its fundamental
principles are that every society, whether capitalist or
socialist, can be divided into those who control and those
who are controlled, and that the character and direction of
society can be understood in terms of the composition,
structure and conflicts of the controlling group.

The main founders of elitist theory were Mosca (1858-
1941) and Pareto (1848-1923).    For Pareto, elites are
formed from those persons who are naturally superior;    a
governing elite is that which is dominant in government
and politics.    There can be elites in other social areas,
and also sub-elites, such as managers, civil servants,
etc., who are often indispensable and sometimes a source
of recruitment.    The non-elite is the mass.    History is
not the story of class struggle but of the replacement of
elites.    Like Pareto, Mosca regarded the domination of
elites as inevitable, but he saw a difference between the
position of elites in a modern political democracy and
previous types of rule.    For him, the political elite
could be conditioned and constrained by other groups in
society, and the necessity of elites depends not on the
facts of human nature, as Pareto argued, but on the needs
of organisation.

A primary concern of Mosca and Pareto was to account
for the survival of elites.    Pareto developed a theory of
the circulation of elites to describe the way that elites
were able to adapt and transform themselves in order to
ensure their survival.    This transformation is made possible by a continual renewal of the elite's legitimacy.
Such legitimacy is central to elite survival and has to be
firmly anchored in concrete achievement which perpetuates
the charisma of the offices held.    Pareto specifies the
characteristics of elite groups which are conducive to

survival.   The elite must remain small in order to ensure
good organisation, and success of the individual members
depends on their corporate organisation to which they must
be loyal.   They must be well trained but avoid narrow
specialisation because specialisation makes it more difficult to adapt to changes in economic, social and political
conditions.   They must avoid rigidity and always be ready
to make concessions and compromises.   Their overriding
priority must be the defence of their corporate interest
rather than attachment to any particular policy.   A
degree of intra-elite competition is of assistance in promoting adaptability.

The important conflicts in society are understood to be
within the elite, not between classes.   And elites
decline when they fail to incorporate new politically
important elements who then organise themselves and the
masses to overthrow the incompetent elite.   Schumpeter
argued that elite power depended not so much on recruitment as on function, on the continuing significance of
their special functions and the degree to which they successfully perform them.   The problem is not reform but
survival.   Mass action can easily destroy, but elites aim
at a moderate and evenly paced circulation of elites based
on flexible recruitment and a readiness to adapt.   This
will dampen criticism and maintain the continuity and
stability of society.   In fact, elite theory (like pluralism) is more concerned with explaining social stability
and continuity than radical change.

Arguments about elite theory have often centred on the
normative question of whether elites exploit and manipu-
late the ruled, or whether their control is beneficial.
Social contract theory sees a voluntary agreement between
rulers and ruled for the general benefit and which need
not be renewed.   Others see elite rule as based on exploitative conquest.   Usually both these elements are present
in elite-mass relationships.   Elitists would argue that
elites have great privileges but they also have great responsibilities.   Either the mass without leaders is unable
to organise, or the mass acts rationally in organising
itself in a hierarchical manner.   Either way, an elite is
necessary for an ordered society.

This view gained support from Michels's studies of political parties in 1911.   Michels concluded, in his
'iron law of oligarchy' that there is a tendency in all
organisations towards a concentration of power in the
hands of a small group of conservative leaders who manipu-

late the organisation in their own interest regardless of
its original purpose.   They are enabled to do this by
their inevitable control over resources, finances, knowledge and communication.   But many commentators have
found it necessary to modify Michels's extreme view for
more general application.   Elites must operate within
certain constraints such as the policy priorities and
political procedures already established, especially when
these are widely accepted like, in Britain, free elections
and freedom of speech and assembly.   They are also limited by the ability of counter-elites to emerge, and procedures like elections which provide some possibility for
replacement.

The social background of elites has often been over-
emphasised as a basis for their power.   Elites depend on
recognition of membership and the maintenance of the
legitimacy of their organisations over against the claims
of other organisations.   For this, the elite has to be
sure that its own standards of competence are recognised
and accepted by society, that is, that it is the elite
which sets the conditions that determine their own recognition as the elite.   It is this, and not middle-class
social origins, which is fundamental to the meaning of
elitism.   So the argument that recruitment from a wider
social background than is usual would help to democratise
the political system is not valid.   Wider recruitment
(for example, from the working class) might well not do
much to help the working class while it would help elite
survival by legitimising it and warding off criticisms.

Attempts have been made to reconcile elite theory at an
ideological level with democracy.   In a mass industrialised society, it is argued, practical difficulties prevent direct participation of the mass in government, so
that some form of representation and leadership is necessary and unavoidable.   The leadership is constrained,
however, by the fact that their position is conditional on
performance and the electoral system is seen as shifting
the balance of power to the electorate, if only from time
to time.   By this means it is thought that rulers must
consider the wishes of the ruled.   But many, including
Mosca and Pareto, have argued that elections make little
real difference because elites have organisation and the
masses do not.   On the other hand, disputes within the
elite will in all probability cause one group at least to
turn to the electorate for support.   Oppositions will
organise against the ruling elite and mass political parties and interest groups will strengthen the position of

the individual voter because they present viable alternatives.   This situation, of course, requires an open
society, another of whose characteristics would be the
principle of constitutionalism, or that the elite, like
the rest of society, are constrained by the laws.


## ELITISM VERSUS PLURALISM

Controversy over whether elitism is a more accurate model
than pluralism for liberal democratic society surfaced in
the United States in the 1950s and stimulated a continuing
debate.   It is important to note that there has been a
shift in the ideological framework of this new school of
elitist thinkers in comparison with the old.   They do not
necessarily claim that elite rule is inevitable, and certainly not that it is desirable.   Indeed, they tend to
accept that a pluralist distribution of power is desirable.
Their main contention is that democratic institutions disguise the real power of a ruling elite in Western democratic states.

   The controversy came to life with the publication of
Floyd Hunter's 'Community Power Structure' (1953), a study
of community leadership based on the reputation of office
holders for exercising power.   Hunter's conclusion was
that it is possible clearly to identify a group of decision-makers who controlled public life.   Hunter's methods
were criticised for failing to distinguish the areas over
which the leaders were supposed to exercise power or the
limits of their influence.   Also, Hunter looked into
those issues in which members of the business elite themselves said they were interested.   On non-business issues
these same leaders were divided and unable and unwilling to
give a lead.   Here there might have been another set of
leaders who were influential.   Much, therefore, depends
in this method on the selection of the issues to be examined.

   C. Wright Mills's 'The Power Elite' (1956) raised the
same issues at a national level.   He maintained that a
ruling elite existed in the United States whose power was
founded in the economic and social structure institution-
alised in the military establishment, business corporations
and the political executive.   This elite is composed of
those who hold office in the hierarchy of these strategic
institutions.   They must have some contact and cohesion
among themselves, ranging from conscious collusion to a
consensus of policies and values.   For Mills, the poten-

tial for the exercise of concentrated power was greater
than at any other period in American history.   The characteristic of American society was elite concentration
and not the diffusion of power as was believed by the
pluralist liberals.

Dahl's 'Critique of the Ruling Elite Model' (1958) is
the best known attack on the Mills thesis.  His main
point was that while Wright Mills asserted the existence
of the power elite, he did not in fact prove its existence, a thing very difficult to do.   Dahl pointed out
that an elite is not (a) merely a potential for control,
as the military may be seen to be;   (b) nor is it composed
of individuals who have more influence than others in the
system;   (c) and nor can one generalise from one area of
influence, for it does not follow that influence will
extend over other areas.   The test of the existence of a
ruling elite was only possible if such a group was well
defined;   where 'there is a fair sample of cases involving
key political decisions in which the preferences of the
hypothetical ruling elite run counter to those of any
other likely group that might be suggested';   and where in
such cases the preferences of the elite regularly prevail.

Dahl set out to propose satisfactory criteria which
could be accepted as a fair test of the hypothesis of the
existence of a power elite.   His major work 'Who Governs?'
(1961) was part of an extensive research programme designed
to re-examine the question and avoid some of Hunter's
dubious methodological approaches.   Dahl's task was to
try to discover who took significant political decisions
in the community (in this case, New Haven).   From a
variety of decision types and potential leaders, data was
produced from which Dahl concluded that power was not confined to an identifiable group but shared among a number
of distinct groups.   If a power elite had ever existed,
its monopoly of power had been broken and all it now had
was social status with little political power.   Different
groups had power in different sectors of government.   If
this was not fully democracy, then it was polyarchy.

Dahl's criteria in their turn soon came under question
in an article (later a book) by P. Bachrach and M.S.
Baratz: 'Two Faces of Power' (1962).   They were not
happy with the concentration by Dahl on the actual taking
of decisions in the community.   Rather, they were interested in an investigation of Schnattscheider's thesis that
the crucial issue was 'the mobilisation of bias' - who
gained and who was handicapped by the established political

procedures, rules of the game, and the dominant values and myths of the community.  Then they looked at the 'dynamics of non-decisionmaking', the way groups influence values and institutions towards the maintenance of the status quo and control the agenda so that 'dangerous' issues do not arise in the agenda for decision.  They thought it vital to identify the 'key' issues which really challenge existing power and authority.  It is these potential issues which must be prevented from becoming actual issues for decision.  Having identified the key and routine decisions based on the above, participation in decision-making on concrete issues could be analysed. Lukes (1974) took this a stage further by emphasising that just as relevant are the ways that potential issues are kept out of politics, disguising the existence of latent conflict in the community.

Although the limitations of the decision-making approach have been revealed and Bachrach and Baratz showed that both elitists and pluralists were biased by their preconceived approach to and behaviouralist assumptions about power, the main difficulty of the non-decision-making and latent conflict approach remains the problem of measurement - how do you measure a non-decision?  While measurability must not be a criterion of relevance, it remains an important factor in assessing the significance of the subjective, negative face of power.


RECENT DEVELOPMENTS

The argument concerning the most appropriate model for the analysis of liberal democratic society may have lost its edge somewhat since the 1960s but it still remains a central issue, even if various modified approaches have now been developed.

Much of the discussion has developed around the role of the state in pluralist and elitist theory.  In pure elitist theory, the political elite is defined as the holders of the major political offices and they are seen to control and direct society.  Traditional marxists see the state apparatus as dominated by the bourgeois class. Pluralist theory has most often assigned to the state a mediating role, a referee in the attempt to reach negotiated compromise agreements with powerful interests.  The exact nature of the relationship of the state to organised interests has had various interpretations.  The degree of authority and involvement of the state attributed by

theorists can vary from positive, authoritative intervention to a minimalist interpretation of 'first among
equals'.   In many analyses, therefore, the state seems to
have very little authority.   It can do little more than
mediate between powerful interests and often seems more or
less at the mercy of these interests with no independent
position of its own.   Recently signs of a reaction against
this extreme view have set in, and corporatist theory
(discussed below) would perhaps see state and groups as in
more of a 'structured' partnership with one another.

One of the ways in which governments may exert their
authority is by crisis management, a concept developed by
Jürgen Habermas (1976, pp. 19-29) to demonstrate how governments develop processes for the containment and neutra-
lisation of opposition and dissent in the interests of
stability.   For Habermas, capitalism is epitomised by the
clash of interests.   But to cope with these conflicts,
major inherent economic crises are reinterpreted as merely
problems of adjustment, as minor contingent events which
do not affect the fundamental structures of society.   The
democratic aspects of the system are reduced simply to the
negative withholding of consent, while the individual is
encouraged to 'privatise' his life and to reduce the significance of his social consciousness and involvement.
The process of depoliticisation is encouraged, whereby
democratic participation becomes merely formal and decisions are taken by means of agreements between pluralistic
elites or by depoliticising the issues into exercises in
the application of technical and bureaucratic principles
instead of open debate and interest group activity.
Problems are redefined in separated ways so that no overall class analysis is possible, and this is reinforced by
an appropriate institutional setting.   Ostensibly neutral
state-appointed bodies like the Commission for Racial
Equality in Britain are sometimes created in order to provide an arena for the defusing of problems by negotiation
rather than conflict.   Legitimacy is maintained by the
promotion of symbolic and personalised activities and
institutions.   Whether and how this balancing act can be
maintained is a major consideration of government.

Another approach is to argue that the entire significant part of the decision-making system is composed of the
interplay of groups and that the government itself is no
more than a collection of groups.   J.J. Richardson and
A.G. Jordan (1979) make it clear that governments can be
constrained to modify their policies by group activity
(such as the burgeoning environmentalist lobby in the

1960s and 1970s) and are heavily reliant on groups for
implementation.   On the other hand, they would agree that
if those with most 'muscle' are not always to prevail it
is necessary for the government to exercise its legitimate
authority, a legitimacy which can enable it to have an
influence over a wider area of events than groups.   But
if we concentrate on the influence of groups vis-à-vis the
government, it is possible to view the system as one in
which the state apparatus has similar characteristics to
those of groups outside the government.   So governmental
institutions can be regarded as very similar to non-gov-
ernmental interest groups, although they may be in a
privileged position by virtue of their 'official' status.
Government institutions - departments, agencies, etc. -
thus become interest groups which compete with one another
because they have different interests and therefore different policy objectives.   So, for Richardson and Jordan,
bureaucracies have interests and there is no difference in
principle between internal government and external interest group pressures.


CORPORATISM

Perhaps the most significant discussion in recent years
has been on whether the pluralist processes in British
government have been developing in the quasi-elitist
direction of corporatism.   Corporatism is a concept susceptible of a variety of interpretations.   Broadly speak-
ing, it involves a positive role for the state in direct-
ing the economy in co-operation with a limited number of
especially important interest groups.   It is opposed to
pluralism in the respect that pluralism is heavily dependent on analogies drawn from the liberal conception of a
perfect market situation.   But it is similar to pluralism
in that it attempts to provide a model on the level of the
political system itself which has as a central feature the
fact of interest group representation.

Wyn Grant (1977) identifies three types of corporatism:

(a)   Classical corporatism, which is anti-parliamentary
and interprets society as a number of 'corporations'.
This form can be linked to medieval understandings of
society and possibly to some more modern theoretical con-
structs like guild socialism.   In particular, it is
linked with the organisation of the Italian fascist state.

(b)   Corporatism as a development of nineteenth-century

policies to ensure the subordination of the workers in the
face of growing worker organisation which was interfering
with market forces.   Ideally, liberal capitalism is seen
to work by the clear separation of the political, economic
and ideological dimensions.   But if this system cannot be
operated, then corporatism is adopted in which the state
organises the economic sphere and other areas of social
life.   Order is maintained by hierarchical control of
organisation.   This type of arrangement is one in which
only the state has the capability to ensure a strong centralised order based on the merger of political and economic spheres.   There has also to be a high degree of ideological agreement - the normative consensus upon which the
hierarchy is based.   Thus, some of the main characteristics and achievements of liberalism are reversed.   The
implications of this analysis is that corporatism takes
its place within the context of class analysis.   It is
the way in which the dominant capitalist class responds to
a challenge at a particular time in its development.
Subordination of labour is its main aim and it is an
alternative strategy to the orthodox capitalist means of
control through markets, when the orthodox means cannot be
pursued or maintained for some reason.

(c)   The third type is what Grant calls 'bargained corporatism' in which the main features of corporatism are
found, but modified by the attempt to combine them with
aspects of the liberal collective bargaining model.   The
most noted student of this type is J.T. Winkler (1976).

    For Winkler, the difference between pure pluralism and
corporatism is that under pluralism the state is supportive in the context of a mixed economy, while under corporatism the state is directive in a regulated economy.
He adumbrates four principles:

unity, in which economic goals are seen as best achieved
through co-operative effort rather than competition;

order, in place of the anarchy of market competition;

nationalism, in which individual rights are subordinate to
national economic achievement;

success - the effective attainment of collective national
goals.

He sees corporatism as representing a new type of political economy which carries the implication that it requires

a new type of political system.   It is created by the
structural changes which have taken place in the economy.
He does not consider in any detail how changes in political ideas and practice could contribute to corporatism's
development.   But Cawson (1982) is prepared to argue that
contemporary democratic theory and especially 'the emphasis on functional participation in a pluralist democracy'
has tended to make corporatist ideas more acceptable.   It
is only because of the fact that interest groups have,
through pluralist analysis, become a recognised and accepted part of the understanding of contemporary democracy,
that corporatist thinking could be so readily accepted by
political parties and public opinion.

So corporatism is the result of economic, political,
administrative and philosophical developments.   Particularly noteworthy is the strong impact of rationalist ideas
on administration and policy-making - planning has become
the norm - and the dramatic changes in the ways in which
major interests are represented in or incorporated into
the political process.   However, corporatism is not an
all-pervasive and all-embracing feature of 'advanced capitalist economy'.   It is more accurate to discern corporatist and pluralist sections of interest group representation, although the former may be a growth area which is
leading to a potential threat to liberal democracy.

Winkler does not relate corporatist ideas to the context of class relationships.   For him, they are entirely
concerned with the relationships of the state to the private economic sector.   Industry is understood as being in
private ownership, but subject to control by the state.
The question he does not seem to ask is:   in whose interest is the state acting and why?   Many would argue that
the state is really operating in the interests of a section of capital.   The idea of the state acting in its own
interests is not easily compatible with a class analysis.

The discussion on the position of the state is of central importance to corporatist theory.   Both the pluralists and the contemporary elitists tend to neglect the
role of the state in creating the conditions necessary for
the maintenance of a particular economic and social order.
Cawson argues that an understanding of the distribution of
power in advanced capitalist society cannot be fully developed from empiricist theories of pluralism or elitism or
from ideological class theories.   It also needs a 'historical and materialist analysis of the changing political

structure' as capitalism develops.   The political structure of corporatism requires specifically corporatist
institutions;  and involves not just co-operation between
government and groups but a high degree of co-operation
between the groups themselves.   The state under corporatism becomes a more important actor than under pluralism.
It is no longer the referee or mediator of competing group
interests but takes important initiatives based on its
interests and policies.   It has a reciprocal influence on
interest groups and it seeks to use them as agents of
social control through their members.   Thus we return to
the point that under corporatism the state has relative
autonomy.

Grant's third type of corporatism is the type likely to
be found in a liberal democracy of the British sort.   In
liberal societies various organisations will retain at
least a relative autonomy, and will never be ideologically
or institutionally subordinate to the state.   They will
always be trying to represent their members in the face of
state activity.   An element of bargaining is always likely
to be a feature of state-group relationships in this sort
of society.   The groups are expected to create social
peace in return for the favours received.   This makes it
very different from the medieval-fascist or class control
models.   Thus capitalist interests in liberal democracies
may not be enthusiastic embracers of corporatist arrangements.   They are likely to be driven to it in the face of
militant labour activity or as a way to deal with economic
problems which are not susceptible to solution through
competitive interest group activity.

In the British context corporatism is linked to the
attempt to develop economic planning and prices and
incomes policy.   There is much emphasis on the 'national
interest' and the interdependence of the different sectors
of society.   A proper relationship between the parts
ensures the health of the whole - using the same organismic analogy as functionalism.   A feature of British society is that some parts are organised more closely than
others on a corporatist model.   Some sectors, like health
administration, water supply and education, show a strong
corporatist tendency, justifying state intervention by
public support.   But in other areas, where state intervention has been less obviously urgent, market forces still
play an important role (for example, in areas dominated by
small businesses).   In non-economic areas (like the cultural) corporatist factors may be less obvious, but
increasing state involvement is likely to require the
development of rationalising corporatist theories.

Perhaps the most obvious corporatist institutional manifestation is 'tripartism', the regular meetings of the
government, the TUC and the CBI in the National Economic
Development Council (NEDC), in order to thrash out an
agreed economic policy.   Grant considers that NEDC is
more operative as a last resort than as a regular policy-
making forum.   For him, the clearly corporatist institutions are such bodies as the Manpower Services Commission
and the Health and Safety Commission which involve government, TUC, CBI and others in the executive operations of
government - an involvement which grants power but also
requires responsibility.   It can only work in areas which
are not too highly politicised.   Critics have pointed out
that the lack of involvement of 'the City' (the financial
centre in London) in corporatist arrangements suggests
quite a serious lack of credibility in the corporatist
system.   In this area market forces are still significantly operative.   An even more serious criticism is that
the elitist leaders of interest groups may plan and co-
operate but they are not sufficiently in control of their
memberships to 'deliver' them in return for the favourable
arrangements they may have arrived at.   Both the TUC and
the CBI have had difficulties over this in recent years.

In the British context, therefore, it is doubtful
whether pluralism, neo-elitism or corporatist developments
of these are fully adequate to describe and explain every
feature of political, economic and social structure.
Different areas of society will manifest characteristics
of one or other of these.   But the reality is not simple
and all takes place within a developing society involving
long-term changes in economic structure, technological
developments and political initiatives.   A gradual trend
in a corporatist direction seems likely, short-term slow-
downs in the process notwithstanding.   But effective,
well-organised political action by the radical left or
neo-liberal right could alter that picture.


RELATIONSHIP TO OTHER THEORIES

Pluralism is often associated with functionalism and neo-
classical economics as conservative theories based on the
maintenance of equilibrium.   There is some truth in this,
but it is important to recognise the different senses in
which these theories are conservative.

Functionalism has a certain ideological neutrality, in
the sense that it can be applied as an anlytical model to

any stable social system, communist, liberal or whatever.
Its conservatism lies in the justification it provides for
the status quo in whatever system it is applied to.

In contrast to this, neo-classical economic theory is
conservative because it presents as an ideal an economic
model that found its most perfect expression in nineteenth-
century Britain and still dominates most western economies.
When classical economic theory was first put forward it
was radical and demanded change.   Only as it became orthodox in theory and practice did it become the ideology of
the status quo.   Today extreme supporters of neo-classical theory regard themselves as 'radical reactionaries',
looking to radical change towards an ideal of the past.

The pluralist model was developed as a tool for the
analysis of political processes in liberal democratic
states and for this reason is limited in its application.
It is conservative, first because as a normative theory it
provides justification for an existing system, but second
because that system is itself conservative in that it may
make radical change difficult.

The relationship between functionalism and the other
two theories can thus be seen to be a contingent one.
They happen to provide a way of analysing the processes by
which existing liberal democratic systems maintain their
equilibrium.   But in other kinds of society, communist,
for example, or feudal, other theories would be more relevant.

The relationship between pluralism and neo-classical
economics is more complex.   It has already been shown how
pluralist theorists treat political processes as analogous
to the competition of the economic market.   Moreover,
Dahl and Lindblom in an early work (1953) provided an
analysis which viewed the private ownership of the means
of production and the operation of the economic market as
important means for ensuring the dispersion of power.
But at the same time the state has a quite different role
in each of the two theories.   In neo-classical economics
the state referees the match, but in modern pluralist
theory the state has an active role in moderating the
results of conflicting interests.

The alliance of pluralism with neo-classical economics
sets it in clear opposition to marxism.   In this context
it may be worth noting that Dahl and Lindblom's (1953)
work was republished in a cheap edition in 1963 under the

auspices of the US Government for export to sustain its
ideological battle with communism.    However, marxism is
not essentially opposed to pluralist ideals.    It merely
argues that pluralism provides an inadequate analysis of
capitalist systems.    At a pragmatic level, marxist parties in several European countries seem to have come to an
acceptance of the general structural and procedural context of liberal democracy, with free speech and assembly,
and contending parties and interest groups.    This has
become known as 'Eurocommunism'.    This has been largely
a resurrection of the long-standing debate over 'revision-
ism' which involved Lenin in a heated argument with such
people as Bernstein, Kautsky and Rosa Luxemburg.    To some
extent, however, this is merely a constructive adaptation
to reality, rather than a genuine agreement about the profound theoretical and practical issues involved.    It
should also be remembered that, unlike pluralism, marxism
is seen by its protagonists as the key to revolutionary
economic and political transformation into a new and
higher form of society.

Turning to the relationship between elitism and marxism,
it was noted earlier that elitism originally developed as
an alternative to marxist analysis of the capitalist
system.    But modern elitists are seen as radical.    The
theory has some affinity with marxism since both regard
pluralist analysis as unrealistic, and both consider that
effective power in western democratic states is held by a
ruling elite.    The major difference seems to be that
elitism takes the elite as given - it is a self-recruiting
oligarchy whose members occupy the higher reaches of the
most powerful structures of western societies.    From this
follows the importance attached to research showing the
interconnections between people holding such positions.
To marxists, however, effective power derives from the
control of the means of production and it is the capitalist
system itself that sustains that power.    Evidence which
reveals the existence of a ruling elite that includes the
industrial barons is interesting but by no means essential
to the marxist thesis.


RELEVANCE TO SOCIAL ADMINISTRATION

Pluralism has always been an important ingredient of the
ideology of the 'welfare state'.    The provision of welfare
by the state is only acceptable if the form and conditions
under which that provision is made can be influenced, or
indeed controlled by the recipients.    Otherwise the power

of government over the lives of individuals is too fright-
ening.   Indeed, even 'paternalism' is used as a deroga-
tory term.   So pluralism as a normative model provided an
ideal while pluralist analysis encouraged the belief that
welfare states conformed to that ideal.

Social administration, as an interdisciplinary field,
was developed first by people like Titmuss and T.H.
Marshall who were committed to welfare provision by the
state within a mixed economy.   They looked to a steady
improvement in provision in response to criticism, and
especially to greater responsiveness to the needs of the
deprived.   So they were also committed to a belief that
incremental change was both possible and desirable.   This
involved an implicit acceptance of pluralist analysis.
However, by the 1970s there was a growing scepticism about
the capacity or willingness of the political and economic
system to respond to pressure for reform based on rational
exposition.   So elitism began to have increasing appeal
as a model of the liberal capitalist state.

Essentially if social administration is to continue to
be concerned with change, it needs an analytical framework
for examining the possibilities of change, and the strategies available for promoting it.   The pluralist/elitist
controversy can provide the outlines of such a framework.
Bachrach and Baratz's study, already mentioned, is one
example of the value of such a framework.   But more pertinent is the use of this framework by Hall, Land, Parker
and Webb (1975), in their book 'Change, Choice and Conflict in Social Policy'.

In this work Hall and her colleagues are concerned 'to
help students of social administration understand why and
how social policies are introduced and modified'.   The
main part of the book is concerned with studies of six
cases where changes in policy at national level have
actually taken place in Britain.   This immediately raises
the criticisms made by elitists of the studies by Hunter
and Dahl, that if one focuses on decisions that are
actually made, one misses the processes that keep other
issues off the political agenda.   This criticism is further heightened by the fact that the authors use Easton's
systems model for their analysis.   However, they are well
aware of the limitations of that model and at an early
stage in the book they present a critical appraisal of the
model and a summary of the main arguments in the pluralist-
elitist controversy.   As a result of this examination they
base their analysis on the conclusion that 'the making of

day-to-day policy on social issues in Britain does operate
within a distinctly pluralist *process*, but that the *limits*
of policy-making are set by elites which for many purposes
are indistinguishable from what Miliband calls a ruling
class' (pp. 150-1, original italics).   Thus the analysis
of the process in the last part of the book is as much
concerned with the factors that enable the issues considered to get on the political agenda, as with the strategies that enable progress to be made.

Since the publication of 'Change, Choice and Conflict
in Social Policy' there has been a shift towards corporatist rather than strictly pluralist analyses of many areas
of decision-making.   For example Klein (1974) argued that
decision-making in the National Health Service is the
result of a corporatist relationship between the government and the medical profession.

FURTHER READING

The student may well feel daunted by the vast amount of
often complex material available on the subjects of this
chapter.   Luckily, one extremely useful book of readings
is available in Castles et al. (1976).   Among many extracts, it includes Dahl, Bachrach and Baratz, and Olson.
Recent studies of contemporary British politics which are
accessible to the non-political scientist are Richardson
and Jordan (1979) and Beer (1982).   Beer is an American
who can bring an enlightening 'outsider's' view.   Most
people will find Lukes (1974) a good short summary of
recent theories, while those interested in a marxist perspective of British politics will discover Ralph Miliband's books (1969, 1972, 1982) to be very readable and
stimulating.   On corporatism Cawson (1982) is perhaps
rather condensed in argument to be easy going, but will
certainly repay the effort.   For those who feel that a
more basic introduction to politics is necessary there are
a number of texts like Ball (1977), Ponton and Gill (1982),
and on British politics specifically is Hanson and Wallas
(1975).

Hall, Land, Parker and Webb (1975) has been referred to
in the text and is particularly recommended to those who
are interested in the pluralist/elitist controversy as a
guide to considering strategies for change.   Part two of
the book not only summarises the controversy, but also
provides a guide to the main parties to the policy-making
process, government departments, parliament and partisan

groups, with relevant references.   The case studies themselves are interesting - the introduction of family allowances, creating the Open University, the development of
health centres, detention centres, the struggle for clean
air, and the abolition of National Assistance.   But the
most important contribution lies in the propositions they
develop in part four.   The same analytical framework is
used to examine the development of Social Services Departments in 1971 in Hall (1976).

BIBLIOGRAPHY

* Recommended.

Bachrach, P., and Baratz, M.S. (1962), Two faces of power,
    'American Political Science Review', vol. 56.
Bachrach, P., and Baratz, M.S. (1970), 'Power and Poverty',
    Oxford University Press.
* Ball, A.R. (1977), 'Modern Politics and Government',
    London, Macmillan.
Barker, R. (1978), 'Political Ideas in Modern Britain',
    London, Methuen.
* Beer, S. (1982), 'Britain Against Itself', London, Faber
    & Faber.
Bentley, A.F. (1908), 'The Process of Government', new
    edn, Cambridge, Mass., Harvard University Press, 1967.
* Castles, F.G., Murray, D.J., Potter, D.C., and Pollitt,
    C.J. (eds) (1976), 'Decisions, Organisations, and
    Society', Harmondsworth, Penguin, 2nd edn.
* Cawson, A. (1982), 'Corporatism and Welfare', London,
    Heinemann.
Crick, B. (1972), The World of Michael Oakeshott, in
    'Political Theory and Practice', London, Allen Lane.
Dahl, R.A. (1958), A Critique of the Ruling Elite Model,
    'American Political Science Review', vol. 52.
Dahl, R.A. (1961), 'Who Governs? Democracy and Power in the
    American City', New Haven, Conn., Yale University Press.
Dahl, R.A., and Lindblom, C.E. (1953), 'Politics, Economics
    and Welfare', New York, Harper & Row.
Dahrendorf, R. (1968), 'Essays in the Theory of Society',
    London, Routledge & Kegan Paul.
Easton, D. (1965), 'A Systems Analysis of Political Life',
    New York, Wiley.
Ehrlich, S. (1982), 'Pluralism - On and Off Course', Oxford
    Oxford, Pergamon.
Grant, W. (1977), Corporatism and Pressure Groups, in
    D. Kavanagh and R. Rose (eds), 'New Trends in British
    Politics', London, Sage.

Grant, W., and Marsh, D. (1977), 'The CBI', London, Hodder
   & Stoughton.
Habermas, J. (1976), 'Legitimation Crisis', London,
   Heinemann.
* Hall, P., Land, H., Parker, R., and Webb, A. (1975),
   'Change, Choice and Conflict in Social Policy', London,
   Heinemann.
* Hall, P. (1976), 'Reforming the Welfare: the politics of
   change in the personal social services', London,
   Heinemann.
* Hanson, A.H., and Wallas, M. (1975), 'Governing Britain',
   Glasgow, Fontana.
Hunter, F. (1953), 'Community Power Structure', Durham,
   NC, University of North Carolina Press.
Klein, R. (1974), The Corporate State, the Health Service
   and the Professions, 'New Universities Quarterly',
   vol. 31.
* Lukes, S. (1974), 'Power - a Radical View', London,
   Macmillan.
Michels, R. (1911, 1959 edn), 'Political Parties', Dover.
* Miliband, R. (1969), 'The State in Capitalist Society',
   London, Methuen.
* Miliband, R. (1972), 'Parliamentary Socialism', London,
   Merlin, 2nd edn.
* Miliband, R. (1982), 'Capitalist Democracy in Britain',
   Oxford University Press.
Mills, C.W. (1956), 'The Power Elite', Oxford University
   Press.
Nicholls, D. (1975), 'The Pluralist State', London,
   Macmillan.
Olson, M. (1965), 'The Logic of Collective Action',
   Cambridge, Mass., Harvard University Press.
* Ponton, G., and Gill, P. (1982), 'Introduction to Poli-
   tics', Oxford, Martin Robertson.
* Richardson, J.J., and Jordan, A.G. (1979), 'Governing
   under Pressure', Oxford, Martin Robertson.
Winkler, J.T. (1976), Corporatism, 'Archives Europeennes
   de Sociologie', vol. 17.

Chapter 7

# The interactionist perspective
## Sandra Walklate

BACKGROUND

The interactionist perspective, often referred to as
symbolic interactionism, unlike other sociological perspectives dealt with in this book, does not consist of a
clearly formulated set of propositions.   It is, as the
title of this chapter suggests, a perspective on the
nature of the individual and his relationship with society
which links together a number of related themes.   It is
consequently important to grasp the structure of this perspective in order to understand its fluidity and frequent
conceptual vagueness.

The historical roots of symbolic interactionism are to
be understood by identifying its links with the American
philosophy of pragmatism and the oral tradition by which
the perspective was perpetuated.   The oral tradition particularly contributes towards the fluid status of this
perspective and its ideas, which alongside the necessary
practical skills were handed down from tutor to student.
In particular the symbolic interactionists seemed to
eschew formal publication, opting to discuss and develop
their ideas in the lecture theatre.   This is particularly
the case with the ideas of George Herbert Mead, whose
students' lecture notes have been a useful source of discovering the essence of his ideas.   This oral tradition
was not only the means of communicating ideas, but also
constituted the means by which such ideas were disseminated
and put into practice.   Thus subsequent developments of
Mead's ideas vary in their emphasis and have affected different areas of sociology differently.   The sociology of
deviance, in particular, has been strongly influenced by
interactionism.   Why this should be the case will be
clarified later.   The effect of this tradition has meant

that there is no coherent body of knowledge which carries
the label 'symbolic interactionism', but there are interpretations concerning the nature of this perspective and
its central area of concern.

The American philosophy of pragmatism is the base which
gives coherence to the work of writers such as James,
Cooley, Thomas, Dewey and Mead who are considered to be
proponents of early interactionist themes.   Such writers
were concerned to develop an image of human beings emphasising their self-conscious creativity.   This concern is
significant given the intellectual climate of the disciplines of sociology and psychology at the turn of the century, both of which were dominated by deterministic images
of human beings, that is, behaviour was viewed as being
either determined by insurmountable instincts, or was
determined by extraneous variables for example, the geographical climate.

The publication of 'The Principles of Psychology', by
William James in 1890, can be seen as a response to such
determinism.   James was anxious to emphasise the importance in understanding human behaviour of recognising the
subjectively meaningful nature of experience and its
creation within an ongoing social process hence what is
referred to as the 'emergent' nature of human beings.
They were to be seen neither as determined nor as deter-
miners of their actions which were to be viewed as being
constructed and reconstructed in the light of individual
experience and interaction with society.   Here attention
is focused on the creativity involved in individual
action, particularly the notion of the potentiality of
individuals.   However, this potentiality is always to be
seen to be realised in an on-going, pre-existing, social
reality which creates the condition for action but does
not determine it.   A dialectical relationship between the
individual and society is being proposed here, which is a
further example of Hegel's influence on modern sociological
thinking.   This central philosophical theme is reflected
in the work of such writers as Cooley and Mead, who have
since been regarded as the founding fathers of symbolic
interactionism.   A further link between interactionism
and more European schools of thought is sometimes made, by
identifying the similarities between the writings of
George Simmel in France and George Herbert Mead in America.
However, the emphasis here will be on the American origins
of this perspective.

The philosophy of pragmatism and the oral tradition

generated a way of analysing human social behaviour in the
first half of the twentieth century which was qualitatively different from the predominant view.    In the post-war
period this influenced a generation of sociologists, enabling them to question the accepted ways of conducting
research and understanding individual action.    The ideas
responsible for this are to be considered, in the first
instance by reference to the work of Charles Horton Cooley
and George Herbert Mead.


CHARLES HORTON COOLEY (1864-1924);    GEORGE HERBERT MEAD
(1863-1931)

Influenced by James and Darwin, the evolutionist, Cooley
developed his own distinctive contribution to the interactionist perspective through the concept of the 'looking-
glass self'.    For Cooley, the individual does not exist
in isolation but can only exist through communication with
others;    there is no separation of the individual from the
social, they exist in a dialectical relationship with each
other.    Hence the self is a looking-glass self because it
emerges in the individual's consciousness through communication with others.    Cooley was essentially concerned
with the process whereby the human personality emerged and
thus he became concerned with the role of the 'primary
group' and its effects.

    Similarly Mead, influenced by James and in some ways
paralleling the work of Cooley, was concerned with the
role of the consciousness in the formation of the self.
Reputedly an excellent lecturer, Mead published little,
and yet he has since become the more influential thinker
in the tradition of interactionism.    More of a philosopher than a sociologist, he spent most of his intellectual
life at the University of Chicago, where, interestingly,
he was a contemporary of the behaviourist, J.B. Watson,
with whom, some of his ideas suggest, he was in dialogue.
There are several themes underlying the work of Mead, in
particular the notions of continuity and flux and the
emergent nature of man.    These are reflected in his basic
concepts of interaction, socialisation, self and mind.

    In considering interaction, Mead wished to make a dis-
tinction between what he called 'human' and 'non-human'
interaction.    Non-human interaction comprised what Mead
called the 'conversation of gestures'.    These gestures do
not constitute subjectively meaningful actions but are
rather patterns of communication controlled by innate

release mechanisms.   So, he argues, animals do not engage
in conscious reflection about their actions.   As far as
human action is concerned, Mead considered the capacity.
for interaction to be the highest of a series of levels of
action which may be correlated with movement along the
evolutionary scale in the Darwinian sense.   The simplest
species are capable of simple reactivity only, e.g. moving
away from something which burns.   At the next level it is
possible to discern a more complex stimulus response
chain, for example, Pavlov's dogs or Thorndike's cats.
Higher primates reflect the capacity for relational responses, identifying cause and effect, shown in the ability
to use tools and solve practical problems in this way.
Only human beings have reached the fourth level of response, which releases them from the stimulus-response
chain of the behaviourists.   Man, he argues, does not
observe the world directly but sees it in terms of labels
which have symbolic meaning for him, i.e. an interpreted
world.   Man, the only species capable of all four levels
of response, is a biological animal freed from the deterministic impulses of his biology and his environment by
his ability to acquire and understand the symbols of the
social world into which he is born, i.e. his language.

The second concept in Mead's framework requiring expli-
cation is the notion of socialisation.   As has already
been suggested, Mead recognised the importance of understanding that man is born into an ongoing set of social
relationships in which the human infant emits a variety of
gestural responses, initially in a disorganised and random
manner.   These random gestures are responded to by those
who are significant in the child's environment, i.e. the
parents.   Through this process meaning is assigned to
these gestures.   For example, a crying baby can elicit
several different responses from an adult.   The adult may
try all of these responses to alleviate the child's condition until the crying stops.   In this way both the child
and the adult learn the meaning to be assigned to such
actions and in what circumstances.   As the child grows
and acquires different mental and physical skills, so the
socialisation process continues and becomes more complex.

For Mead, socialisation has three main stages;  preparatory, play and game.   In the preparatory stage the child
acquires the rudimentary abilities to explore its environment;  language, physical movement, etc.   During the play
stage, the child orients himself towards different forms
of role-playing, not being able to pursue this skill fully
in a consistent and organised manner until the game stage

of development.   Such games as 'playing school' or
'doctors and nurses' indicate the child's growing awareness of the role of 'self' and 'other' in the process of
interaction and the technique of sympathetic introspection, the ability to put oneself in the role of other.
This skill is a crucial acquisition in developing the
ability to engage in interaction with others.   The concept is also very important in understanding how shared
meanings are created in the process of interaction.   Such
an interpretation of the socialisation process may suggest
a cultural as opposed to a biological or environmental
determinism.   Mead avoids this in two ways.   On the one
hand, he stresses the interactive process of socialisation,
and on the other, his concept of 'the self' gives a positive role to individuals in structuring this interaction.

The 'self' is perhaps the most important of Mead's concepts and is also the most vaguely formulated.   For Mead:

> the self has a character which is different from that
> of the physiological organism proper.   The self is
> something which has a development, it is not initially
> there at birth, but arises in the process of social
> experience and activity, that is develops in the given
> individual as a result of his relations to that process
> as a whole and to other individuals within that pro-
> cess. (Mead, 1934, p. 135)

Mead is here drawing our attention to a number of features
of the individual.   First, that it is possible to distinguish between experience and the organisation of that
experience into the self;   i.e. the self is a construction
of our consciousness without which we merely experience
feelings of pain, pleasure, etc.   Consequently, it is
possible to distinguish the self from the body.   In
making this distinction, Mead is also emphasising the re-
flexive nature of the self, i.e. that an individual may
act towards himself as he does towards others and can
therefore become both the subject and object of his own
actions, again emphasising the importance not only of consciousness in action but also of self-consciousness.   In
this process of self-experience, however, the individual
experiences himself not directly, but indirectly, through
his relations with others.   It is interesting to note the
parallels here with Cooley's 'looking-glass self'.   Thus
the self emerges from a process of experiencing self as
subject, as object, and as inferred from interaction with
others.

This emphasis on process is further developed by Mead
in his subdivision of the self into the 'I' and the 'me'.
The exact interpretation of these two categories is not
entirely clear.   It would appear, however, that Mead is
attempting to encapsulate the unpredictable nature of man
alongside the internalised norms acquired in the process
of socialisation.   The 'I' can be considered to be the
impulsive, spontaneous, undirected, tendencies of the
individual, whereas the 'me' constitutes the sets of
social expectations which the individual has internalised
through interaction with others.   An example may serve to
illustrate the relationship intended between the 'I' and
the 'me'.   In a game of football, all the players on the
pitch are aware of the rules of the game.   Each team may
also have worked out various 'set' moves in, for example,
free kick situations.   These dimensions of the game would
constitute those sets of expectations which each player
has of the others during the course of the game.   However, how any one particular player performs on the day,
or whether a player opts to play the set piece or to
pursue an attack individually depends upon that individual's interpretation of the situation, i.e. is dependent
upon the interaction between the expectations of his
fellow players and his own response to those expectations.
This gives an insight into the kind of relationship Mead
envisages between the 'I' and the 'me'.   It is in essence
a dialectical relationship the product of which is never
totally predictable.   Thus the actions of the self need
to be seen as the product of the interactions which take
place between the 'I' and the 'me'.

There are several implications of conceptualising the
self in this way.   In some ways, Mead is creating a
society in miniature within the individual, making possible interaction with oneself as well as with others.
By implication, this gives expression to the possibility of
of inner experience which may never reach overt expression, as we think through alternative courses of action,
i.e. a mental life or mind.   The individual is consequently viewed as an active rather than a passive agent
able to direct and control responses in the light of
interactive processes.

Mead's writings on 'mind', in contrast with the work of
his contemporary at Chicago, Watson, reflect a concern to
understand the contribution of the thinking process to the
production of action.   It is his understanding of the
relationship between the 'I' and the 'me' which allows for
the existence of the 'mind' and thought processes.   This

is not enough, however, to understand the complexity of
mental processes envisaged by Mead.  His 'philosophy of
the present' adds a further dimension to this resulting in
an emphasis on what is referred to as the 'indexicality'
and 'reflexivity' of action.  Mead expresses this as
follows:

> If we had every possible document and every possible
> monument from the period of Julius Ceasar we should un-
> questionably have a truer picture of the man and of
> what occurred in his lifetime;  but it would be a truth
> which belongs to this present, and a later present
> would reconstruct it from the standpoint of its own
> emergent nature. (G.H. Mead, 1934, p. 214)

Although individuals have the ability to select action
actively and creatively using their previous experience as
a guide, such actions are simultaneously developed out of
and are a part of a social process already present, i.e.
are context-bound.  In other words, an understanding of
any action requires an understanding of the present in
which that action was constructed as well as an understanding of the definition of the situation and the interpretation employed by the actors involved.  Consequently,
there are limits to the extent to which complete understanding is achievable.  For one present cannot be transferred to another - 'indexicality'.  Neither can one
individual's understanding be completely transferred to
another - 'reflexivity'.

In summary, Mead's work provides us with a particular
view of the individual as neither being determined nor
being the determiner of his action.  Individuals are a
product of their interaction with ongoing social reality
and the ongoing interaction within themselves between the
'I' and the 'me'.  The essence of these interactions is
dialectical in nature.  Further in order to grasp the
process of producing action it is necessary to appreciate
the actors' perspective and the circumstances in which it
was constructed.


DEVELOPMENTS OF G.H. MEAD

The theoretical formulations of Mead handed down to his
students, largely because of the oral tradition associated
with this perspective, have been interpreted in very different ways.  Consequently, rather than there being an
agreed framework identifiable as symbolic interactionism,

a number of related interactionist *themes* have developed,
all of which lay different emphasis on aspects of Mead's
work.   Four of these will be discussed here, the work of
the Chicago school, of Erving Goffman, of the Iowa school
and ethnomethodology.

This first and possibly the most well known of these
themes is seen in the work of Chicago school of thought.
This school follows Mead's work in the classical manner
and is primarily associated with the work of Herbert
Blumer (a student of Mead's) and Howard Becker, a key
figure in what is referred to as labelling theory.
Blumer (in Rose, 1962), expresses interactionism in the
following way.   First, human beings act towards objects,
situations, others, on the basis of the meaning that these
circumstances have for them.   Second, these meanings are
a product of social interaction.   Consequently, they are
modified and interpreted by the individual in the course
of situations they encounter.   Finally, participant
observation must be the main research tool for understanding this process.   As a consequence a wide variety of
participant observation studies have been conducted,
designed to get inside the actors' reality.   This is seen
to be the key to understanding the nature and structure of
social life.   A classic study conducted within this tradition, is contained in the work of Howard Becker, 'The
Outsiders' (1963), in particular the essay on 'Becoming a
Marihuana User'.   In this essay Becker extends interactionist thinking into what was to become known as 'labelling theory'.

On the basis of his empirical work Becker produced the
following typology as a means of understanding the interactive process.

TABLE 7.1   Types of deviant behaviour

|  | Obedient | Rule-breaking |
| --- | --- | --- |
| Perceived as deviant | Falsely accused | Pure deviant |
| Not perceived as deviant | Conforming | Secret deviant |

As can be seen, Becker's main area of concern was with
those who fall outside what constitutes acceptable behaviour in society;   but in expressing this concern he draws
our attention to understanding how, through an understanding of the processes of interaction, some individuals
acquire the label deviant and others do not.   As the

typology suggests, this depends on the way in which we are perceived by others.   Viewing what is referred to as rule-breaking behaviour in this way had considerable impact, in particular on the sociology of deviance.   Previously dominated by the functionalist mode of analysis, this was extended into understanding the processes involved in the formation of the rules of society.   Hence Becker's further concern in 'The Outsiders' with the relationship between changes in the law concerning marihuana and the use of it as being defined as deviant behaviour. The implications of these developments for understanding the impact of various sorts of social policy legislation will be dealt with shortly, but the importance of understanding such processes of definition and how they operate in the context of social administration would seem significant.

A further school of thought is referred to as the dram dramaturgical school, clearly represented in the work of Erving Goffman.   The essence of Goffman's work lies in his development of the notion of role and role-playing in the portrayal of self to others.   His earliest work, 'The Presentation of Self in Everyday Life' (1959), outlines this development in its most extreme form which he has later refined and modified.   However, it does reflect the importance with which role playing is endowed by Goffman, and its relationship with the thoughts of Mead.   For Goffman, the individual is an actor putting on a performance in front of an audience.   Consequently, as an actor the individual's concern is with the management of his identity, with competent role-performance;   particularly with conveying to others that he is a capable performer. Thus much of our interaction is governed by 'impression management', in which we offer idealised, misrepresented, images of our 'selves', intended to mystify others, as to our 'true' nature (though in Goffman's perspective since we are all actors putting on performances all of the time the notion of a 'true' self becomes rather problematic). This model is extended in his book 'Asylums' (1968), in which we are given an insight into 'The Moral Career of a Mental Patient', i.e. on how the structure of an organisation, here a mental institution, controls and defines the role(s) that inmates are required to play.   They are stripped of their former identity and acquire a new one in the light of the demands and expectations of the institution and its members.

Much of Goffman's later writing is concerned with similar processes in less 'closed' surroundings.   'Stigma:

Notes on the Management of Spoiled Identity' (1968),
introduces a further dimension to impression management,
i.e. examining the way in which stigmata serve to identify
those who are different and who may either be 'discredited' or 'discreditable'.   The discredited are those whose
exclusion or inclusion in certain groups is obvious, i.e.
the blind, the handicapped, etc., and the impact that this
has on processes of interaction.   The discreditable are
those about whom discrediting information is not obvious,
e.g. the successful businessman who might also enjoy wear-
ing ladies' clothing.   Here Goffman is concerned with how
such information is managed in different circumstances.
Goffman's more recent works reflect a move towards ethnomethodology in that 'Relations in Public' (1972) is concerned with the significance of fundamental techniques of
interaction for the maintenance of public order and 'Frame
Analysis' (1975) transfers the analogy from the theatre to
the cinema, where he is concerned to understand the organisation of experience - how some situations are defined as
real and others not, hence the use of the term frame.

The nature of language becomes his explicit concern in
his recent publication 'Forms of Talk' (1981) in which he
states:   'In what follows then I make no large literary
claim that social life is but a stage, only a small technical one, that deeply incorporated into the nature of talk
are the fundamental requirements of theatricality' (p. 4).
Goffman's work contributes significantly to our understanding of the processes of interaction and the tactics that
are available for both the communication and the censoring
of information about ourselves.

Ethnomethodology, as already mentioned, has connections
with symbolic interactionism through the concepts of indexicality and reflexivity.   It is these that the ethno-
methodologist is keen to take account of in the attempt to
study everyday activity.   In doing so, attention is drawn
to the ways in which individuals, as members of society
(hence ethno-) devise their own methods (hence methodology)
for engaging in everyday interaction.   Thus ethnometho-
dologists are interested in people's methods for engaging
in competent interaction.   Interest in this, by implication, means that the individual's account of the processes
of interaction assumes prior importance, and that fundamental concern is with the way in which members of society
acquire the competence to assign meaning to their environment.   Importance is also attached to the role that language plays in this process.   Again a link can be made
here with the thoughts of Mead, since language is the

technique used to assign meaning to the world, and enables
articulation of the rules and norms of a particular social
situation in word and action.   Consequently, attention is
focused on that which 'everyone knows';   that which in our
everyday conversation every speaker and hearer assumes,
i.e. how the 'gaps between words' are filled so that communication can proceed.   From this follows the need to
stress the context-bound nature of such communication,
since part of its understanding will be contained within
the situation in which the communication occurred, and
also the need to stress the subjective understanding
attached to the communication by the individuals concerned, since part of the meaning will remain with them.
Ethnomethodology, therefore, is concerned with the rules
which lie behind our communications, i.e. the assumptions
on which we operate which make everyday interaction possible.

Empirical investigation of such rules by ethnomethodol-
ogists has been varied.   However, they have primarily
used tape recordings to analyse conversational practices,
and more recently have used videotape recordings to cap-
ture the non-verbal as well as the verbal communication in
interaction.   Such techniques have been used in contexts
such as doctors' surgeries, in an attempt to discover the
normal practices that operate in doctor-patient interaction.   The extent to which any complete understanding
or explanation can be gained from such studies is obviously limited given the nature of the conceptual starting
point.   For it implies that the researcher's account of
the proceedings is not necessarily any more valid than the
participants', and also that the researchers themselves
will be using rules of interpretation to understand the
data available and that these rules themselves are a topic
of study in their own right.   In this way, a major difficulty arises with respect to ethnomethodology for those of
a more orthodox sociological persuasion, that of infinite
regress, i.e. the question of where the interpretive procedures stop.   The theoretical and empirical implications
of ethnomethodology have certainly contributed to the ongoing debate on the appropriate nature of sociological subject matter.   However, ethnomethodology shares with other
interactionist schools methodological weaknesses which are
discussed below.

The final school of thought to emerge from the thoughts
of Mead has been referred to as the Iowa school, characterised by the work of Manford Kuhn (1964).   Perhaps the
main concern associated with Manford Kuhn's work could be

characterised as a concern to render Mead's rather indeterminate concepts operational and empirically testable.
In their original formulation, and as adopted by the
Chicago school, Mead's concepts have certainly shown
themselves to be rather vaguely formulated and open to
different interpretations.   Kuhn's work constitutes an
attempt to render these concepts researchable in the traditional sense of the scientific, i.e. that they be testable.   Thus Kuhn particularly developed what is referred
to as 'self theory' with an associated method of rendering
the self researchable, the Twenty Statements Test.   This
test is designed to elicit the individuals' verbal repre-
sentations of their selves and compares this with the rep-
resentations of others on this self.   By implication one
can infer that in Mead's terms, we are concerned with a
self that consists of the 'me' which has been denuded of
the influences of the 'I'.   In this way Kuhn removes a
level of indeterminacy from Mead's work creating from it a
more determinable and scientific perspective.

Alongside this kind of definition of the self, i.e. a
prime concern with its social formation, go concomitant
concerns with the notion of role and reference group and
their impact on the individual.   This kind of interpretation does not necessarily contradict the Meadian perspective.   As was stated earlier, Mead was more of a philosopher than a sociologist and consequently was perhaps more
concerned with proposing an image of the human being which
might lead to empirical investigation than offering a
blueprint as to how interactionist work was to be conducted.   Indeed, Mead himself does recognise the valuable
knowledge to be gained from laboratory research and the
light this might throw on human behaviour.   However, what
is open to question is whether Kuhn's interpretation legit-
imately retains the spirit of Mead's work.   This constitutes the essence of the debate between the Chicago and
the Iowa schools of thought.

It can be seen that symbolic interactionism, in its
various forms, has a number of themes which give these
schools of thought a certain coherence.   First, they are
all perspectives which take as their starting point the
individual in interaction with others, i.e. they are all
micro-sociological perspectives.   This starting point has
implications for the level of explanation that such perspectives can offer and the kind of empirical research
that is generated by them.   Explanations of behaviour are
offered in terms of the individuals taking part and the
definitions and interpretations of the situation they are

operating with.   This involves the empirical imperative
of sympathetic introspection (however this is interpreted),
i.e. of 'getting inside the actor's head'.   These issues
distinguish symbolic interactionism from functionalism and
marxism, in that they render it a perspective characterised
by 'methodological individualism' as opposed to 'holism'
(see chapter 1, pp. 16, 20).   This, however, has not
inhibited attempts to marry interactionism with a macro-
perspective, and also suggests what is often regarded as
the main limitation to this perspective, its limited understanding of macro-processes.


## RELATIONSHIP WITH OTHER THEORIES AND CRITIQUE

It has often been observed that macro-sociological analyses of society have to make what might be considered to be
unreasonable assumptions about the motivation of individual action.   It is a common comment, for example that
Marx lacked an understanding of social psychology.   It is
functionalism, however, not marxism which has been married
with the social psychology of symbolic interactionism, and
it is the ease with which this marriage is accomplished
which also constitutes a criticism levelled at interactionism to be dealt with shortly.

   The most explicit formulation of this relationship can
be found in Kai Erikson's 'Wayward Puritans' (1966).
Erikson was concerned here with the mechanisms of social
control which were in operation in the pioneering American
Puritan communities of the seventeenth century.   These
communities established their own particular characteristic social order based primarily on a literal interpretation of the Bible.   However, in order to understand fully
how social order was maintained in these communities,
Erikson argues that it is necessary to understand how the
processes of interaction operated at an interpersonal
level, to identify those who deviated from the rules and
simultaneously served to maintain the boundaries of what
was acceptable and unacceptable behaviour within the community.   Such boundary maintenance was functional to the
survival of the wider community and the maintenance of law
and order.   Such an analysis may appear quite reasonable
given the time and context in which Erikson is presenting
his ideas.   However, in complex modern societies it is
perhaps more difficult to see how interaction at the interpersonal level has such a direct impact on the maintenance
of social order.   It is also possible to suggest that
Erikson's version of interactionism as portrayed here is a

distortion of the Meadian tradition since it moves towards
a determinism which Mead was anxious to avoid.

Despite this proviso, Erikson's work reveals the main
weaknesses inherent in the interactionist tradition.   In
the first instance, it draws attention to the status of
interactionism as a theory.   As has been indicated
earlier, the concepts associated with interactionism do
not necessarily form a coherent theoretical perspective in
the same way that functionalism or marxism might.   This
arises for two reasons.   First, it stems from the nature
of Mead's thoughts.   Mead is perhaps best seen as part of
an older tradition of armchair theorising, in which he was
more concerned to create a meaningful image of man as a
response to alternative ideas of the time.   This, combined with the oral tradition also associated with interactionism, has meant that the perspective relies on an
intuitive grasp of its ideas rather than a formal set of
operational propositions.   The total effect of these two
factors has meant that interactionism is left open to a
good deal of ambiguity.   There is no widespread agreement
as to the interpretation of its concepts or as to how they
might be investigated empirically;  this is illustrated by
the difference, for example, between the Chicago and Iowa
schools of thought.   Mead's ideas give little guidance
with respect to such issues because they leave room for
diversity.

A second issue is the scientific status of interactionism.   This, of course, depends on one's interpretation of
'scientific' (see chapter 1).   The main issue seems to be
the extent to which interactionist concepts are empirically testable, but this also involves a deeper methodological issue.   The Iowa school of thought is concerned to
render Mead's concepts researchable, hence the development
of a test which would be considered both valid and reliable, i.e. would provide the same results repeatedly and
would be measuring what it intended to measure.   In contrast, the Chicago school adopted the methodological
imperative of 'getting inside the actor's head' by the use
of participant observation.

Participant observation, as its label might imply,
requires the researcher to become actively involved with
the individuals he or she is researching.   As such it is
an overly subjective research tool.   It requires that the
researcher, through participation, reveals those shared
understandings on which the interaction proceeds.   In
this way it is hoped that the taken-for-granted meanings

of the interactive process can be identified to others.
The ultimate goal of such research is to produce a 'blueprint' of interaction;  revealing the basis of the relationships under study.   Hence many studies using this
technique have provided useful insights into the world of
the homosexual, the drug-taker, the street-corner gang
(for example Liebow, 1966).   Such research is guided by
an open theoretical perspective;  i.e. that the theory be
allowed to emerge from the data, that which Glaser and
Strauss call 'The Discovery of Grounded Theory' (1968).
The more traditional methods of testing hypotheses are not
considered of use and consequently this leads to the criticism that it cannot fulfil the criteria of either relia-
bility or validity since it is dependent upon acceptance
of the researchers' interpretation of the social world
they have been involved in.

As has already been stated, what is being reflected
here is a much wider debate as to the nature of science
and what constitutes being scientific.   What is clear is
that this means different things to different symbolic
interactionists and the extent to which the charge of not
being scientific is applicable depends upon which school
of thought is being referred to.   Goffman's work adds a
further dimension to the debate, in that his work is for
the most part rooted in the intuitive writing of a well-
informed novelist or diarist.   Yet this has not lessened
the impact that Goffman's work has had.   Thus this criticism needs to be carefully considered before accepting or
rejecting symbolic interactionism on these grounds.

Perhaps a more significant limitation to the perspective lies not in its scientific status but rather its conceptualisation of the structure of society.   For Mead and
his followers, human beings are born into an ongoing social
situation about which they learn through the socialisation
process.   Their relationship with the social process is a
dialectical rather than a deterministic one.   Their
actions are to be seen as an outcome of constant interaction between the individual and the social process.
Symbolic interactionists go no further than to conceptual-
ise society in this way.   Interactionism has no theoretical ability to understand society as a series of structures historically produced with distorted and unequal
power relationships between social groups.   But neither
would it make claims to understand such processes.   Goffman expresses the following reply to his critics:

The analysis developed does not catch at the differences

between the advantaged and the disadvantaged classes
and can be said to direct attention away from such
matters.   I think that is true.   I can only suggest
that he who would combat false consciousness and awaken
people to their true interests has much to do because
the sleep is very deep.   And I do not intend here to
provide a lullaby but merely to sneak in and watch the
way the people snore. (1975, p. 14)

It may be that in the closed environment of a mental
institution or in the process of interpersonal relationships some individuals do have the power over others to
assign labels to others and make those labels stick.
However, the success of such power needs to be related to
such individuals' positions in the social structure to be
understood fully, since the role they play is ultimately
derived from this.

Interactionism not only assumes equality of social
position, but also assumes consensus reached as a consequence of the interactive process.   A definition of the
situation is agreed upon by all parties.   Consequently,
interactionism cannot address itself to issues of social
change, since it is not equipped to understand the mechanisms of change occurring above and beyond face-to-face
interaction.   To understand such mechanisms requires a
theoretical perspective which incorporates an understanding of power relationships in society in their political,
social and economic manifestation, i.e. a macro-sociological perspective.   So those with a macro-sociological
orientation are often led to dismiss interactionism as
social psychology and by implication of limited use to the
sociologist.   This criticism may appear rather unfair,
since it could be argued that interactionists do not
intend to address themselves to such a level of analysis.
It is a criticism, however, which does limit the possible
usefulness to which this perspective may be put in its
relevance to social administration, as will become clearer
shortly.

Interactionism not only fails to satisfy sociologists,
it also fails to satisfy psychologists.   This is due to
the image of human beings employed by interactionists and
the kind of qualities attributed to them.   Human beings
are viewed as possessing qualitatively distinct attributes
from other species;   firstly in that they possess a language, and secondly in that the interaction which takes
place between the 'I' and the 'me' acknowledges a mind.
This latter quality in particular renders people capable of

imaginative conscious thought which is seen as the means
by which alternative courses of action are thought through
and the appropriate action chosen.   At this point two
problems emerge.   In the first instance, it implies a
being governed by conscious processes.   The influence of
unconscious processes is not fully considered.   This
criticism is important from the psychological viewpoint if
comparison is made, for example, with the Freudian
approach in which unconscious processes are given central
importance.   It is difficult to assess how far this is a
valid criticism since it is unclear from Mead's writings,
in particular, the extent to which the 'I' and the 'me'
are to be considered conscious or unconscious.   However,
it is clear that interactionists have failed fully to
explore the implications of this issue.

The second question which is raised from this view of
individuals concerns the role that emotions play in the
construction and reconstruction of interaction.   Not only
are people seen to be consciously motivated animals but
they are also seen to be rational in their decision-taking.
Rational behaviour may be that kind of behaviour which is
more highly evaluated, but as far as interpersonal interaction is concerned, it is also necessary to understand
humans as emotional animals;   beings who experience anger,
rejection, etc., as real feelings.   This is an element
not fully grasped by interactionism.

It is also necessary to be aware that as individuals we
are not all equally capable in the manipulation and interpretation of shared symbols.   Some have physical disabilities which make a difference to interactive abilities (for
example Scott, 1969).   Others do not have the same memory
abilities, or perceptual apparatus.   These sorts of factors, which draw attention to the significance of individual variation, are possibly the kinds of variable one
might feed into the 'I'.   Whether this was the Meadian
intention is open to debate, what they do confirm, however,
are the difficulties faced by this perspective in its
attempt to formulate some meaningful relationship between
the individual and society.

There remains one further area of contention surrounding interactionism.   This involves a consideration of the
ideological tendencies and implicit value-judgments of
which interactionists stand accused.   One of their main
critics in this respect is Alvin Gouldner (1970).   One
characteristic of interactionism which distinguishes it
from other sociologies is its professed value commitment.

Becker, in particular, stands forcefully for sociologists
being committed in their values.   The commitment which
Becker and others profess is for a particular section of
society, namely the 'underdog'.   This, for Gouldner, is
where problems arise.   For although Gouldner is not
necessarily against sociologists making value commitments,
he considers that there is an acceptance of the status quo
in accepting society's definition of the underdog.   Such
a commitment may prevent a critique of society, which for
Gouldner is the essence of being a sociologist.   Indeed,
interactionist studies do seem to focus on those who have
already been labelled and are 'the outsiders' of the
social system.   Such studies reveal a good deal of interesting information about the lifestyles of homosexuals,
drug-takers, etc., but really fail to take any further the
way in which such a labelling process might be alleviated
or changed and in doing so have real consequences for the
individuals concerned.   Interactionism may have laudable
humanitarian and liberal tendencies but for some, particularly Gouldner, this is not enough.   The easy marriage of
interactionism with functionalism, based on a common failure to question the status quo, makes interactionism
equally vulnerable to criticism.   Again, given the nature
and structure of interactionism as a theoretical perspective, it is not difficult to see how it moves towards such
ideological tendencies.   Issues of structure, the political and historical formations of societies, do not fall
within its area of analysis.   This ultimately leads to an
acceptance of the ongoing social structure.


RELEVANCE FOR SOCIAL ADMINISTRATION

The criticisms discussed in the previous section indicate
where symbolic interactionism can and cannot be relevant
to social administration.   In contrast to macro-sociological theories like marxism and functionalism, it cannot
throw light on the broad structural issues that influence
the role of welfare provision in society.   It can, however, illuminate the ways in which policy and practice in
the social services affect the individual directly.   In
so far as it is concerned with middle ground between sociology and psychology, symbolic interactionism provides a
useful set of bridging concepts between them.   Concepts
such as 'self', 'role', and 'socialisation', facilitate an
understanding of the relationship between the individual
and his social environment that is not made available by
mainstream sociology or psychology.   It thus makes possible consideration of three questions relevant to social
administration.

First, by focusing on face-to-face interaction it enables one to see more clearly the effects of policy decisions in practice and the way in which well-intentioned
policies may be subverted by the manner of their implementation.   Goffman's work, such as 'The Moral Career of a
Mental Patient' (1968, part 2), reveals the way in which
labelling procedures result in the patient conforming to
the behaviour expected of the resident of an institution.
Once defined as mentally ill, the person's own account
carries little weight.   In the same way, the complaints
of offenders in prison and children in school are treated
as if of no account.   King, Raynes and Tizard (1970),
used Goffman's concept of a total institution to examine
various residential homes for mentally retarded children.
They showed how in some homes the procedures that Goffman
identified reinforced by an appropriate bureaucratic
organisation, resulted in failure to develop the children's full potential.

In the penal field it is being increasingly recognised
how the labelling process combines with the court's
tarriff system, under which successive offenders receive
heavier penalties, to ensure that more offenders receive
custodial sentences.   For example, in 1969 encouragement
was given under the Children and Young Person's Act to
procedures that would keep children out of court and so
avoid labelling.   However, Ditchfield (1976) found that
one of the procedures recommended, the use of the police
caution, actually resulted in more children coming before
the courts and more children being removed from their
homes.   This happened because some offences which had
been previously dealt with by an informal warning were now
dealt with by a formal caution which was recorded so that
children found themselves more quickly registering a
record of previous convictions.

Such processes as these throw light on the second level
in which interactionism proves useful.   By focusing on
interaction at ground level, attention is drawn to the
ways in which officials influence legislation.   In the
examples cited above, those with official positions are
operating under policies and legislation which help define
their role.   The policies set out the conditions under
which help can be given and this usually involves giving
the person a label - 'offender', 'suspected non-accidental
injury', 'blind', 'mentally ill', and so on.   But the
legislation and the policies are normally influenced by
the officials or professionals who are to execute them.
So they feed into the policy-making process their defini-

tions of the problems and then act within the framework created by the policies and interpreted in the light of their own experience.

Third, in adopting the actor's point of view as a meaningful way of analysing a social situation, it allows the conventional view to be questioned.   This has two implications.   The client is seen as an individual whose view of the situation needs to be taken seriously if communication is to be established and if any meaningful change in the client's perspective and behaviour is to be achieved.   It is in this sense a radical perspective. Consequently, it allows the social service workers to operate with some meaningful view of their practice as being radical, albeit on a micro as opposed to a macro scale, should they so wish.


CONCLUSION

Symbolic interactionism presents a view of human beings which stresses the indeterminate nature of their behaviour, laying emphasis on the individual's own interpretation of the situation.   It provides a way of analysing the processes and procedures of welfare provision, in turn illuminating the way in which bureaucratic powers may sustain the interests of the status quo as the ultimate labelling power always remains in the hand of officials. In this way it provides a critique of welfare provision as it is experienced by both clients and officials, since both sets of interpretations need to be considered, but it does not provide an analysis of the wider social structure which sets the limits on the changes which can be achieved on the interpersonal level.


FURTHER READING

The student wishing to obtain a more thorough grasp of interactionism should refer to one or more of the general texts marked with two asterisks.   Meltzer et al. (1975) is particularly recommended, and for those interested in a more philosophical approach, Rock (1979) is very good. Becker's and Goffman's works have been particularly influential in social administration and should be read if only as a check on how they are used by other writers.   Of Goffman's work, 'Asylums' (1968) and 'Stigma' (1968) make particularly good reading and may prove relevant.

Participant observation studies generally make enjoy-
able reading and give the flavour of the interactionist
perspective.  Liebow (1966), Humphries (1970), and Becker
(1963) are recommended, with McCall and Simmons (1969)
providing a good overview of the issues involved in participant observation as an empirical method.

The general readers give a good overview of the criticisms often levelled against symbolic interactionism.
Gouldner (1970), however, provides some interesting comment not only on interactionism, but on sociology in
general.

BIBLIOGRAPHY

*   Recommended.
**  Recommended for easier reading.
* Becker, H. (1963), 'The Outsiders', Chicago, Free Press.
Becker, H., Geer, B., and Hughes, E.C. (1968), 'Making the
    Grade: the Academic Side of College Life', New York,
    Wiley.
Becker, H., Geer, B., Hughes, E.C., and Strauss, A. (1961),
    'Boys in White', Chicago, Free Press.
Ditchfield, J.A. (1976), 'Police Cautioning in England and
    Wales', London, HMSO.
Erikson, K.T. (1966), 'Wayward Puritans', London, John
    Wiley.
Garfinkel, H. (1967), 'Studies in Ethnomethodology', Engle-
    wood Cliffs, NJ, Prentice-Hall.
Glaser, B., and Strauss, A. (1967), 'The Discovery of
    Grounded Theory', Chicago, Aldine.
Goffman, E. (1959), 'The Presentation of Self in Everyday
    Life', New York, Doubleday.
* Goffman, E. (1968), 'Stigma: Notes on the Management of
    Spoiled Identity', Harmondsworth, Penguin.
* Goffman, E. (1968), 'Asylums', Harmondsworth, Penguin.
Goffman, E. (1972), 'Relations in Public: Microstudies of
    Public Order', Harmondsworth, Penguin.
Goffman, E. (1975), 'Frame Analysis', Harmondsworth,
    Penguin.
Goffman, E. (1981), 'Forms of Talk', Harmondsworth,
    Penguin.
* Gouldner, A. (1970), 'The Coming Crisis of Western Socio-
    logy', New York, Basic Books.
* Humphries, L. (1970), 'Tearoom Trade', Chicago, Aldine.
King, R.D., Raynes, N.V., and Tizard, J. (1970), 'Patterns
    of Residential Care: Sociological Studies in Institu-
    tions for Handicapped Children', London, Routledge &
    Kegan Paul.

Kuhn, M. (1964), Major Trends in Symbolic Interaction
    Theory in the Past Twenty Five Years, 'Sociological
    Quarterly', Winter.
* Liebow, E. (1966), 'Tally's Corner,' Boston, Little,
    Brown.
** Manis, G., and Meltzer, B.M. (1978), 'Symbolic Inter-
    action', Boston, Allyn & Bacon, 3rd edn.
* McCall, G.J., and Simmons, J.L. (1969), 'Issues in Par-
    ticipant Observation', London, Addison-Wesley.
Mead, G.H. (1934), 'Mind, Self and Society', Chicago Uni-
    versity Press.
** Meltzer, M., Pehas, J., and Reynolds, L.T. (1975),
    'Symbolic Interactionism: Genesis, Varieties and Criti-
    cisms', London, Routledge & Kegan Paul.
Polsky, N. (1966), 'Hustlers, Beats, and Others', Harmonds-
    worth, Penguin.
** Rock, P. (1979), 'The Making of Symbolic Interaction-
    ism', London, Macmillan.
** Rose, A.M. (ed.) (1962), 'Human Behaviour and Social
    Processes', London, Routledge & Kegan Paul.
Scott, R. (1969), 'The Making of Blind Men', London, Sage.
Speier, M. (1973), 'How to Observe Face to Face Communica-
    tion', Santa Monica, Ca, Goodyear.
Turner, R. (1974), 'Ethnomethodology', Harmondsworth,
    Penguin.

Chapter 8

# Two theories of social justice
## Anthony Forder

It has already been made clear in the introduction and
elsewhere in this book that issues of value are inherent
in all current social science theories and in the concept
of 'welfare'.   It could therefore be expected that philosophical theories would have some contribution to make to
the consideration of welfare.   In practice, although
students of social administration have often received some
introductory teaching on political philosophy, there has
in the past been little reference to philosophy in the
literature of social administration.   Issues of value
have been discussed without reference to philosophy.

This situation was changed somewhat by the publication
of Rawls's 'A Theory of Justice' in 1973, and the earlier
use of some of Rawls's ideas by Runciman (1965 and 1966).
Rawls's book received wide public interest (Daniels, 1975,
pp. xii-xvi), partly at least because it tackled a subject
of crucial importance to current political controversy,
namely the principles that are relevant to:  'the way in
which the major social institutions distribute fundamental
rights and duties and determine the division of advantages
from social co-operation' (Rawls, 1973, p. 7).   Part of
its interest also lies in its attempt to relate the philosophical concept of social justice to social science
theory, and particularly to the neo-classical theory of
the market.

Rawls's theory has been selected for discussion here
because of the frequent reference to it made in the literature of social administration, and because the criticisms
made of it by philosophers and others throw considerable
light on the problems of identifying an approach to social
justice that can be regarded as having universal validity.
A contrast is provided by the discussion of David Miller's

'Social Justice' (1976).   Miller considers that different
and conflicting concepts of social justice have a validity
in their own right, but can only be fully understood in
the context provided by wider views of society, which are
particularly relevant to different social structures.
Where Rawls uses economic theory to examine the possible
role of an economic market in promoting just distribution,
Miller uses a sociological analysis to relate different
theories of social justice to different social structures.

## RAWLS'S THEORY OF SOCIAL JUSTICE

Rawls is a philosopher in the liberal tradition.   His
primary objective in presenting 'A Theory of Justice' is
to provide an alternative to utilitarianism, on the one
hand, and 'intuitionism', on the other.

Utilitarianism has already been briefly discussed in
chapter 1.   There it was pointed out that utilitarianism
is concerned with 'happiness' or the satisfaction of wants.
But it deals with this on an aggregative principle, 'the
greatest happiness' of people as a whole, without having
anything to say about the distribution of happiness or
satisfaction between different individuals, which is the
subject of social justice.   Utilitarianism also, as Rawls
points out, is a 'teleological' theory in the sense that
it starts by determining what is good (i.e. happiness) and
then defines as right whatever actions serve that end.
Rawls is concerned to present a theory in which what is
right and what is good are mutually dependent.

'Intuitionism' begins from the acceptance that there
are different principles for the determination of what is
just and these principles may be in conflict with one
another.   These conflicts can only be resolved by intuition, the subjective balancing of one principle against
another in the light of the circumstances of the particular case.   Rawls is concerned to apply the principles of
liberal philosophy to the problem of social justice in a
way that allows different principles (including that of
'utility') to be put in order of priority.   In this way
the need to use intuition is minimised even if it cannot
be wholly avoided.

Rawls describes his theory as 'justice as fairness', by
which he means that 'the principles of justice are agreed
to in an initial situation that is fair'.   The theory is
a 'contract' theory, that is to say, it is based on the

idea that the principles of justice are decided by people
who are imagined to be negotiating a binding agreement.
The theory is in two parts.    The first describes the conditions of the original position which ensure its fairness.
The second part concerns the principles that Rawls argues
would be agreed in that situation.    As Rawls says:  'the
two parts of the theory are not ultimately dependent on
one another.    It is possible for a person quite rationally to accept either part without necessarily accepting
the validity of the other' (p. 15).    The original position in which the contract is made is a device:  'to make
vivid to ourselves the restrictions that it seems reasonable to impose on arguments for principles of justice, and
therefore on the principles themselves' (p. 18).    He asks
us to imagine that the people engaged in negotiating the
contract are rational, capable of moral judgments, equal
in their right to contribute to the choice of principles
and mutually disinterested.    By 'mutually disinterested'
Rawls means that they are neither altruistic nor envious.
They are unwilling that their interests should be sacri-
ficed to the interests of the others, but they may have a
personal commitment to other individuals and a concern for
the next generation.    Equally, they would not propose an
arrangement that might reduce their own circumstances
merely to ensure that someone else was no better off then
themselves.

In order to avoid the dangers of bias, and to make
unanimous agreement possible, each participant would be
under a veil of ignorance about the future.    All participants would be ignorant about their own personal endow-
ments - whether they would have high or low abilities for
example - and their own place in society - whether they
would be among the socially superior or inferior.    They
would know that they would each have a concept of the good
and a life plan, but not the nature of the concept or plan.
They would all be ignorant about the nature of the society
for which they were legislating in matters such as its
technological development and the resources available to
it.    But they would have a general knowledge of economics,
politics and sociology and know that there would be conflicting interests and moderate scarcity of resources.
They would be ignorant of the chances of different sets of
circumstances arising (for example the chances of being
born mentally handicapped).

Rawls argues that this veil of ignorance would predis-
pose the people involved to invoke what is called the
'maximin' rule in determining priorities between different

principles.   The maximin rule requires that one ranks
alternatives according to their worst possible outcomes
and adopts that alternative for which the worst outcome is
superior to the worst outcome of the others.   This minimises the risks of a negative outcome at the cost of
ignoring the possibility of outcomes that might in other
ways be much more satisfactory.   For example, one might
imagine that one alternative might result in the social
rejection and physical starvation of a mentally handicapped person and a high measure of prosperity for a large
number of other people.   This alternative would be rejected for a solution that gave a better deal to the mentally
handicapped at the expense of a reduced total prosperity
(pp. 152-3).

Rawls argues that in these circumstances the following
general principle would be agreed (p. 303):   'All social
primary goods - liberty and opportunity, income and
wealth, and the basis of self respect - are to be distributed equally unless an unequal distribution of any or all
of these goods is to the advantage of the least favoured.'
This general conception of social justice is then spelt
out in two principles (p. 302):

> *First Principle*
> Each person is to have an equal right to the most
> extensive total system of equal basic liberties compat-
> ible with a similar system of liberty for all.
> *Second Principle*
> Social and economic inequalities are to be arranged so
> that they are both:
> (a)   to the greatest benefit of the least advantaged,
> consistent with the just savings principle, and
> (b)   attached to offices and positions open to all
> under conditions of fair equality of opportunity.

The 'just savings principle' is concerned with justice
between different generations, and the need for investment.
I shall not discuss this principle here, but it may be
worth noting that Rawls does not consider that intergenerational justice requires the constant expansion of
the economy that is demanded by utilitarianism.

These principles are put in 'lexical order';   that is
to say, the first principle takes precedence over the
second, and the second clause of the second principle over
its first clause (known as the 'difference principle').
At the same time, the principles of justice are given priority over efficiency.   These priorities are expressed in
two priority rules:

*First Priority Rule* (The Priority of Liberty)
The principles of justice are to be ranked in lexical
order and therefore liberty can be restricted only for
the sake of liberty.   There are two cases:
(a)   a less extensive liberty must strengthen the total
system of liberty shared by all;
(b)   a less than equal liberty must be acceptable to
those with the lesser liberty.
*Second Priority Rule* (The Priority of Justice over
Efficiency and Welfare)
The second principle of justice is lexically prior to
the principle of efficiency and to that of maximising
the sum of advantages, and fair opportunity is prior to
the difference principle.   There are two cases:
(a)   an inequality of opportunity must enhance the
opportunities of those with the lesser opportunity;
(b)   an excessive rate of saving must on balance miti-
gate the burden of those bearing this hardship.

The general conception of social justice appears very
like a socialist or communist conception of social justice
- from each according to his ability, to each according to
his need.   The more detailed presentation of the principles begins to look much more like a liberal philosophical statement.   First, there is the priority given to
liberty, and then the emphasis on equality of opportunity
in the competition for offices and positions to which
higher social and economic rewards are attached.

For the purposes of the first principle, Rawls tries to
avoid a definition of liberty (p. 201), but it is clear,
from the examples, that he chooses to discuss that he is
using a liberal concept.   He is concerned with liberty of
thought and conscience, freedom of expression, freedom of
the person and of property, and freedom of participation
in political affairs.   These are the liberties whose
equality is to be enshrined in the principles of justice
and the structure of the just society.   On the other
hand, he accepts that there will be inequalities in the
ability of different people to take advantage of these
liberties as a result of poverty, ignorance and a lack of
means generally.   But he regards these as inequalities of
the worth of liberty to different individuals not as inequality of liberty as such (p. 204).   Rawls argues for
the priority of the principle of liberty through the
application of the maximum rule under the veil of ignorance.   For he considers that nobody would be prepared to
risk these liberties because the loss of liberty has such
potentially disastrous consequences.

With regard to the second principle, Rawls considers a properly regulated economic market as a primary institution for the allocation of income and wealth.   He considers such a market as an example of an instrument of 'pure procedural justice'.   By this he means that the justice of the institution lies in the fairness of the rules rather than the equality of the distribution it produces.   He compares it to a game of roulette in which equal opportunities using an unbiased machine nevertheless result in an unequal distribution of rewards.   He accepts the economic market as an allocation system because of its contribution to efficiency and its potential for improving the situation of the worst off.

Rawls is, of course, aware of the limitations of the economic market as a system for allocation, if taken in isolation.   So Rawls envisages four branches of government, concerned with distributive justice.   First the allocative branch has the tasks of keeping the price system workably competitive, preventing the formation of unreasonable market power, and compensating for externalities by suitable taxes and subsidies.   The stabilisation branch is concerned with the maintenance of full employment.   The transfer branch has the responsibility for ensuring that everyone receives the social minimum.   This would presumably include provision for ensuring fair equality of opportunity through, for instance, the provision of education.   Finally the distribution branch has two main tasks.   The first of these is concerned with limiting inheritance and gifts so that the accumulation of wealth does not endanger political liberty and equality of opportunity.   Second, it must raise in a fair manner the money necessary for the provision of public goods and the transfer arrangements necessary to ensure the social minimum and the application of the difference principle.

Rawls considers that this model is compatible with socialism as well as capitalism.   But his analysis of its relevance to socialism is relatively superficial, and consists largely of an acceptance that a market economy is compatible with the social ownership of land and capital. What must strike any reader is the similarity between Rawls's institutions and the institutions of 'democratic-welfare-capitalism'.   Essentially, the implications of his theory of justice is that those institutions should be reformed to give justice, defined in liberal terms, a higher priority.

CRITICISMS OF RAWLS'S THEORY OF SOCIAL JUSTICE

Having noted the similarity between Rawls's just institutions and a reformed system of 'democratic-welfare-capitalism', the question arises as to the source of this similarity.  Is Rawls's theory an objective concept of social justice which happens also to provide a defence of democratic-welfare-capitalism?  Or does the content of Rawls's theory depend on certain basic assumptions that are common to other apologies for the system?

Crucial to this issue is Rawls's description of the original position under which the contract is developed. Rawls uses this in two different ways.  First, it is an analytical device for defining the restrictions on legitimate arguments.  Second, Rawls considers that it has a role in justifying the acceptance of the principles derived from it - or, as Daniels (1975, p. xix) puts it: 'that the conditions and constraints embodied in the original position constitute a model of procedural fairness and, as such, they should be acceptable to everyone on due consideration.'  Both these uses are put in doubt by criticisms that the conditions of the original position introduce bias into its procedures and the conclusions derived from it.  Such a bias may spring either from the characteristics that Rawls attributes to the negotiators or from the veil of ignorance under which they operate.

Rawls describes the negotiators as rational, free, equal and mutually disinterested.  This is a very individualistic approach to human nature, very much in the liberal tradition.  It is therefore not surprising that Rawls should argue that people like this would devise a system of justice which gives priority to the ability of people to pursue their own individual life-plans.  So liberty becomes the first principle, and the equality of the second principle is modified to leave room for incentive.

The effect of these characteristics is reinforced by 'the veil of ignorance'.  Clearly, objectivity demands that people should be unaware of their future position in society.  But why should they be ignorant of their concept of the good?  One would certainly expect this to have some influence on their concept of justice.  However, this was introduced by Rawls to deal with a real problem in the development of the contract.  He was well aware that differences over the concept of the ultimate good could not be resolved by universal agreement.  So if decisions about the principles of justice were made dependent on prior agreement about the nature of the good, the principles of justice would never be agreed.   So Rawls limited knowledge of what was good to certain primary goods which could be used for a variety of different ends. But the principles of justice that he elicits are in fact much more efficacious in the pursuit of some life-plans than of others.   They are less useful in achieving life-plans that depend on certain kinds of social structure as opposed to individual effort.   Ignorance of wider concepts of the good seems to bias the results in the direction of individualism.   In a similar way, ignorance of the nature of the society in which the principles will be put into practice rules out concepts of justice which may be particularly relevant to particular social structures - an argument discussed more fully in looking at the work of David Miller.

Another aspect of the veil of ignorance that may introduce bias is the ignorance about the chances of different misfortunes occurring.   It is on this that Rawls founds the adoption of the 'maximim' rule.   But people are frequently disposed to take risks - gambling takes place in many different kinds of societies and not only among people whose livelihood is secure.   Even if they were ignorant of the odds against misfortunes, the original contractors might have been disposed to take some risks. This would have been even more likely if they were able to calculate their chances.   If this resulted in the abandonment of the maximin rule, then less attention would be given to the needs of the worst off, and the difference principle might be abandoned.   It has also been argued by Lyons (1975, p. 161) that knowledge of the probabilities of different chances occurring would lead to a policy of maximising expectations and that in turn could lead to the adoption of utilitarianism.   Hare (1975, p. 103) comes to the same conclusion.

Finally the question arises whether equality of liberty is compatible with inequality of income and wealth - whether Rawls's first principle is compatible with the inequalities that may arise under the difference principle. Daniels (1975, pp. 153-82) argues that they are not compatible.   First he contends that there is nothing in Rawls's institutions of social justice that would prevent the differences in wealth being very extensive.   Moreover, in existing societies where there are extensive differences in wealth, these contribute to inequalities in liberty, for example in the ability to participate in pol-

itical processes.    Since the mechanisms by which the one
set of inequalities influences the other is not known, it
would be impossible for the original participants in the
contract to be sure that they could be avoided.    So the
arguments that are relevant to their choice of the first
principle would also be relevant to a decision not to
allow large differences in wealth, even if these were con-
sonant with the difference principle.    In Daniels's view
Rawls's distinction between liberty and the use of liberty
is irrelevant if not invalid.

Daniels's argument accepts Rawls's definition of
liberty.    If liberty is defined in broader terms to include other means that are important to the furtherance of
a person's life-plan, then the influence of wealth on
liberty becomes even stronger.

Thus it can be seen that biases in the formulation of
Rawls's theory tend to rule out the more obvious alternatives to the mixed economy of the 'welfare state'.


## MILLER ON SOCIAL JUSTICE

Like Rawls, David Miller is opposed to utilitarianism as
providing a basis for a concept of social justice and for
similar reasons.    But he is also very critical of Rawls's
theory which he sees to be:    'less a radical alternative
to utilitarianism than a modification of the utilitarian
theory, differing from that theory chiefly in demanding
the maximum benefit for one particular group in society -
the worst-off - instead of the maximum benefit of society
at large' (p. 50).

Miller himself returns to earlier views of social justice involving three conflicting bases:    rights, deserts
and needs.    Runciman (1965, 1966) describes these as the
conservative, liberal and socialist principles of social
justice.    Miller does not believe it is possible to
reconcile these three principles or to find any overriding
principle that puts them in priority.    Instead, he considers that each concept can best be understood in its
relationship to different views of society and each tends
to be particularly appropriate to different forms of
society.    He sums his thesis up (p. 342):    'Men hold con-
ceptions of social justice as part of more general views
of society and ... they acquire these views through their
experience of living in actual societies with definite
structures embodying particular kinds of interpersonal

relationship.'  Miller's method is first of all to explore the meaning of the three different concepts of
social justice.  Then he gives an account of the views of
three philosophers each of whom has a different principle
of social justice at the centre of his philosophy - Hume
who defines social justice in terms of rights, Spencer in
terms of deserts and Kropotkin in terms of need.  Finally
he examines the views of social justice expressed in words
or actions in four types of society - primitive societies,
feudal societies, market societies and various kinds of
communes.

In considering social justice based on rights, Miller
makes a distinction between positive and ideal rights.
Positive rights are those rights which are actually acknowledged in a society.  They can be demonstrated as
empirical facts if people assert these rights and others
acknowledge their legitimacy by their response.  They may
be legal rights enshrined in law, or moral rights like the
fulfilment of promises.  In contrast, ideal rights, like
the right to free speech, must be defended by moral argument not empirical investigation, and can be regarded as
'rights' whether or not they are socially recognised.
Some ideal rights may become socially recognised, and
therefore be positive rights so there is overlap between
the two categories.  Miller argues that ideal rights are
always justified by reference either to deserts or needs
so he confines his consideration to positive rights.

A theory of social justice based on positive rights
must be conservative in its implications.  The value of
positive rights lies in the predictability they give to
life.  Miller suggests that this predictability gives
security and freedom.  The security comes from being able
to rely on one's expectations being fulfilled; the freedom from the fact that one can plan one's actions within
known limits - not perhaps a common definition of freedom,
but a legitimate definition that equates freedom with
'functional autonomy' (Forder, 1974, pp. 104-7).

Hume is the philosopher selected to illustrate this
approach to social justice.  Hume has an essentially
pessimistic view of the nature of human beings as social
animals.  It is not that he regards them as wholly ego-
tistic, for they are capable of kindness and affection,
but only for a limited group of people whose interests
they pursue.  This 'partiality' is destructive of the
larger society.  It is restrained by three separate
causes, government and law, custom and habit, and love of

reputation.   Of these custom and habit are far the strongest, and therefore must be defended to the last ditch.   Any breach is liable to be enlarged to produce chaos.   Hume's opposition to desert as a basis for social justice lies in the impossibility of developing a rational and workable system that would command sufficient support to avoid destructive conflict.   Equally, he regards distribution on the basis of need as unrealistic in the light of his view of human nature.

In considering desert as a basis for social justice, Miller begins by pointing out the wide range of qualities and activities that may be rewarded and the wide range of different rewards that may be given.   All of this complicates the general consideration of the subject.   However, he concentrates his argument chiefly on the question of 'economic desert' that is to say, 'the desert of monetary and other rewards for socially useful work - for doing one's job, in a society which has such a division of labour' (p. 102).   He quotes three principles which have been seriously put forward as possible determinants of economic desert:

contribution which a person makes to social welfare
    through work activity;

effort expended in work activity;

compensation for costs incurred in work activity.

Miller regards compensation only as an additional factor to be taken into account when determining desert on one of the other two criteria.

Both effort and contribution are difficult to define in principle and to measure in practice.   So Hume's objections might have been generally sustained had not the classical theory of the economic market given reason for thinking that the market would produce wages and prices that would give a rough approximation to reward in return for contribution.   This seems to be the only way of getting round the problem of evaluating contribution in conditions where production is undertaken by joint action.

Spencer is the philosopher used by Miller to illustrate the role of this concept in a view of society.   Spencer expresses the fundamental principle of justice as that: 'each individual ought to receive the benefits and the evils of his own nature and consequent conduct.'   To

Spencer this is an absolute principle and not dependent on
its contribution to incentives, and the production of
happiness, as utilitarians would propose.   Closely associated with this fundamental principle is another concerned
with freedom:   'Every man is free to do that which he
wills, provided that he infringes not the equal freedom of
another man' (quoted by Miller, p. 190).   So close is the
connection between these two in Spencer's thought that
Miller says that he uses them as equivalent statements of
justice.   The point is that the validity of the criterion
of desert depends on freedom of choice.   Spencer is
against an attempt to allocate rewards on the basis of
human judgment about desert.   What he wants is a natural
mechanism that will allocate on the basis of desert according to 'natural' laws, acting like natural selection in
the evolutionary process.   He finds this mechanism in the
economic market, although he is ambivalent about the private ownership of land.   Thus he has little respect for
rights that are not established as a result of a contract
freely entered into by the parties.   He is more clearly
opposed to distribution on the basis of needs, as an extension of the ethics of the family to the state, primarily on the grounds that it is unjust in depriving the
deserving of their just reward.   This breach of the principles of the economic market would ultimately lead to the
assertion of people's basic egoism and the breakdown of
society.   Thus Spencer, like Hume, was pessimistic about
human nature and its egoism, but accepted the economists'
view that this egoism could be channelled into good by the
mechanisms of the market.

In considering needs as a basis for distribution, Miller
has to begin by defining needs.   He rejects the view that
needs are the same as wants.   Instead he proposes the
equation (p. 130):

A needs X = A will suffer harm if he lacks X.

This leads him on to the definition of harm.   Here he
quotes a story about the philosopher Brentano, who became
blind in his later life.   When friends commiserated with
him he denied that the loss of sight was a bad thing
because it had enabled him to concentrate on his philosophy
in a way that he had found impossible before.   This is
used as an illustration of the way in which we can only
understand what is harmful to a person in the context of
his own plan of life.   So Miller defines harm and needs
in the following way (p. 134):   'Harm, for any given individual, is whatever interferes directly or indirectly with

the activities essential to his plan of life and correspondingly, his needs must be understood to comprise whatever is necessary to allow these activities to be carried out.'   It should be noted that by defining 'need' in this way Miller is stressing the individual's own definition of his needs ('felt need') as against the definition by experts that encourages paternalism.

Despite the flexibility of the concept of a plan of life, Miller still attempts to put limits on individual needs.   For example, he rejects the idea that a need for status can make for constantly expanding needs, suggesting that such a need generally means only a need to be respected by one's social group.   Since needs can be limited he is left with a surplus for distribution after essential needs have been met.   After considering various alternatives for distributing this surplus he finally takes the view that consistency can only be achieved if the surplus is distributed on egalitarian principles related in some way to the plans of life of individuals.

Miller's choice of philosopher to illustrate a philosophy of social justice based on need is Kropotkin.   This seems an odd choice, since, as Miller says, Kropotkin was more of a pamphleteer and a propagandist than a philosopher.   But Miller considers that a consistent philosophy can readily be discerned in Kropotkin's political writings and that the relationship between his philosophy of justice and his view of society is more explicit than for the other two because of his interest in political ends. Kropotkin was also a scientist, committed to the inductive-deductive method and wished to derive an understanding of morality from a similar scientific study of human beings within a natural environment.   In this he resembled Spencer.   But unlike Spencer, Kropotkin denied that there was evidence that man was basically egoistic.   Instead, he emphasised the evidence for the existence of sympathy, solidarity and altruism.   He found this evidence not only in primitive societies but also in the way in which mutual aid associations, and institutions for distribution on the basis of need ('museums, free libraries, free schools') grew up even in the hostile environments of the laisser-faire market economy.   These basic attitudes of sympathy, solidarity and altruism had survival value for man as they had for other species.   Hume and Spencer each acknowledged that need was an appropriate basis for social justice in the family where affection, friendship, generosity and altruism predominated, but considered it inappropriate in the wider society where other principles predominated.

Kropotkin considered that a wider society could be so
structured that these virtues could be given their full
play, and distribution could be made on the basis of need.
His view of need was an expansionist one that grew with
the expansion of production.   This ideal distribution
would find its expression in an anarcho-communist society.

Kropotkin was an anarchist because he believed that the
law supported the claims of a dominant group, and was
essentially inegalitarian and unjust, as well as being unnecessary.   In this way he opposed distribution on the
basis of rights.   Distribution on the basis of desert he
opposed as a dilution of his central principle of equality.

It is important to recognise the extent to which the
arguments of different philosophers are based on practical
questions, sometimes related to views about human nature.
Both Hume and Spencer seem to accept that need provides an
appropriate principle for social justice within the family
and similar small closed groups.   But both believe that
human nature is such that the same principles cannot be
extended to the wider society.   The same point is made by
other writers such as Phelps Brown (1977), reviewing the
evidence about the basis for earnings differentials discussed in the next chapter, and Pinker (1979), examining
the limitations of altruism as a basis for social policy,
On the other hand, Kropotkin believes that given the right
social conditions human beings are capable of constructing
a society based on altruism, and so sees need as a proper
basis for social justice.

Similarly, in considering desert as a basis for social
justice, Hume's arguments appear to depend, at least
partly, on the impossibility of determining desert.
Presumably for the same reason neither Spencer nor Rawls
give much attention to desert as the reward of effort as
opposed to the reward of contribution.   Instead, for both
desert is rescued as a principle by the belief that the
economic market provides a valid measure of the contribution that people make to society.   But if the validity of
this measure is questioned, as it is by some people, then
desert is still immeasurable.

A crucial difference between the three philosophers,
which flows partly from their views about human nature, is
their attitude to the importance of controlling human
behaviour.   To Hume, this was a paramount consideration,
and leads to his emphasis on rights.   To Spencer, human
egotism could be harnessed to the social good through the

economic market.    Kropotkin believed that given the right
social situation, control would be unnecessary, but of
course creating the right situation is itself problematic.

Given this relationship between moral and practical
issues, it is logical to look at the situations in which
the different philosophies have found practical expression.    This leads Miller to an examination of the expression of social justice in different societies:  primitive
societies, feudal societies, capitalist societies and
communes.

Miller begins this part of his study with a consideration of primitive societies.    He concludes from his study
of literature on such societies that they have no concept
of social justice as such because they lack the concept of
an individual with an existence separate from that of the
community of which he is a part.    Ultimately, he concludes, decisions are made on the basis of what is best
for the common good, and this applies also to decisions
about the distribution of rights and goods.    Miller
attributes this to two main causes.    First, the relationship between members of a community are personal.    Second,
the economic circumstances of these communities are such
that they are preoccupied with social survival and the
avoidance of starvation.    However, it should be said that
Miller's arguments for the absence of an implicit concept
of social justice are not entirely convincing.    First of
all, Miller is trying to make generalisations about primitive societies as a whole when these societies are very
different from one another.    The examples are selected
from individual societies, and other examples might have
led to different conclusions.    Even the examples that he
does choose suggest a basic structure of rights, which
includes need and to a much lesser extent desert, but
which can be overridden where the common good is at stake.

Feudalism supplies an excellent example of a society
which bases social justice on rights.    Feudal society was
hierarchical and different rights were given to different
levels in the hierarchy.    These rights included the use
of land, claims on people's labour, and claims to the
fruits of labour.    However, unlike a caste system, the
hierarchy was based on personal allegiance (although
generally inherited) and there was sufficient mobility to
ensure that people at different levels were not regarded
as being completely different species.    Desert was given
some recognition through mobility.    Need was recognised

in that people were expected to distribute any surplus
above what was needed to maintain a person's status.
This surplus might be distributed to sustain the needy or
to sustain the church, which also had a role in sustaining
the needy.   The church itself was organised on somewhat
different principles yet was closely integrated into the
feudal hierarchical structure.   Miller sees certain characteristics making rights an appropriate principle for
social justice in such a society.   First, there was the
existence of a surplus product above subsistence;   then
the hierarchy was based on personal allegiance and the
existence of limited mobility which encouraged a recognition of common humanity and a sense of mutual obligation;
finally the segmented nature of society led to real danger
dangers of a dissolution into chaos, which did indeed
happen from time to time.

The relationship between a capitalist economic market
and a concept of social justice based on a principle of
desert interpreted as a reward for contribution to society
hardly needs further enlargement.   Miller, however, draws
attention to the influence of the remnants of an earlier
order in the continued role of the landed aristocracy and
the defence of their rights.   He also comments on the
ambiguous position of workers who have tended to accept
the principles of the market economy in their work role
but have also developed trades unions and co-operatives on
different principles to protect themselves against some of
its consequences.   He compares them in this respect to
the merchant guilds under feudalism.   Relevant factors in
the interdependence of the market economy and social justice based on desert are the existence of plenty, by earlier standards;   rapid economic development, which was
furthered by and itself supported an individualistic
ideology;   the impersonality of market relationships and
a belief that egoism could be channelled into productive
social ends by the operation of a free market economy.

More recently there has been a considerable shift away
from a pure theory of desert towards greater emphasis on
need with wages and salaries determined less by the principles of supply and demand than by a  customary concept
of fairness.   Miller relates this to a shift from the
classical market economy to 'organised capitalism'.   In
the classical market economy individual entrepreneurs,
owning and managing their own firms, made contracts with
'free' workers according to the conditions of the labour
market.   In organised capitalism the growth of large
bureaucratic firms and trade unions means that typically

the worker contracts with management through the inter-
mediary of a collective organisation, while the manager
himself works as a member of an organisation not an individual decision-maker.   In this situation the declining
importance of the exchange relationship tends to undermine
individualism.   There is a hierarchy of status, power and
economic reward but based on capacity and talent rather
than custom and birth.   There is a greater belief in the
possibility of motivation by social responsibility and
even altruism.   Nevertheless profit and wage differentials are still defended on the basis of desert and contribution.   In some ways there is the basis for a new
synthesis between desert and needs.   Rewards are distributed on the basis of desert, but desert is assessed on
the basis of contribution to need.   Miller suggests that
Rawls's theory has achieved wide support largely because
it encapsulates this synthesis.

Finally, Miller looks briefly at communes as an example
of communities basing social justice on need.   The communes that he looked at have had very different origins.
There were religious communities of dissenting sects in
fifteenth and sixteenth century Germany.   There were communities set up mainly in the period 1820 to 1850 either
on religious principles (like the Shaker communities) or
Owenite or similar principles.   Then there were the very
varied communes of the 1960s and after, and finally the
kibbutzim in Israel.   Despite their very different
origins all these communes tended to base distribution on
need and equality.   But Miller considers that whether or
not their original members started with egalitarian
beliefs, their primary motive for joining lay not in this
but in seeking a new form of relationship between people.
The egalitarianism results from the close-knit community
that they establish, in a situation in which membership is
voluntary.   Few communes have lasted for a long time and
this may be due to inherent limitations in human nature.
But one must also recognise that all such communes have
been enclaves in societies organised on different principles and have therefore been subject to great pressure.


CRITICISMS OF MILLER

The way in which Miller has developed his case is not
beyond criticism.   His choice of philosophers may at least
partly have been dictated by the needs of his argument - a
limitation of all case studies as a basis for developing
generalisations.   Similarly, the selection of material

for his studies of particular types of society may also be
biased.    As has been pointed out, this is particularly
obvious in his consideration of primitive societies.

As an example of the operation of selection, the choice
of Hume may account for the fact that Miller deals somewhat inadequately with the moral justification of rights
as a basis for social justice, concentrating instead on
the more pragmatic issue of the role of rights in maintaining a stable society.    There are two moral arguments that
are relevant.    First, from the point of view of individuals their established rights can be likened to the rules
of a game, but a very serious game.    They make decisions
about their lives and their life plans on the basis of
these rules, and will object if the rules are suddenly
changed in the middle of the game in a way that adversely
affects their position.    This is a similar case to that
used against retrospective legislation.    It is particularly strong in societies where all change tends to be
slow.    But, second, it would be difficult to contend that
the continuance of all systems of rights can be morally
justified by such arguments - for example, the rights
given to owners in a system of chattel slavery.    This is
why Miller draws attention to the personal nature of the
allegiance in feudalism, and the fact that different
classes were not seen as different species.

Runciman takes these aspects of feudalism to build his
concept of a conservative system of social justice:

In the conservative theory, social justice consists in
a social hierarchy, but a hierarchy governed by a
stable system of inter-connected rights and duties.
Those at the top are the holders not merely of privi-
lege but of responsibility for the welfare of those
below;   and through the recognition that different
strata in society have different functions to fulfil,
the hierarchy is accepted without dissension or envy as
long as the responsibilities imposed on each class are
in fact properly exercised.

If a system of social justice based on rights is justified on such grounds as these, rather than its value in
maintaining the stability of society in its existing form,
then change is not necessarily ruled out.    For if the
obligations laid on different people change, then so
should the rights that they enjoy.    Now it is clear that
the expectations laid on all adults, whatever their place
in society, have changed radically throughout the last two

centuries and are still changing.   This can be seen in
their roles as citizens, workers and parents as well as
in the general expectation that they make their own decisions about their lives in a complicated and constantly
changing environment.   So in changing circumstances
rights based on obligations can become very like rights
based on needs.   Both may be concerned with facilitating
the formulation and pursuit of individual life-plans.

Again with regard to Spencer, it is difficult today to
regard his philosophy as anything other than an aberration
produced by the extreme individualism of the nineteenth
century.   Its validity depends on faith in the economic
market first of all as a means of giving free rein to
egoism yet harnessing it to the common good, and then as
providing a just reward for people's contribution to
society.   It ignores the extent to which some social contributions are not rewarded in the economic market (for
example, good parenting) and treats as irrelevant the
extent to which rewards in the economic market may reflect
the natural injustices of chance rather than effort, skill
or personal quality.   So Rawls, although accepting the
economic market as a system exhibiting 'pure procedural
justice', introduced the difference principle to ensure
that some account was taken of the need to give protection
against unpredictable mischances.

However, Miller's general case is certainly convincing.
Social justice may be an important value in most complex
societies but it is not necessarily the primary value as
Rawls proposes:  'Justice', he maintains (p. 3), at the
opening of his book, 'is the first virtue of social institutions, as truth is of systems of thought ... laws and
institutions no matter how efficient and well-arranged
must be reformed or abolished if they are unjust.'   In
practice social justice must take its place in a pattern
of social values and the form it takes in any society will
depend on broader aims, like survival, growth, maintaining
order and promoting co-operation.   These in turn will
attain their priority according to the level of threat
under which people feel themselves to live and the possibilities they see for change in human behaviour, in the
relationship between the individual and society, and in
the control of the environment.

This does not mean that the concept of social justice
can be stretched to accommodate any system of rights that
fits a particular society.   There are surely minimum requirements that can be laid on a society before it can be

considered just.   First, it must acknowledge that individuals have some rights, such as the expectation of
security in their social relationships, and the ability
to maintain self-respect.   It follows that arbitrary
subjection to the whims of others - as in chattel slavery
- must be excluded;   that self-respect should not depend
on the fulfilment of obligations which cannot be met for
various reasons over which the person has no control.
Thus every socially just system must take some account of
obligations, needs and deserts.   Our own society makes
high demands on everyone, and makes self-respect dependent
on meeting those high demands.   Hence the increasing
expectation of greater equality in the distribution of
resources.

FURTHER READING

There is really no alternative to reading the originals as
a basis for assessing the issues.   On the other hand,
Wolff's critique of Rawls, which I read after writing this
chapter, gives a particularly clear account of the development of Rawls's thinking.   This helped me to understand
many issues more clearly, including Runciman's use of his
earlier writings.   Bernard Ackerman (1980) represents an
alternative liberal view of social justice based on a contract, which is more readable and, perhaps because of this,
more convincing, but it has attracted less attention.
So it is probably more useful in visualising for oneself
the implication for social justice of a liberal philosophy
but is less useful for understanding the critical literature.

BIBLIOGRAPHY

* Recommended.

* Ackerman, B.A. (1980), 'Social Justice in the Liberal
    State', New Haven, Conn., Yale University Press.
* Daniels, N. (ed.) (1975), 'Reading Rawls: Critical
    Studies of "A Theory of Justice"', Oxford, Blackwell.
Forder, A. (1974), 'Concepts in Social Administration',
    London, Routledge & Kegan Paul.
Hare, R.M. (1975), Rawls' Theory of Justice, in Daniels
    (ed.) (1975).
Lyons, D. (1975), Nature and Soundness of the Contract and
    Coherence Arguments, in Daniels (ed.) (1975).
* Miller, D. (1976), 'Social Justice', Oxford University
    Press.

Phelps Brown, H. (1977), 'The Inequality of Pay', Oxford University Press.

Pinker, R. (1979), 'The Idea of Welfare', London, Heinemann.

* Rawls, J. (1973), 'A Theory of Justice', Oxford University Press.

Runciman, W.G. (1965), Social Justice, 'The Listener', 29 July.   Republished in Eric Butterworth and David Weir (eds) (1970), 'The Sociology of Modern Man', Glasgow, Fontana/Collins.

Runciman, W.G. (1966), 'Relative Deprivation and Social Justice', London, Routledge & Kegan Paul.

* Wolff, R.P. (1977), 'Understanding Rawls: a reconstruction and critique of "A Theory of Justice"', Princeton University Press.

Chapter 9

# Explanations of poverty
## Anthony Forder

DEFINITIONS OF POVERTY

The purpose of this chapter is to relate the theories discussed earlier to a specific social problem.  The problem
selected is that of poverty because of its wide implications and its centrality to social administration.

To describe a condition as a 'social problem' implies
that the condition is undesirable and should, if possible,
be eliminated or alleviated through collective action.
It therefore involves value-judgments about what is desirable or undesirable and whether collective action should
be taken to change the situation.  The latter judgment
will depend among other factors on how one evaluates the
undesirable condition against other effects of attempts to
alleviate it.

Few people would deny that poverty is an undesirable
condition.  There are, however, crucial differences of
opinion about what constitutes poverty and in particular
the level of poverty that demands collective action for
its alleviation.  This raises the question of the definition of poverty.

Poverty can be defined narrowly or broadly to varying
degrees.  The narrowest definitions concentrate on monetary income, which has the advantage of being relatively
easily measurable.  The broadest definitions see poverty
as the denial of life chances to people.

Within definitions that relate to monetary income there
are two different approaches.  The first is based on the
determination of a level of income necessary to meet some
minimum standard of living.  The second is a comparative

approach that relates the income of the poor to average income.

The first and classic use of a minimum standard, or poverty line, in the definition of poverty was in Rowntree's study of York (Rowntree, 1901).   Rowntree's standard was a deliberately low one covering the minimum diet required for 'the maintenance of merely physical health,' the cheapest clothing plus the actual cost of the rent paid by a household.   He purposely ignored expenditure 'needful for the development of the mental, moral and social sides of human nature' or even sick clubs and insurance (p. 87), not because he regarded them as unimportant, but because they were difficult to measure and were not necessary to make out his case for action. Equally, Rowntree was well aware that people living on the income he set as his standard were unlikely actually to receive a diet that would maintain their physical health because of culturally determined patterns of expenditure, as well as inefficiency and misspending.   In his later studies Rowntree made rather more allowance for social expenditure (Rowntree, 1941;  Rowntree and Lavers, 1951) but this was still too meagre to ensure that the minimum diet would actually be achieved (Townsend, 1954 and 1979, p. 34).   More recently it has been recognised that a minimum standard should aim at a broader goal of social participation involving family and neighbourhood interaction and meeting the standards of appearance and parental support expected by schools.

The comparative approach to the definition of poverty starts from this recognition that social factors are of vital importance in determining whether an income of a particular level gives people an adequate standard of living.   The social factors that influence individual expenditure are themselves influenced by average income in the communities in which people live, and, in these days of communication and advertising through the mass media, in the society in which people live.   Thus comparative poverty is defined as an income per head of a household that is lower than a fixed proportion of average income per head, say two-thirds or half.

For practical reasons many British studies use a rather arbitrary compromise between these two definitions.   They start from the officially approved scale rates for Supplementary Benefits, which are designed to provide on a means test a subsistence minimum for those unable to work.   The origin of these scales lies in Beveridge's adaptation of

Rowntree's poverty line of 1936.    However, when Beveridge's proposals were put into effect, the scale rates
were lower than Beveridge proposed.    Over the next ten
years the scale was periodically updated to allow for increases in the Retail Price Index, a rather crude index of
the cost of living when applied to those with low incomes
because their patterns of expenditure are different from
households with higher incomes.    After 1959 until 1979
adult scale rates were increased to take account of increases in average earnings if these were higher than increases in the Retail Price Index but the children's rates
were only adjusted for changes in the RPI.    In view of
its arbitrary nature, the only justification for using the
Supplementary Benefit scale is its official character and
practical convenience.    Frequently the poverty line is
defined as the Supplementary Benefit scale increased by a
proportion, usually 20 or 40 per cent.

All these standards confine themselves to monetary
income and ignore factors such as the quality of housing
and the environment which also affect the standard of
living.    Rowntree did concern himself with these matters
but could not include them in a single index of poverty
and the same difficulty has influenced other investigators.

The broadest definitions see lack of income as one
among a whole range of deprivations which are shared by
the same people and tend to reinforce each other.    The
term 'relative deprivation' is sometimes used as a synonym
for this kind of definition of poverty.    Runciman (1966)
for example, examines the conception held by manual
workers of their relative deprivation in a historical
study from 1918 to 1962 and in a contemporary survey.    He
makes use of Weber's view that a person's social position
must be plotted on three dimensions - class, status and
'party' - although interpreting the concepts rather differently from Weber.    In examining these dimensions of
deprivation, Runciman interprets class as meaning income,
while acknowledging that this is a narrow interpretation
of class.    Status he interprets as the respect with which
people are regarded.    He used the word 'power' rather
than 'party' and interprets it as the exercise of trade
union power in the work situation.

Baratz and Grigsby (1972) in America consider that:
'"poverty" is best viewed as a condition involving those
*severe deprivations* and *adverse occurrences*  that are
closely (but not necessarily exclusively) associated with

"*inadequate economic resources*"' (original italics).
Thus the essence of poverty is seen to lie in the actual
conditions of life, not the low income that contributes to
this condition.    These deprivations and adverse occurrences are then classified under five headings:

severe lack of physical comfort;

severe lack of health;

severe lack of safety and security;

severe lack of welfare values;

severe lack of deference values.

These last two correspond to Runciman's use of lack of
status and power as elements of relative deprivation.
'Welfare values' include all those elements that affect a
person's self-perception, including, for example, 'inability to perform a socially valued function (e.g. paid work)'
and 'lack of a good quality education'.    'Deference
values' include those elements of a person's life situation that have a bearing on society's view of him or her
and the extent to which he or she is taken into account in
the actions of others, such as 'exclusion from participation in the political process (especially powerlessness)'
and again 'lack of a good education'.

Townsend (1979) is putting forward a similar wide view
when he suggests that there are five priorities in developing an understanding of the causes of poverty (pp. 87-8):

1.   The division of resources and not only income in
     society.
2.   The methods, principles and systems by which these
     resources are produced and distributed.
3.   The styles of living with which the differential
     ownership in the population of these resources cor-
     respond (and hence the forms of deprivation which
     lack or denial of such resources denote).
4.   The social classes who mediate the relationships of
     people with systems of production and distribution,
     and who share relatively distinct standards and
     styles of living.
5.   The minority groups who are liable to have an un-
     equally small share of available national resources.

If one compares these different ways of defining

poverty, it is evident that the broader the definition,
the larger the implications for possible explanations.
If poverty is defined narrowly in terms of income, and
especially a subsistence minimum income, it is conceivable
that economic theory alone can explain its continuation.
If status and power are also included in the definition,
then explanations must cover the social and political
structure as well as economic influences.   Indeed, those
who use such broader definitions tend to assume that the
interrelationship between these different deprivations
makes it impossible for economic explanations alone to
explain even income poverty.


THE PHENOMENON OF POVERTY

Before turning to alternative explanations of poverty, it
is necessary to say something more about the phenomenon of
poverty that needs explaining.

   Taking income poverty first, what one is dealing with
is an unequal distribution of income that leaves some
people - the number varying according to the definition
taken - unable to meet their physical needs and the social
demands made on them.   Such inequality has tended to per-
sist in industrialised countries despite massive growth in
average income per head of the population.   For example,
for the USA Hunt and Sherman (1978, pp. 220-2) quote official figures showing that in 1947 the poorest 20 per cent
of the population received 5.1 per cent of total personal
income before taxation.   By 1974 this had risen to 5.4
per cent, implying that on average the poorest fifth of
the population received a quarter of the national average.
At that date almost all these incomes were below the official poverty line.   In Britain the Royal Commission on
the Distribution of Income and Wealth (The Diamond Committee) (HMSO, 1975) found that in 1972 the poorest 20 per
cent of the population received 8.4 per cent of total personal income before tax, and 9.6 per cent after tax - an
improvement on the American figures but still leaving those
people with on average less than half the national average
income.   Looking at it in another way, in 1972 it was
estimated officially that no less than 1,860,000 persons,
or 3.5 per cent of the population were actually living
below the Supplementary Benefit level.   While the majority
of these could presumably have claimed benefit but did not
do so, 250,000 persons in 88,000 families had income of
this low level despite the family head being in full-time
employment (Forder, 1975, p. 114).   The Diamond Committee

(HMSO, 1975) using the more generous standard of the supplementary benefits scale plus 40 per cent found 25 per
cent of the population in poverty.

Most studies of poverty, including Rowntree's and that
undertaken on behalf of the Diamond Committee (Layard et
al., 1978) have found poverty falling on similar groups.
The two major categories are households dependent on
people with low earnings and on people unable to earn.
Both categories include households dependent on people
with limited skills and education, with irregular employment, with disabilities or chronic or severe illness and
households dependent on women.   In Layard's study it was
noticeable that a substantial number of households was
kept out of poverty because they had two earners, so that
single-parent families were particularly likely to be in
poverty.   So were families with a higher than average
number of dependent children and, of course, the retired.

It is worth mentioning at this point one theory about
poverty that is solely concerned with explaining some
aspects of its incidence.   This is Rowntree's theory of
the life-cycle of poverty, which traces the way people,
and particularly low earners, move in and out of poverty
through their lives.   The single worker and the young
married couple without children are comparatively well off.
When children are born to the marriage, the wife is likely
to stop working and the needs of the family increase as
the children grow in age and numbers.   In middle-class
families the main wage-earner's income generally increases
annually over the years, but not to the extent of the
demands on it.   The manual worker reaches a maximum
quickly and there is little increase in earnings as family
responsibilities grow.   Later, as the children grow up
and become more independent, the demands on the parents'
income is reduced, while the income may be increased by
having two earners.   This comparative affluence lasts for
a few years but is suddenly terminated by retirement.
The pattern is complicated by periods of temporary unemployment and sickness.   Obviously as Rowntree recognised,
this life cycle is in some ways less fundamental than the
low earnings that make it impossible for many workers to
cover their needs over their lifetime.

The importance of this theory for social administration
in Britain is that it was the starting point for the
Beveridge Plan (Beveridge, 1942) which provided the basis
for the British social security system.   The central
feature of Beveridge's plan was a system of compulsory

insurance to cover unemployment, sickness, widowhood and
retirement.   The contributions were to be heavily subsi-
dised out of taxation to ensure that low earners were not
put into permanent poverty, and the benefits were to be at
a basic subsistence level.   The insurance scheme was to
be supported by children's allowances at subsistence level
for all children (except the first child in the family)
and by an assistance scheme on a means test for the minority of people not covered by the insurance scheme.   If
the social security scheme in post-war Britain has not
succeeded in abolishing subsistence poverty, it is largely
because successive governments have been reluctant to put
into it the resources required for its fulfilment (George,
1968;   Atkinson, 1969).

Since most people in industrial countries are dependent
on earnings for the greater part of their income, inequality in the distribution of earnings is a major influence
on the incidence of poverty.   In explanations of poverty
three aspects of earnings distribution have to be taken
into consideration;   the pattern of distribution, the
stability of differentials and the relationship between
status and pay.

There is considerable evidence to show that in industrialised countries the distribution of earned income
tends to follow a particular pattern.   This pattern is
shown in Figure 9.1.   This distributional curve is in the
general shape of the normal curve of distribution but
strongly skewed to the left and with a long tail to the
right.   The implication of this is that a high proportion
of earned incomes are concentrated among low earners.
Because this is so, it is likely that whatever definition
of poverty is taken, unless it is a very low subsistence

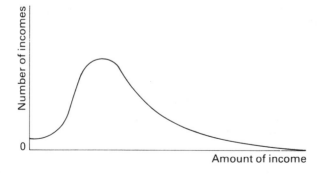

FIGURE 9.1  Typical pattern of income distribution

level, a relatively high proportion of earners will be
either in poverty or on the borders of poverty.   Since
households dependent on non-earners are unlikely in a
market economy to receive higher incomes than those dependent on earners, the distribution of incomes as a whole
will be even more skewed to the left leaving an even
higher proportion on the edges of poverty.   So one way of
examining the causes of poverty is to seek explanations of
the leftward skew in the distribution of incomes.

A second aspect of the distribution of income that has
to be considered is the relative stability of the differentials between different occupational groups and between
men and women.   This stability has been shown to exist in
many different countries, both socialist and capitalist
although the extent of the differentials will vary from
country to country and from one industry to another.

A classic study illustrating this is that undertaken by
Routh of occupational earnings in Great Britain from 1906
to 1960 (Routh, 1965).   Routh examined the average earnings of men and women in eight occupational groups - higher
professional, lower professional, managers, foremen, cleri-
cal and skilled, semi-skilled and unskilled manual workers.
This agglomeration into broad groups does disguise some
changes that took place within occupational groups, but
the general stability shown is remarkable.   For example,
over the whole period the average earnings of male unskilled workers remained within a point or two of 86 per
cent of the average earnings of all male workers.   Similarly, the earnings of women in each occupational group
were consistently lower than the earnings of their male
counterparts, and the earnings of unskilled manual women
remained at about 66 per cent of the average earnings of
all men and women throughout the period.   There were
changes, for example a narrowing of differentials of
higher professionals and of skilled workers, but these
tended to take place over brief periods of time, mainly
during the two world wars.   After the wars there was some
increase in these differentials, but not to their previous
level.

A third consideration is that surveys of public attitudes to different occupations has shown a consistent correlation between status and pay.   While the surveys have
generally taken place in industrialised capitalist societies, occupational pay differentials tend to follow the
same pattern in socialist countries as in capitalist countries.   The existence of this correlation still leaves

open the question of whether status determines pay, or pay
determines status, or both are determined by some other
factor.

Inequalities of income due to earnings differentials
are intensified by inequalities in the distribution of
wealth, on the one hand, and the existence of substantial
numbers of non-earners.

In most capitalist societies, wealth is highly concentrated.   In Britain the Royal Commission estimated that
between 80 and 90 per cent of wealth was held by 20 per
cent of the population (HMSO, 1975, p. 87).   For the purposes of looking at income poverty, the importance of the
distribution of wealth lies in the way in which wealth
produces income.   Although not much more than 10 per cent
of personal income in Britain comes from this source, most
such income goes to those who have high incomes.

The numbers of non-earners is particularly seriously
affected by industrial recession with its effects on unemployment although the numbers of retired people represent
a larger figure.   It is important to note that whether
non-earners are in poverty or not depends on the scale of
the income transfers under schemes such as social security
and pensions plans.

Turning to the question of life-chance poverty, the
evidence is less precise, and to some extent ambiguous.

First of all, there is a good deal of evidence showing
the correlation between different forms of deprivation
(e.g. Townsend, 1979).   As Baratz and Grigsby (1972)
point out, low income goes with poor health, poor education, poor conditions at home, at work, and in the environment, poor pension rights, and in every case both as
cause and effect of that low income.   This correlation
can be seen in many community studies, and it is in these
that the correlation between material poverty and low political power are also seen most clearly.   This relationship is particularly exemplified by the failure of the
poverty programmes in both Britain and the USA.   The failure of these projects will be discussed later in the context of the theory of poverty causation that gave rise to
them.

However, these correlations of different kinds of
deprivation exist side by side with intergenerational
mobility both between social classes and into and out of

poverty.   The evidence on the latter will again be examined in the context of theoretical exposition.   The evidence on class mobility is examined by Parkin (1972).   He
estimates (p. 49) that:  'between about a quarter and a
third of those born into the manual working class in
modern Western countries will move into the ranks of the
middle class'.   Downward mobility also occurs, but on a
somewhat lesser scale because of the increase in middle-
class occupations compared to manual occupations over the
years.   Parkin, however, takes the view that much of this
mobility takes place on the margins of the social classes
leaving largely untouched the lowest manual classes.


NEO-CLASSICAL ECONOMIC THEORY AND THE EXPLANATION OF
POVERTY

Neo-classical economic theory is a normative theory as
well as a positive theory - it sets out to describe the
conditions which will produce the best possible outcome,
as well as to explain the actual distribution of production and consumption.

As a normative theory, neo-classical economics proposes that the operation of a free competitive economic
market with prices determined by supply and demand will
ensure the most efficient use of resources.   This applies
to the prices paid for labour as well as for other factors
of production.   Distortions in the market, due to political or other social factors, will tend to make the system
less efficient, reduce growth and make the problem of
poverty worse.   This ideological orientation influences
the definition of poverty which is usually in terms of a
minimum standard of subsistence.   For such a definition
minimises the need for state intervention.

As a positive theory, neo-classical economics tends to
see the causes of poverty not in the economic system, but
in the performance of the individual within that system.
So the major immediate causes of poverty are seen as:

(a)   low earnings due to lack of the abilities that are
valued in the economic market;

(b)   a consequential inability to insure against misfortune and old age;   and

(c)   personal irresponsibility leading to such behaviour
as unwillingness to compete in the economic market, or to

insure against future misfortune, and failure to restrict family size in accordance with income.

Now there is considerable evidence that supply and demand plays an important role in determining wage differentials not only in Western capitalism, but in other systems.   Phelps Brown (1977) provides a thorough review of this evidence, drawing on research from many different countries including the Soviet Union, China, Cuba and Israel, as well as Western industrial countries.   His general conclusion is that, except in relatively small enclosed communities like the Israeli kibbutzim, some differentials appear to be necessary to provide incentives where there is freedom to choose employment.

However, the fact that the 'laws' of supply and demand require earnings differentials does not explain the actual pattern of differentials generally found and illustrated in Figure 9.1.   Indeed this distribution pattern provides a major discrepancy with the theory.   Neo-classical theory leads to an expectation that earnings differentials will be related to levels of ability.   Since it is generally assumed that the distribution of abilities within the population will follow the normal curve of distribution, it would be expected that the distribution of earnings would be similar.   So considerable efforts have been made by economists to find an explanation for the skew in the distribution of earnings.

Some economists consider that the discrepancy is primarily due to imperfections in the labour market (e.g. Bosanquet and Doeringer, 1973).   In this view, known as the dual market theory, it is possible to distrinquish two distinct labour markets, one covering highly unionised or professionalised occupations, the other covering a range of occupations, mainly unskilled or semi-skilled and often performed by women, where unionisation is weak or non-existent.   These occupations are particularly likely to be subject to competition from unskilled people on the margins of the normal labour market - migrants from rural areas or foreign countries, the unemployed from declining industries, and married women.

An alternative explanation is put forward by Lydall (1968).   He made a statistical analysis of the distribution of the earnings of adult men in full-time employment and concluded that most of the leftward skew in the distribution of earnings could be accounted for by the distribution of ability in the population in combination with

certain related factors.    He assumed that 'ability' was
the product of three main factors, genetic endowment,
social class (through the home environment) and education.
He considered that genetic endowment would tend to follow
a normal curve of distribution, but those with higher
genetic abilities would be more likely to come from a
higher social class and to receive a better education, so
that the curve of distribution of 'ability' would be
skewed to the left with a tail to the right.    This tendency would be increased by choice of occupation and by
the tendency of men in their later years to have lower
earnings.    However, Lydall's statistical analysis could
not account for all of the long tail to the right, which
he attributed to the need in large organisations for a
hierarchical structure, in which each level of the hierarchy had to be paid more than the level below it.    When he
went beyond his data to consider the differences in earnings between men compared to women and black workers compared to white, he felt bound to ascribe this to social
rather than economic factors.    Lydall did not consider
the possibility that these organisational or social factors might be able to explain the whole shape of the distribution.


SOCIAL PATHOLOGY AND INDIVIDUAL ABILITY

If Lydall and the neo-classical economists are right, then
the problem of differentials is shifted back one stage to
an explanation of the extent of differences in ability.
A permanent reduction of poverty will depend on reducing
differences in ability by improving the abilities of the
less able, while amelioration would be achieved by some
form of compensation.    Two common explanations of poverty
are consistent with this theoretical view.    They are
based on the intergenerational cycle of poverty and the
culture of poverty.    These explanations are not mutually
exclusive.    Each of them suggests the possibility of a
solution to at least part of the problem of poverty
through the development of social services.

The first of these two theories attributed the continuation of poverty to an intergenerational cycle, in which
the characteristics that ensure poverty are handed down
from one generation to another within the family.    This
theory has been associated in Britain with the Conservative
politician Sir Keith Joseph (Jordan, 1974), but Holman
(1978) has argued that it was as clearly espoused by Roy
Jenkins when he was a leading spokesman of the Labour

Party.   The reason is perhaps that both politicians at
the time accepted the rightness of the welfare state with
its mixed capitalist economy, despite other political differences.   The argument runs on these lines.   For almost
thirty years after the Second World War there was an expanding economy, with full employment and the provision of
many universal social services, including those covering
health, education and social security.   In these circumstances low earnings and poverty must be due to those
factors in the environment of the poor that prevented them
from taking advantage of the opportunities offered by the
welfare state.   The most obvious cause of this was inadequate socialisation in childhood.   The solution was
therefore seen to lie in breaking this cycle by improved
education together with the offering of special help to
the parents.   It should be noted that this explanation of
poverty attributes some of the causes of poverty to the
failure of the social services to meet the special needs
of these families.

The evidence for and against this thesis was examined
by Rutter and Madge (1976) looking at intergenerational
continuities in a wide range of disadvantages, not just
income poverty.   They concluded that moderate continuities do occur over two generations with respect to intel-
ligence, educational attainment, occupational status,
crime, psychiatric disorder and 'problem family' status.
There are substantial continuities in the case of some
severe forms of parenting such as child battering.
Almost no information was available at the time with
regard to income poverty or poor housing.   However, even
with forms of disadvantage where family continuities are
strong, discontinuities are also striking: 'At least half
of the children born into a disadvantaged home do not
repeat the pattern of disadvantage in the next generation.
Over half of all forms of disadvantage arise anew in each
generation' (p. 304).

Since the publication of Rutter and Madge's work, the
intergenerational inheritance of income poverty has been
explored by Atkinson, Maynard and Trinder (1983), as part
of the same programme of research into poverty sponsored
by the Social Science Research Council.   Atkinson, Maynard and Trinder based their study on a follow-up of Rowntree and Lavers's third study of poverty in York (1951).
As many as possible of the original sample were traced and
information obtained about their children in 1971.   The
analysis of the results was complex, because of the need
to take into account changes that had occurred in the

social and economic situation in the intervening twenty
years.    However, the authors' conclusions were broadly in
line with those of Rutter and Madge with regard to other
deprivations and also Parkin's account of the evidence
about class mobility mentioned earlier.    The authors
found considerable intergenerational continuities but also
discontinuities.    However, the discontinuities tended to
show shifts between neighbouring income and class categories rather than major intergenerational change.

   A second explanation of poverty is Oscar Lewis's theory
of the culture of poverty (Lewis, 1961 and 1966).    Lewis
is an anthropologist who studied slum communities in
Mexico and Puerto Rico.    As an anthropologist he was
interested in the total pattern of life in the communities
that he studied.    He found that the people exhibited many
of the attitudes, values and characteristics that Sir
Keith Joseph attributed to 'problem families'.    But he
could see that these were a response not just to faulty
socialisation within the family, but to the whole environment in which they lived.    This response was in many ways
realistic.    Living from day to day may be the only way to
live if disaster is always round the corner;    political
apathy is an appropriate response to constant failure to
obtain improvement.    But in Lewis's view changing the
situation except in the most profound and permanent way,
would not be sufficient in itself to enable the members of
the community to take advantage of new opportunities
because the responses are too deeply ingrained.    Lewis
gives as an example of a successful change the Cuban
revolution.

   Lewis has been challenged for his methodology and his
conclusions (Valentine, 1968).    Madge and Rutter
(1976, p. 30) consider that this explanation is unlikely
to be relevant to Britain.    But weaker versions of the
theory, combining it with the intergenerational cycle of
poverty, have provided the basis for poverty programmes in
Britain and the USA.    These weaker explanations start,
like the culture of poverty theory, from the concentration
of poverty in specific areas and from some of the attitudes
that tend to produce alienation in these areas from other
parts of society.    They include, however, an optimistic
belief that a combination of improved services and a community programme that encourages participation in social
and political processes and self-help would make a radical
difference to the situation.

   Underlying these views is an implicit acceptance of a

functionalist view of society and a pluralist theory of
Western political processes.  It is assumed that the
poverty of these communities is dysfunctional to society,
which will therefore respond positively to the revelation
of its existence.  Similarly pluralist political processes will be sufficiently sensitive to the expression of
these needs for appropriate action to result.

A whole series of demonstration projects was instituted
in Britain and America in the 1960s and 1970s, ostensibly
to examine the validity of these assumptions, with a view
to an expanded programme if they were successful.  The
results are summarised by Higgins (1978).  In one way
these projects challenged the pessimism of the culture of
poverty theory, if it had any relevance to the areas
chosen for the projects.  People tended to respond to the
opportunities offered by the projects.  However, the projects were unsuccessful in two ways.  First, they appeared
to make no permanent change in the areas where they were
tried out.  This was partly because they were inadequately funded and were carried on for a relatively short time
- three to five years.  But the main reason appears to
have been the political opposition stirred up by the pros-
pect of a permanent shift of power.  But they also failed
in a second way in that where they were successful, there
was no political commitment to changing policy, and commit-
ting more resources to an expansion of similar activities.


CUSTOM AND RELATIVE EARNINGS

One of the facets of earnings differentials that may need
explaining is the relationship between status and income.
This relationship exists not only between status and pay
but also between status and a whole range of other per-
quisites that are part of a person's real income, like
pension rights and the physical comfort of his or her surroundings.  To neo-classical economists, this relationship between income and status is seen as due to the fact
that both are a product of competitiveness within the
economic market.  The superior skills which enable people
to gain a high income also enable them to gain high
status.  On the whole functionalist theories also tend to
accept this view (e.g. Davis and Moore, 1945), although
Parsons himself (1964, p. 84) questioned whether the economic explanations of the relationship between status and
pay were adequate for the complexity of the issue.

A more direct attack on the neo-classical view was made

by Wootton (1955), who was concerned with the contrast
between economic explanations of wage determination and
the actual processes that could be observed in Britain.
Much of her evidence came from the operation of voluntary
and statutory machinery for wage negotiations.   The arguments of both employers and employees were directed primarily to the question of fairness based on customary differentials and comparisons with the earnings of people in
similar employment elsewhere.   Economic arguments based
on the supply and demand for particular kinds of labour
were rarely used and were generally marginal to the central issue of fairness based on customary relationships.
Thus in Wootton's view it is the traditional status of an
occupation that determines its pay rather than both pay
and status being dependent on the economic value attached
to skills.

Phelps Brown (1977) attempts to integrate theories of
earnings differentials based on supply and demand with
those based on the importance of custom.   He concluded,
as indicated above, that the laws of supply and demand
have a basic role in determining differentials in the long
term, but social factors operate in two ways.   First,
trade unions and professional associations, as in the dual
market theory, can control supply and can also use other
forms of power to create or maintain differentials.
Second, custom is of great importance in maintaining differentials in the face of changes in supply and demand.
It is particularly influential in the resistance to reduc-
tions when supply increases in relation to demand.   Thus
a sort of ratchet effect tends to operate, since increased
demand for particular skills produces an improvement in
the position of those who possess them, but custom resists
the downward change when supply increases or demand falls.


RADICAL EXPLANATIONS OF POVERTY

Radical explanations of poverty tend to focus on the role
of power in determining income, of which 'market power',
the ability to compete in the economic market is only one
aspect.

In marxist economic theory the capitalist economic
system is essentially exploitative, and poverty is primarily a result of this exploitation.   What is at issue is
the disposal of 'surplus value', the difference between
the costs of the reproduction of labour and the value of
its product (see pp. 43-4).   Under a capitalist system most

surplus value will be extracted in the form of profit and
rent, so that earnings will tend to be no higher than is
required to meet the costs of the reproduction of labour,
which would of course be somewhat higher for skilled than
unskilled labour.    This could certainly explain the leftward skew in the distribution of earnings.    There is,
however, some possibility of flexibility in the distribution of the surplus value between profits, earnings and
government expenditure on the basis of a political and
economic power struggle.    Gains from this struggle by a
minority of workers with high bargaining power could help
to explain the long tail to the right in the distribution
of earnings.    However, it is important to note that this
pattern of earnings distribution is evident in communist
as well as western industrial states, so an explanation
confined to capitalist exploitation is not wholly adequate
(Phelps Brown, 1977).

In so far as the appropriation of surplus value is a
major cause of inequality of income and therefore of
poverty, it is the power of those who control the means of
production which makes this possible.    It is, moreover, a
central tenet of marxism that economic power cannot be
separated from other forms of power.    Thus the political
system reinforces the power of those who control the means
of production, landlords, capitalists and their allies in
the social and economic structure.    So, in marxist theory
the distribution of income and status tends to follow the
distribution of power in the widest sense of that term.
It is easy to see this reflected in the relationship
between earnings and the hierarchical structure of industrial and government organisations.    This echoes Lydall's
explanation of higher earnings in terms of the need for an
administrative hierarchy.    It is also easy to see the
importance of all forms of power in creating the deprivations involved in the broadest definitions of poverty that
include life-chances as well as income.

One objection to the marxist view that surplus value is
largely appropriated by capitalists is the remarkable
growth of government expenditure as a proportion of gross
national product (GNP) throughout the twentieth century.
In most industrial countries it is beginning to approach
50 per cent.    However, it has been suggested (e.g. Taylor-
Gooby and Dale, 1981) that most of this growth can be
understood as support for capitalism and capitalists
rather than a charge on profits.    Most government spending can be categorised under three heads:

a contribution to the costs of the reproduction of labour, for example through the social security system, including child allowances, through education and training programmes and through the health service. This makes possible the payment of lower wages, below the minimum required for the reproduction of labour;

a contribution to the costs of the reproduction of capital, through maintenance of demand, especially in areas of high technology, including defence; through the maintenance of the industrial substructure like roads and the subsidy of fuel; through various forms of capital grant;

the maintenance of law and order and national defence.

In this way the profits of capitalists in general are maintained, even if some industries pay more than they receive directly. If the expansion of government expenditure and its distribution is strongly influenced by the needs of capitalists, it is hardly surprising if the social security system remains attached to a minimum subsistence standard of poverty, and the poverty programmes made little progress through lack of commitment.

Marxist theory does not deny entirely the validity of the explanations of poverty in capitalist states set out earlier. But it does suggest that attempts to end poverty that are based on these explanations will generally fail because they do not take into account the more fundamental causes that lie in the distribution of power.

Before leaving the subject of radical explanations of poverty, mention must be made of what is often called the 'radical functionalist' explanation. This theory was first put forward in an article by Gans (1972). Gans suggested that while poverty was dysfunctional for the poor, its existence had a number of positive functions for the wider society and especially for the dominant groups in it. These positive functions included ensuring that dirty, dangerous, menial and undignified work was performed; upholding the legitimacy of dominant norms by providing examples of deviance that was punished; and reinforcing the status of the non-poor. This explanation is radical in only a limited sense. It does make overt the anomalous status of poverty as a problem and leads to a questioning of the status quo in the writings of people like Holman (1978). But radical functionalism suggests no solution to the problem, and like other functionalist theories can be used to support a conservative stance.

CONCLUDING SUMMARY

The explanations of poverty discussed in this chapter can
be seen as alternatives that conflict with one another;
but they can also be seen as complementary, as presenting
different perspectives on the same problem.   The conflicts can be seen most clearly when they are examined in
their ideological commitment to different solutions, reactionary, reformist or revolutionary.   But before looking
at these ideological conflicts it will be helpful to summarise the arguments in the chapter which show how the
relevance of different theories depend in part on the
narrowness or breadth of the perspective taken.

The narrowest approach is to treat the problem of
poverty as primarily an economic problem, and to focus on
differentials in monetary incomes.   Neo-classical micro-
economic theory proposes an explanation of these differentials based on bargaining power within a competitive
market economy.   This bargaining power affects income
from investment as well as wages and the relationship
between the two, but in looking at poverty the returns to
investment are taken for granted and it is on wages that
the theory focuses.   Economic power in the labour market
is seen first of all as a function of individual ability
and second, particularly in the dual market theory, as a
function of trade union power.   It is difficult to fault
this as an immediate explanation of the wide wage differentials operating in a capitalist economic market.   Moreover, if Phelps Brown's analysis of the evidence is correct, then it also operates to some extent in non-capitalist countries.

However, even in capitalist countries, and perhaps more
so in non-capitalist countries, there is evidence of
'custom' operating to maintain differentials (Wootton,
Phelps Brown).   'Custom' suggests the influence of a
belief in social justice based on rights, which are generally regarded as 'earned rights'.   Skilled workers, for
example, have developed their life-plans on certain
assumptions about the rewards they will receive, and
resent as unjust attempts to take away those rewards.

However, competitive power in the economic market also
needs explanation.   It is not just governed by genetic
endowment, but depends on social factors such as family
background, membership of particular sub-cultures and
access to education and other services that pave the way
to higher employment.   Evidence can be found for all

these influences contributing to the causation of poverty,
and they take their place in the explanations of Lydall,
of the intergenerational theory of poverty and in Lewis's
theory of the culture of poverty.   This analysis immediately draws attention to the role of the social services
in developing competitive ability in the labour market.

The social services have two roles in combating poverty.   One is in counteracting the factors that contribute
to low bargaining power in the labour market;   and the
other is in compensating for that low bargaining power
particularly for those unable to obtain paid employment.
In both roles the performance of the social services
depends on political power.   So theories of political
power are relevant to the reduction of poverty, even if
one defines poverty in a way that excludes power itself.
The first response to the rediscovery of poverty in the
1960s in the USA and in Britain was made on the assumption
that poverty could be conquered by mobilising the poor to
make the social services more relevant to their needs.
It was assumed that the pluralist analysis was valid, so
that a direct assault on the disabilities of the poor
would be effective.   The failure of the poverty programmes and other reformist movements, such as the Child
Poverty Action Group in Britain, drew attention to the
limits within which pluralist political processes operate,
and widened again the framework within which a solution
needed to be sought.   So lack of power may be included in
the definition of poverty, and explanations of poverty
looked for in the structure of power in society and the
pervading influence of the capitalist system.

In terms of explanation all the theories discussed here
have some explanatory potential and in that sense provide
complementary perspectives.   The conflict between them
comes when the explanations are translated into programmes
for change and the ideological implications of the theories
are brought into debate.   Here the issues revolve around
the extent to which policies should be reactionary, conservative, reformist or revolutionary.

The neo-classical-monetarist theoretical approach can
be regarded as reactionary since it involves moving back
from post-war welfarism to a new emphasis on the economic
market in the distribution of resources.   The acceptance
of the ideology associated with neo-classical economics
leads to a definition of poverty in terms of minimum subsistence, and explanations of income differentials in
terms of individual pathology and the operation of economic

laws.   Social explanations of income differentials are
largely ignored except in so far as they are necessary to
account for deviations from the results predicted by the
economic theory.   In consonance with an ideology of minimum intervention in the economic market, proposals to deal
with poverty keep such intervention to a minimum.

At the other extreme, explanations of poverty from the
radical left, and particularly marxist explanations, see
income poverty as part of a wider phenomenon of multiple
deprivation.   Poverty is defined in comparative terms
taking into account the life-chances that people have.
Poverty is identified as the condition of life of a very
substantial proportion of the population, at least in
capitalist countries.   The fundamental explanation of the
causes of poverty is found in the structure of capitalist
societies and the unequal distribution of power within
that structure.   The kind of piecemeal tinkering with
different facets of deprivation advocated by reformists is
seen as being helpful for some, making marginal and probably worthwhile improvements.   But ultimately such
changes make no fundamental difference to social inequality.   While fewer people will be below the minimum standard, more will be poised on the brink of poverty.   They
will be inside the poverty trap where the overlap between
income and other taxes with means-tested benefits makes
movement into a position of comfort almost impossible.

Between these two extreme positions are those who are
ideologically committed to a reformist position.   Accepting that there are benefits accruing from the capitalist
economic market, and doubtful that radical change will
bring unalloyed improvements, they believe in the capacity
of western democratic social systems to respond to some
degree at least to the needs of the poor.   Implicit is
either a functionalist theory of the social system or,
more frequently, a pluralist political theory.   Functionalist theory (except for radical functionalism) defines
poverty as socially pathological and assumes that the
system is able to respond to such pathology.   Pluralist
political theory provides an explanation of how the system
can be influenced to respond through its political processes.   Reformists are likely to be committed to a range of
intermediate causal theories and related solutions.   A
central problem they have to face is the evidence that
there are quite tight limits to the changes that have
actually been achieved.   These limits are more explicable
through a functionalist than a pluralist theory but even
more easily explained by marxist theory.   However, which-

ever theory reformists espouse, they still have to consider the basic questions.   Are these limits due to in-
exorable economic laws which cannot be disregarded without
paying a heavy cost in loss of liberty and restriction to
growth?   Are they due to a social and economic structure,
which is potentially changeable but perhaps only through
violence?   Or is it just a matter of presenting the case
better and developing new techniques for tackling specific
problems?


## FURTHER READING

The easiest book to read to look further at the main
theories of poverty is Holman (1978).   It deals in more
detail with several of the theories discussed here, ending
up by supporting a radical functionalist explanation.   It
does not, however, set these theories in the context of
broader theories.   The first two chapters of Townsend
(1979) also provide a useful extension of and a somewhat
different perspective on the matters discussed here.   The
rest of Townsend's book describes a sample survey in 1968-
9 of poverty in Britain, whose breadth provides constantly
new perspectives on the phenomenon of poverty.

   Higgins, Phelps Brown, Madge and Rutter and Layard et
al. have been mentioned in the text, but the summaries do
no justice to the value of the works.   Atkinson (1975)
provides a broader discussion than Phelps of the economic
roots of inequality.

   Coates and Silburn is a community study which is useful
for grasping the meaning of poverty for people living in
such areas.

   The social security system and its failures is such an
important aspect of poverty that its study should not be
neglected.   George (1973) provides a particularly
thorough critique.   Jordan (1978) provides a similar but
more restricted critique.


## BIBLIOGRAPHY

* Recommended.

Atkinson, A.B. (1969), 'Poverty in Britain and the Reform
     of Social Security', Cambridge University Press.
* Atkinson, A.B. (1975), 'The Economics of Inequality',
     Oxford, Clarendon Press.

Atkinson, A.B., Maynard, A.K., and Trinder, C.J. (1983),
  'Parents and Children: income in two generations',
  London, Heinemann.
Beveridge, W. (1942), 'Social Insurance and Allied Services', London, HMSO.
Bosanquet, N., and Doeringer, P. (1973), Is there a Dual
  Labour Market in Britain?, 'Economic Journal', vol. 83.
Baratz, M.S., and Grigsby, W.G. (1972), Thoughts on Poverty
  and its Elimination, 'Journal of Social Policy', vol.
  1, pt 2.
* Coates, K., and Silburn, R. (1967), 'St. Ann's: poverty,
  deprivation and  orale', Nottingham University (Univer-
  sity Dept of Education).   Republished with an expanded
  theoretical section as 'Poverty: the forgotten English-
  men', London, Allen Lane.
Davis, K., and Moore, W.E. (1945), Some Principles of
  Stratification, 'American Sociological Review', vol. 10,
  no. 2.
Forder, A. (1975), Income and Need, in J. Mays, A. Forder
  and O. Keidan (eds), 'Penelope Hall's Social Services of
  England and Wales' (9th edn), London, Routledge & Kegan
  Paul.
Gans, H. (1972), The Positive Functions of Poverty,
  'American Journal of Sociology', vol. 78, no. 2.
George, V. (1968), 'Social Security - Beveridge and After',
  London, Routledge & Kegan Paul.
George, V. (1973), 'Social Security and Society', London,
  Routledge & Kegan Paul.
* Higgins, J. (1978), 'The Poverty Business: Britain and
  America', Oxford, Blackwell.
HMSO (1975), Royal Commission on the Distribution of
  Income and Wealth (Diamond Committee), 'No. 1 Initial
  Report on the Standing Reference' (Cmnd 6171).
HMSO (1978), 'No. 6 Lower Incomes' (Cmnd 7175).
* Holman, R. (1978), 'Poverty: explanations of social
  deprivation', Oxford, Martin Robertson.
Hunt, E.K., and Sherman, H.J. (1978), 'Economics: an intro-
  duction to traditional and radical views', New York,
  Harper & Row, 3rd edn.
* Jordan, B. (1978), 'Poor Parents: social policy and the
  cycle of deprivation', London, Routledge & Kegan Paul.
* Layard, R., et al. (1978), 'Causes of Poverty: back-
  ground paper no. 6 for the Royal Commission on the
  Distributon of Income and Wealth', London, HMSO.
Lewis, O. (1961), 'Children of Sanchez', London, Secker &
  Warburg.
Lewis, O. (1966), 'The Culture of Poverty', San Francisco,
  Freeman.
Lydall, H. (1968), 'The Structure of Earnings', Oxford
  University Press.

Parkin, F. (1972), 'Class, Inequality and Political Order: social stratification in capitalist and communist societies', London, Paladin.

Parsons, T. (1964), 'Essays in Sociological Theory', Chicago, Free Press.

* Phelps Brown, H. (1977), 'The Inequality of Pay', Oxford University Press.

Routh, G. (1965), 'Occupation and Pay in Great Britain, 1906-1960', Cambridge University Press.

Rowntree, B.S. (1901), 'Poverty: A Study of Town Life', London, Macmillan.

Rowntree, B.S. (1941), 'Poverty and Progress: A Second Survey of York', London, Longmans.

Rowntree, B.S., and Lavers, G.R. (1951), 'Poverty and the Welfare State', London, Longmans.

Runciman, W.G. (1966), 'Relative Deprivation and Social Justice', London, Routledge & Kegan Paul.

* Rutter, M., and Madge, C. (1976), 'Cycles of Disdadvantage: A Review of Research', London, Heinemann.

Taylor-Gooby, P., and Dale, J. (1981), 'Social Theory and Social Welfare', London, Edward Arnold.

Townsend, P. (1954), Measuring Poverty, 'British Journal of Sociology', vol. 5.

* Townsend, P. (1979), 'Poverty in the United Kingdom: A Survey of Household Resources and Standards of Living', London, Allen Lane.

Valentine, C.A. (1968), 'Culture and Poverty: Critique and Counter Proposals', Chicago University Press.

Wootton, B. (1955), 'Social Foundations of Wages Policy', London, Allen & Unwin, 2nd edn 1962.

Chapter 10

# Conclusion
## Anthony Forder

The main purpose of this book has been to set out as
clearly as possible in the limited space available the
different theories that are most frequently referred to in
the literature of social administration or implicitly
assumed in what is written.    It is hoped that students
will be given some basis for judging the soundness of what
is said through an understanding of the implicit and explicit assumptions that underlie the theories and the sort
of criticisms that have been made of them.    This chapter
is intended to summarise some of the central issues in a
way that will enable the student to move forward with more
confidence and a bit less confusion.


IDEOLOGY AND THEORY IN SOCIAL ADMINISTRATION

In considering these theories in relation to the literature of social administration, it is important to remember
that social administration has for most of its existence
as a discipline been justly accused of being pragmatic and
atheoretical.    As a discipline it has been mainly a
British invention, in the sense that in the USA and to
some extent elsewhere social policy in general and the
social services in particular have usually been studied
within the frameworks provided by the separate more traditional disciplines within which the theories discussed in
this book have largely been developed.    In Britain the
discipline grew up in parallel with the development of
what came to be called 'the welfare state', particularly
in the twenty-five years after the Second World War.    It
managed without any real commitment to explicit theories
of society and its parts because it was implicitly built
on the theories and ideology on which the welfare state
itself relied.    Because the acceptance of these theories

was implicit rather than explicit, writers within the
discipline had great difficulty in getting away from a
pragmatic approach to an objective examination of the
wider implications of what they were saying and doing.

What was the ideology of the welfare state on which the
discipline was founded?   Marshall (1970) draws attention
to the fact that 'the welfare state' could more accurately
be described as the 'democratic-welfare-capitalist state'.
It involved three different systems built on different
principles - the democratic political system, the capitalist economic market and the welfare system.   This concept
of a divided polity gives some clues to the theories on
which the ideology was based.   First of all, there was a
belief that the compromises involved were based on a broad
consensus that recognised the common interests of the
people of the country.   Second, there was a belief that
the political system was effectively pluralist and that
real and fundamental change could be achieved through
incremental reform.   Third, there was a basic acceptance
of the role of the capitalist economic market as a system
for production and distribution as modified in accordance
with a Keynesian model for the maintenance of full employment.   The capitalist market economy was valued for promoting individual choice and economic growth.   The welfare system was designed to counteract the worst effects
of an unregulated market economy and could safely be left
to the technical decisions of professionals, provided
there was some accountability to democratic processes of
government.

Most writers on social administration seemed to accept
this ideology and the related theories.   They implicitly
accepted a functionalist framework to explain the welfare
state.   This was seen as a response to the expression of
the needs of the social system and its sub-systems, including communities and families, within a general consensus about the sort of society we should be aiming for.
Writers recommended reforms on the basis of a rational
analysis of problems.   While it might take time to engage
the attention of government, in the long run a pluralist
democratic process would ensure that the needs of all
groups would receive attention.   It was also implicitly
accepted that a Keynesian management of the economy would
ensure the continuance of economic growth so that redis-
tribution could take place without too much heightening of
conflict.   There was an eclectic use of other micro-
economic and micro-sociological theories to examine particular problems.   Reactionary neo-classical economic

theories and radical marxist theories were largely
ignored.   It is perhaps symptomatic of the level of
optimism of writers in social administration that so
little was done to promulgate a wider understanding of
these issues to the general public and particularly in
the schools.

The general optimism among academics and others about
the nature of the welfare state first began to break with
the recognition that post-war reforms had not abolished
poverty.   Abel-Smith and Townsend's (1965) 'The Poor and
the Poorest' was a turning point in this respect in
Britain.   This study showed that poverty defined in comparative terms had been increasing during the 1950s and
that 'of all *persons* in the low expenditure households as
many as 34.6 per cent were in households whose head was in
full-time work' (p. 30).   Even so, it was assumed that
political action within a pluralist process would effect
change.   Abel-Smith and Townsend established the Child
Poverty Action Group with the expectation that it could
use political pressure to raise family allowances sufficiently to ensure the abolition of child poverty, within a
short period.   Twenty years later that objective had
still not been achieved.

Disillusion with a functionalist/pluralist model deep-
ened with the failure of the poverty programmes in the USA
and Britain discussed in chapter 9.   Even more serious
was the failure in the 1970s of Keynesian policies to deal
with international economic recession.   As a result, what
had previously been a positive sum game, in which co-operation produced some rewards for everyone, became a zero
sum game in which one person's gain had to be someone
else's loss.   The belief that there was a consensus on
the values of the welfare state was no longer tenable.

The resulting conflict may have been intensified by a
recognition that in any case constant economic growth
might eventually run up against limits to the expansion of
resources - that our growing prosperity, which had dissi-
pated potential conflicts, might have been based on con-
suming capital in the form of natural resources that could
not be replenished for the next generation.   At the same
time attempts by individual countries to solve their own
problems by expanding their economies often failed as a
result of a deterioration in their trading position with
other countries.   If they are forced to obtain credit
from the International Monetary Fund to cover an adverse
balance of trade, the conditions attached to the loan

involved a reversal of the expansionary programme and
often a cut back in the development of the welfare programme.    This occurred in Britain on several occasions
as well as in numerous other countries.    Governments have
also frequently found that to attract investment, particularly from multi-national companies, it is necessary to
create the economic conditions which make such investment
profitable, and this too sets limits to economic and welfare policies.

The result of these failures from 1970 onwards was a
questioning of the theories and ideology on which the welfare state was based.    Among academic writers on social
administration there was a more considered examination of
theoretical issues.    Pinker's (1971) 'Social Theory and
Social Policy' was the first major British book in the
field of social administration to examine the theoretical
perspectives underlying the study of the subject.    Since
then there has been a steady trickle of such books mainly
written from a radical perspective (George and Wilding,
1976;    Gough, 1979;    Mishra, 1977;    Taylor-Gooby and Dale,
1981).    There was a breakdown of consensus in political
as well as academic circles, and more extreme paradigms
were espoused more widely.    On the one hand, there was a
reversion by way of monetarism to a more dogmatic acceptance of the neo-classical theory of the market, exhibited
most clearly in the politics of government by Reagan in
the USA and Thatcher in Britain, but evident in most other
western countries.    Indeed, the very generality of the
adoption of monetarist policies made it difficult, if not
impossible, for individual countries to adopt a different
solution.    On the other hand, there was a mounting interest mainly in academic circles but also in some political
parties in marxist theories.    The failure of reform
seemed to confirm marxist analyses of political and economic power, while the intractability of the recession suggested that Marx might have been right about the inevitability of the demise of capitalism.

The increased interest in the theoretical analysis of
social administration included a new concern about its
philosophical basis.    This was reflected in the wide
interest aroused by Rawls's theory of social justice.
This theory appeared to provide a philosophical justification for the mixed economy of the welfare state as well as
indications for its refinement.    However, subsequent
criticisms led to a recognition of the bias created by its
basic assumptions.    In contrast, Miller's analysis was
more fundamental in its examination of criteria for social

justice, rights, merit and need, and in relating these to
the structure of societies and to broader issues in the
environment.   So if Rawls provides a rationale for the
post-war ideological consensus, Miller makes it easier to
examine the philosophical bases for the conflicting ideologies that replaced that consensus.


DIMENSIONS OF THEORETICAL VARIANCE

This brief account of the theoretical development of
social administration as a discipline is a reminder of two
aspects of theoretical variance that have already been
discussed.   First, there is the ideological continuum
from reactionary to revolutionary theories discussed at
the end of the previous chapter - using 'reactionary' to
cover theories that look to an ideal in the past, and
'revolutionary' for theories that aim at a new form of
society.   Second, there is the connection between functionalism, pluralism and neo-classical economic theory
discussed at the end of the chapter on pluralism and
elitism.

The reactionary-revolutionary continuum is the dimension of theoretical variance that is most frequently discussed.   One aspect of this continuum is presented by
George and Wilding (1976) who classify theorists and
writers on social policy on a continuum from 'anti-collectivists' on the extreme right (Hayek, Friedman and Enoch
Powell) through 'reluctant collectivists' (Keynes, Beveridge and Galbraith) and 'fabian socialists' (Tawney and
Crosland) to the marxists (Laski, Strachey and Miliband).
George and Wilding are concerned with analysing different
visions of the ideal society.   Another aspect of this
continuum is the speed of change.   The conservative wants
limited change.   The reformist looks for incremental
change.   The radical reactionary or the revolutionary may
look for rapid change but towards different ideals.   The
revolutionary may also believe that rapid change is the
only sort of change that is possible.

The relationship between functionalism, pluralism and
neo-classical economic theory is a reminder of the complexity of the reactionary-revolutionary continuum in contrast to the way it is frequently presented.   All three
theories can be regarded as 'conservative', but in different senses.   Functionalism is conservative because it
explains the structure of a society in terms of the functions currently performed.   This implicitly justifies the

status quo with only minor adjustments, whatever the particular form the society takes.   Pluralism is conservative partly because it presents the current form of liberal
democracy in a favourable light, and partly because a political system based on pluralist processes is likely to
give support to the existing power structure or to lead to
a political impasse.   The conservative or reactionary
nature of orthodox economic theory is more a matter of
contingency.   Once Adam Smith's presentation of classical
theory was radical in its proposals for an economic system
freed from political control, but its wide acceptance as a
normative model for the economy has resulted in it becoming conservative.   However, all three theories provide
prescriptive support for the continuance of the capitalist
system, one of the major subjects of ideological debate
for the last 150 years, although they all allow for some
modification of capitalism by welfare provision.

A more systematic way of considering theoretical variance is to examine theories in relation to the different
levels of society to which they refer and to see what they
have to say about change.   The levels to be considered
are society as a whole, the role of government, intermediate institutions and, briefly, the individual.   Change
is particularly important for social administration
because the discipline has a reformist bias.   So consideration will be given to the way different theories make
different propositions about what can be changed, what
should be changed, and how changes can and should be made
at the institutional levels to which they relate.


THEORIES OF SOCIETY

The two major theories of society considered in this book
are functionalism and marxism.   Both of these theories
stress the difficulties of achieving major changes within
our present social system but for rather different reasons.
Functionalism stresses the complexity of the inter-relationships within society and the tendency for countervail-
ing forces to reassert old patterns of interaction when
changes have taken place.   Marxism stresses the importance of the power of the owners of the means of production
and the dominance of the economic system within society.
In these respects the theories are not basically contradictory, and there is a good deal of evidence that both are
correct.   For example, if one considers the attempts of
successive British governments since the Second World War
to find a smoother path to economic growth, both the com-

plexity of the inter-relationships within the system and
the dominance of the capitalist market seem obvious.
However, functionalism stresses the role of consensus and
a shared ideology in maintaining stability, while marxism
sees the apparent consensus as based on a 'false consciousness', particularly on the part of those living under
domination.   It disguises the reality of conflict.   Most
marxists also lay emphasis on the role of constraint as
well as ideological indoctrination in maintaining stability, linking up with Dahrendorf's analysis (p. 139).

Both theories are essentially deterministic because,
looking at society holistically, they are unable to take
into account individual will.   Yet both leave some room
for the influence of people.   Most marxists consider that
the action of individuals, albeit acting in concert, can
influence the speed of change, although the direction of
change may be fixed.   Functionalism leaves room for
shifts in direction - after all the consensus is not
immutable - except in the more extreme version of convergence theory (p. 122), but assumes that the speed of
change must be slow.

It is in this area of the prediction of the nature of
the changes that can or will take place that the two
theories are in most disagreement.   Functionalism is concerned to explain stability and has no place for revolutionary change.   Solutions for the problems revealed by
conflict have to be found within a fairly rigid framework.
Conflict is seen as an indication of pathology, a symptom
of malfunctioning.   Marxism is a theory of change based
on conflict, which is seen as inevitable within all social
systems except the true communist state.   By assuming the
inevitability of conflict, it widens the range of changes
that are seen as feasible, since the social system itself
is capable of fundamental change.   It makes clear predictions about the nature of the changes that will take
place, although there may be differences of opinion among
marxists about the time-scale and the processes involved.

These differences between marxism and functionalism are
well illustrated by the contrasting views about the nature
of the present economic crisis in the west.   Functionalists tend to define the crisis as a technical problem and
look for a solution to macro-economic theory.   They
assume that a solution can and will be found which need
not require any fundamental change in the structure of
society.   Macro-economists also assume that the problem
is a technical one for which a solution is available.

The crucial differences between macro-economic theorists lie in the role proposed for the state in the solution of the problem, and the importance attached to state provision of social services as a support for, or drag on, capitalist expansion.   In contrast, marxism sees the crisis as a social as well as an economic crisis.   It reflects essential conflicts and contradictions within the system that will ultimately lead to its demise.

In these areas one moves into the realms of faith. There are ultimately no firm reasons for believing either that the social system will or will not reach a point of breakdown or that, if such a breakdown does occur, the final result will be a communist society that accords with Marx's ideal.   Functionalists can point to previous crises overcome and suggest that this crisis is not essentially different.   Marxists can point to evidence of class conflict in the failure to resolve recent economic problems - for example, the difficulty in enforcing incomes policies- and to numerous revolutions or wars of revolution against capitalism throughout many parts of the world.

## THEORY AND THE ROLE OF GOVERNMENT

In looking at theories of the role of government it is important to distinguish between normative theories which suggest the role that governments should take, and positive theories which attempt to describe the roles that governments do actually perform in western democratic societies.   There are only about three or four different roles that are regarded as ideologically acceptable today. Some people consider that the role of government should be limited to that of referee, separating political control from as many areas of economic and social life as possible and ensuring only that the minimum necessary rules are obeyed.   Some neo-classical economists, particularly of the monetarist school, take this view.   Some pluralists take a similar view but they are more likely to see the role of referee extended into a somewhat more active mediation between conflicting parties, seeking a compromise as well as enforcing the rules.   Other theorists again would want the government to take an even more active role in the promotion of co-ordination, in discovering needs and responding to these.   Such a role is implicit in functionalist theory and Keynesian macro-economics.   Finally, one can go a stage further and see the state as the protector of minority interests in competitive economic and political systems.

Positive theories of the role actually taken by governments in western democracies suggest a wider range of
possibilities than are actually regarded as desirable.

Marxism sees these governments as the tool of capitalism.   It is not so much that governments respond to the
power of capitalists, but more that the logic of the capitalist system demands that governments behave in particular ways.   From this would follow the common approaches
of governments of different political persuasions and in
different countries to the economic expansion of the
1950s and 1960s and the economic recession of the 1970s
and 1980s.   Wyn Grant's second type of corporatist theory
also sees governments taking this role (pp. 149-50).

Elitism sees governments as the tool of a dominant
elite, which includes other interests than those of capitalists.   Views differ among elitists about whether the
position of the elite is maintained purely by the control
over resources of various kinds (military, economic, information) or whether it also requires some means of legitimation, and some ability to recruit the most able of its
opponents.   They also differ on whether democratic elections provide a restraining influence.

Government may also be seen as a group operating among
other groups.   Some of these theories regard the government as the most powerful of the groups as in some forms
of pluralism, where government acts as mediator, or in
bargaining corporatism (pp. 150-1).   Other theorists see
government as having much less power.   Richardson and
Jordan (pp. 148-9) see government itself as being composed
of groups which are only assisted in their bargaining with
other groups by their official status.   Beer sees this
lack of power as leading to 'the paralysis of public
choice' and 'pluralist stagnation' (pp. 140-1).

Finally, government can be viewed as actually fulfilling the normative role ascribed to it of co-ordination,
and of discovering and responding to need.   Functionalism
assumes that government is one of the sub-systems of society that takes this role and that a pluralist political
process enables it to do so.

None of the positive theories of the role of the government rules out the possibility of change through the
influence of people other than those whose interests are
directly served by government.   Pluralist theories,
except for Beer's, tend to be more optimistic than the

others in believing that such change can be obtained
through direct influence.   Other theories tend to stress
the limits placed on change by the role of government in
actively espousing particular dominant interests or in
maintaining the system in equilibrium.   But within these
limits change can still be obtained.   For example, elitism allows for some responsiveness to influences outside
the elite.   Even marxism leaves room for the exploitation
of the power of the labour force, and the threat of social
unrest to gain concessions from government and the capitalist system.

   Equally, none of these positive theories can be wholly
written off as a model of actual behaviour.   There are
clearly important limits to the power of government to
effect change.   These limits are set by the existing
structure of power and by the ideological framework within
which those who have power (including voters) consider
that solutions to problems must be found.   How the power
structure operates to limit what governments can do will
vary according to the matters at issue and the way they
impinge on those who hold power.   This was evident in the
dialectical interchange between pluralists and elitists
(pp. 145-7).   There are many issues where the agenda is
set by acceptance of a need to maintain the capitalist
economic market, as is apparent when economic crises are
met;   others where the power of wider elite groups is
relevant, as in the failure of the poverty programmes.
In some issues corporatist power sets the agenda;   in
others no major interests are threatened and the interests
of comparatively weak groups can receive attention.   Over
some issues government will appear relatively monolithic,
perhaps where dominant interests are threatened;   in
others different groups within government will appear
divided.

   The implications of this are that when planning or proposing changes, it is not sufficient to rely on rational
argument based on a simple functionalist analysis of the
needs of systems and sub-systems.   It is also necessary
to develop a strategy that takes account of the power
structure among those whose interests may be affected.
The wider and more powerful the interests adversely affected, the more radical the strategy that will be required
to effect change.   Above all, one should never assume
that governments will act impartially in weighing up conflicting demands.   Governments are affected by the realities of power, as they perceive them, and by the ideological framework they adopt.

Having looked at positive theories of the role of government, it may be worth returning to look briefly again at normative theories.   Here one must recognise that if in practice the role of government is limited by the structure of economic and other forms of power, then normative theories may be used as a means of disguising the actual role undertaken.   The concept of government as a referee or as co-ordinator-responder suggests a neutrality that may be unrealistic.   If a boxing match takes place between a heavyweight and a flyweight, the neutrality of the referee will hardly ensure a fair fight.   Nor will it do so if the rules have been devised to favour the interests of one party, particularly if he is intrinsically the stronger.   Similarly, a government acting as co-ordinator-responder is bound to be influenced by the realities of power which are likely to skew its responses towards those who are more rather than less powerful.

## THEORIES AT INTERMEDIATE LEVEL

Social administration as a discipline is biased towards the consideration of change, and particularly incremental change.   As a result much of the focus of its studies will be on institutions at an intermediate level between society and government on the one hand and individuals and families on the other.   In general the nature of society and the role of government set the limits within which changes in social policy are possible.   At the other end, social administration is not concerned directly with changing individuals or families, but rather with creating an environment in which they can develop.   All the theories discussed in this book have some relevance at this intermediate level.

Functionalism once again provides a useful basis for the analysis of the barriers to change.   Given a strong rational case for change and a failure to achieve it, or for change in one direction and a persistent move in another, functionalism suggests a fuller examination of latent as well as manifest functions performed by the system under consideration.   Similarly, Gouldner's (1959) account of strategies for increasing functional autonomy also throws light on the methods used to maintain professional and organisational autonomy in the social services (Forder, 1974, pp. 104-18).   While such an analysis can lead to a conservative approach, it may be an essential preliminary to a search for alternative proposals which will ensure that all necessary functions are taken into account, thus making change more likely.

While functionalism suggests that all the functions
undertaken by systems are likely to be necessary, and
therefore justifiable, marxism questions the validity of
some of these functions by drawing attention to the extent
to which they may be supportive of an exploitative capitalist system.   For example, Navarro's (1978) analysis of
the health service draws attention to the possibility that
the development of a capital-intensive, technologically-
oriented medical service may owe as much to the needs of
the capitalist system, as to the needs of medical care or
even the career interests of practitioners.   Similarly it
may be important to recognise the extent to which the provision of public housing by British local authorities is
interlocked with and dependent on the capitalist economic
system (Berry, 1974).   The borrowing of money and the
purchase of land takes place in competition with demands
from private industry;  the building and often the maintenance of public housing is undertaken by private contractors.

Whether a functionalist or a marxist analysis is used,
the pluralist-elitist-corporatist debate has relevance to
the power structure at intermediate levels, and therefore
to decision-making processes.   For example, the analysis
by Hall et al. (1975) of policy changes at national level
resulted in the derivation of principles that are also
relevant to changes in local government policies and to
some extent to changes within organisations.   Similarly,
Klein's (1974) corporative analysis of the relationship
between the government and the medical profession has
implications for the possibilities of change at more local
levels.

Neo-classical micro-economic theory, particularly welfare economics, and the interactionist perspective provide
complementary perspectives on the conditions which enable
individuals to influence their environment and to make
their own decisions.   Both attempt to feed into complex
decision-making processes the perspective of the individual at the receiving end.

Neo-classical micro-economic theory sets an ideal of
individual choice in its analysis of economic markets.
There can be no doubt that there are large areas of consumption in which human welfare is more effectively maximised by delegating choice to individuals through the
operation of an economic market than by centralised and
paternalistic methods of distribution.   Welfare economics
as a development of neo-classical theory provides ways of

extending the principles of rational choice shown in the
economic market to areas of consumption which may be more
efficiently served by a more centralised provision.    A
system of evaluation which weighs up costs and benefits or
adds up the preferences of the different people affected
by a situation is an obvious aid to rational decisions,
although it cannot remove all need for judgment.    Critics
of cost-benefit analysis like Self (1970) object that such
analysis tries to disguise political issues as technical
issues.    This is clearly a danger as Habermas points out
(p. 148) and as is evident from the functional analysis of
Thoënes (1966).

The interactionist perspective is concerned with the
analysis of social relationships at the face-to-face
level.    As a result it focuses attention on the exercise
of power in such interaction, particularly by those with
power deriving from their official or professional status.
Such power enables the person possessing it to ensure that
his own or the official interpretation of the situation
prevails.    This can happen when professional services are
provided through the economic market, as in private legal
or medical practice or in private schools, as well as in
state services.    By looking at this exercise of power,
the perspective throws light on the connections between
the larger institutional patterns of society and the state
and the experience of individuals of the services they
receive.    It draws attention to the latent as well as the
manifest functions of the exercise of this power, and so
suggests some of the barriers to change as well as some
means of achieving it.    In this way the interactionist
perspective provides a qualitative analysis that comple-
ments the quantitative analysis of welfare economics.
It suggests alternative ways of providing services rather
than just allowing a choice between existing alternatives.

However, it should be remembered that there are many
other intermediate theories that are relevant to this
level of analysis, which are not discussed in this book.
Rutter and Madge (1976) are referring to such theories
when, at the end of their study of the evidence about the
intergenerational cycle of deprivation, they conclude that
there are many causes of deprivation and that the problems
associated with it should be tackled on that basis.    The
theories discussed here have been selected for consideration because of their wider implications for the organisation of society and the meaning of welfare.

CHANGE AND THE INDIVIDUAL

None of the theories given major attention in this book
has been concerned with individual behaviour as such,
although reference has been made to psychological theories
in chapter 1 and to beliefs about the fundamental nature
of human beings in the chapter on social justice - whether
they are essentially capable of a wide altruism or not.
On the whole the literature of social administration takes
little count of psychological theories although, as with
philosophy, students of social administration often undertake a course in psychology.

Perhaps it is appropriate that psychology is mainly
left to the practitioners at the coal-face - the social
workers, teachers, nurses, and so on.   Perhaps it is
necessary that social administration, in concentrating on
the middle ground between society and individuals, where
change is most likely to be achieved, should accept the
limits set by society as it is now and by individual human
nature as it appears in the social context in which we
find people.   Yet it is clear that even the definition of
welfare requires that assumptions are made about human
nature which are as important for social policy as the
theories of society and government discussed in this book.
The web of interaction between the policies of government
at one end and the face-to-face interaction between officials and individuals at the other shown by the discussion
of the interactionist perspective, confirms the importance
of this.   It is as necessary to examine the implicit
assumptions about individual psychology made by practitioners of social administration as it is to examine their
implicit assumptions about society and government.

Probably Maslow's (1954) theory of personality, discussed in chapter 1 (pp.19-20), because of its commitment to
personal development and individual will, provides the
implicit psychology of social administration.   However,
if this book has largely ignored that area, it is perhaps
because the materials are not readily to hand and the connections have not been made.   Perhaps there is a need for
a book on the psychology of welfare?

BIBLIOGRAPHY

Abel-Smith, B., and Townsend, P. (1965), 'The Poor and the
    Poorest', London, Bell.
Berry, F. (1974), 'Housing: the great British failure',
    London, Knight.

Forder, A. (1974), 'Concepts in Social Administration', London, Routledge & Kegan Paul.

George, V., and Wilding, P. (1976), 'Ideology and Social Welfare', London, Routledge & Kegan Paul.

Gough, I. (1979), 'The Political Economy of the Welfare State', London, Macmillan.

Gouldner, A.W. (1959), Reciprocity and Autonomy in Functional Theory, in L. Gross (ed.), 'Symposium on Sociological Theory', New York, Harper & Row.

Hall, P., Land, H., Parker, R., and Webb, A. (1975), 'Change, Choice and Conflict in Social Policy', London, Heinemann.

Klein, R. (1974), The Corporate State, the Health Service and the Professions, 'New University Quarterly', vol. 31.

Marshall, T.H. (1970), 'Social Policy', London, Hutchinson, 3rd edn.

Marshall, T.H. (1972), Value-Problems of Welfare-Capitalism, 'Journal of Social Policy', vol. 1, pt 1.

Maslow, A.H. (1954), 'Motivation and Personality', New York, Harper & Row, 2nd edn, 1970.

Mishra, R. (1977), 'Society and Social Policy', London, Macmillan.

Navarro, V. (1978), 'Class Struggle, Medicine and the State', Oxford, Martin Robertson.

Pinker, R. (1971), 'Social Theory and Social Policy', London, Heinemann.

Pinker, R. (1979), 'The Idea of Welfare', London, Heinemann.

Rutter, M., and Madge, C. (1976), 'Cycles of Disadvantage: a review of research', London, Routledge & Kegan Paul.

Self, P. (1970), Nonsense on Stilts: the futility of Roskill, 'New Society', vol. 16, no. 405.

Taylor-Gooby, P., and Dale, J. (1981), 'Social Theory and Social Welfare', London, Edward Arnold.

Thoënes, P. (1966), 'The Elite in the Welfare State' (ed. J. Banks), London, Faber & Faber.

# Author Index

# Subject Index

Abilities, 176, 213-16, 221

Access, to decision makers, 136

Accountability, 17, 23, 228

Adaptation, 114-16; modes of, 119-20

Agricultural Policy, Common, 32

Alienation, 88, 89, 92-4, 216

Altruism, 19, 49, 140, 184, 258-9, 263

Apparatuses: ideological, 96, 105, 126; repressive, 96

Assumptions: in elitism, 142, 143, 144; in functionalism, 11, 113-14, 117, 118-19, 123-4; in interactionism, 161 et seq., 174-7; in macro-economics, 55-6, 58, 62-3, 79-80; in marxism, 62-3, 88-9 et seq.; in model-making, 11-13, 23; in neo-classical economics, 12-13, 28-9, 39-42, 44-5, 46-7; in pluralism, 133-5, 135-6 et seq., 138, 139-40; in social administration, 228-31

Attitudes, public: to status, 210-11

Autonomy, 15, 49; functional, 124-91, 237; see also 'decision-making', 'choice'

Behaviour, human: and social sciences, 1; complexity of, 13-17; influences on, 10; see also 'human nature', 'individual'

Behaviourism, 8, 12, 19, 162-3, 165; in political theory, 147

Bias, mobilisation of, 146-7

Biological analogy, 16, 21, 111, 113, 117-18, 124, 133-4, 152

Blacks, see 'race'

Capital: accumulation, 91, 93, 99; as factor of production, 35, 44-5; marxist definitions of, 91; reproduction of, 78

Capitalism, 10, 27-8, 45, 89-90 (see also 'economy', 'market'); advanced, 40-1, 151-2; and corporatism, 150-2; demise/survival of, 90, 230, 232, 234 (see also 'crisis'); democratic - welfare, 228 (see also